Corona
the circle city
AN ILLUSTRATED HISTORY OF CORONA
By Diann Marsh

First Edition
Copyright ©1998 by
Heritage Media Corporation

ISBN Number: 1-886483-15-9

Library of Congress
Card Catalog Number: 97-078263

Author: Diann Marsh
Photo Editor: Diann Marsh
Publisher: C.E. Parks
Managing Editor: Lori M. Parks
Editorial Coordinators: Betsy Blondin
                        Susan Ikeda
                        Betsy Lelja
National Sales Manager: Ray Spagnuolo
Project Sales Manager: Merrilyn Fleming
Corp. Development: Bart Barica
Production Manager: Deborah Sherwood
Asst. Production Manager: Christa De Martini
Project Art Director: Gina Mancini
Production Staff: Janet Craven
                 Sean Gates
                 Darlene Kocher
                 Steve Trainor
                 Ray Williams
Operations Manager: Marla Eckhoff
Administration: Michael Bayon
                 Regina Read
                 Scott Reid
                 Diana Russell

Sponsored by:
Corona Historic Preservation Society
P.O. Box 2904
Corona, CA 91718

Friends of Corona Public Library
Heritage Committee
650 South Main Street
Corona, CA 91720

Published By

6354 Corte del Abeto, Suite B
Carlsbad, CA 92009
www.heritagemedia.com

Printed in the United States of America.

Corona
the circle city
AN ILLUSTRATED HISTORY OF CORONA
by Diann Marsh

Dedication

To our daughter,
Robin Marsh Patrick
(1959-1997). She enjoyed
her years at Garretson
Elementary School and
Corona Junior High.

To Gloria Scott Freel,
Curator of the Heritage
Room of the Corona Public
Librar. Starting as a volunteer at the library in 1979,
she became a full-time
librarian in 1980. She has
devoted many years to the
gathering and
preservation of Corona's
unique history.

Table Of Contents

Introduction

Corona has a special beauty. Built on an alluvial plain which rises gently to the foothills of the Santa Ana Mountains, the city rapidly became a stable community with schools, churches, a Victorian hotel, and downtown stores. It was a good place to raise a family. Perhaps that recognition is part of the reason Corona has grown by leaps and bounds since the early 1980s.

When Heritage Media was looking for an author for their book about Corona history, I was eager to be selected for the job. Our family had lived in the Corona-Norco area from 1962 to 1974, and have many fond memories of our years spent in both cities.

First of all, let me express my gratitude and appreciation to Gloria Scott Freel and the staff of the Heritage Room of the public library. Everyone who comes through the door is welcomed, and the person at the desk tries her best to provide answers to the wide variety of questions. They have at their fingertips hundreds of maps, thousands of pictures, treasured memorabilia, important documents, and shelves of local history books to help you explore Corona's unique history.

Gloria Scott Freel, Curator of the Heritage Room, is well known for her dedication and her cheerful, friendly attitude. In charge of the Heritage Room since 1983, she was honored by the Riverside County Historical Society for her part in the county Centennial Celebration.

She serves as liaison to the Heritage Preservation Society. She has been honored by the Society for raising the City's consciousness in the field of historic preservation. Her enthusiasm and knowledge of Corona's fascinating history helped make researching this book fun and interesting.

Second, let me thank Steve Nathan, President of the Norco Historical Society. Extremely knowledgeable about both Norco history and politics, he has been active in civic affairs for many years. He served on the City Council for a number of years and was Mayor of Norco in 1981-82. He graciously helped me select the photos for Chapter Six from among the hundreds of excellent ones in the Society's extensive collection. He led an exciting and unforgettable tour of the Norco Rehabilitation Center, Lake Norconian and the Casino building. It is evident that Steve's heart will always be in Norco.

In 1962, seeking a more wholesome life for our family, we moved from Garden Grove to a three-quarter-acre mini-ranch in Norco. We wanted our children, Elaine (age 8 at the time), Randy (6), Robin (3), Kevin (2), and Eric (1) to have plenty of room to run and play. During the seven years we lived there, Virginia and Rodney were born. Our family had the usual chickens, goats, pigs, peacocks, dogs, cats, turkeys, ducks, rabbits and a couple of steers.

In the early 1960s Norco was just beginning to grow. New ranch-style houses, complete with small barns and half-acre-plus lots, were being built as the larger parcels were being subdivided. Our house, for example was one of three new houses built on an old vineyard. As the new houses were built, people who loved horses and animals found Norco the ideal place in which to settle.

In 1969 we moved to 1510 Dana Street in Corona, and our children went to Garretson School and Corona Junior High. We had begun to look at old houses in Corona, and were considering selling our contemporary house to fulfill our "old house" dream of many years. Life in Corona was truly great for our family. The neighborhood was pleasant, the schools excellent, and there was little crime to worry about. We would probably have remained Coronans for the rest of our lives if it had not been for the gas shortage of 1973-74. My husband, Robert, was driving 110 miles round trip to work in those days. It was with regret that we had to move to Orange County, closer to his job, in 1974.

We still belong to the Starlighters Club from the First Methodist Church, and have many fond memories of the great parties, trips and events we attended with our friends there. A close-knit group of Christian people, many of the members of the club have been active for more than 40 years. Several of them had first-hand knowledge of important events in Corona. The Corona Art Association, of which I was once a member, has continued to be an important cultural force in the City.

Our daughter, Robin Marsh Patrick, the other person to whom this book was dedicated, loved Corona. Because we lived in a house close to Corona Junior High, her friends would come to our house every morning to pick her up, gathering in the bathroom to talk and fix their hair. Corona was a great place to raise children, and Robin, with her enthusiasm, was always in the middle of some activity. She passed away, at the age 38, while I was writing this book. It seemed particularly appropriate to dedicate it to her. She is survived by her husband, Tom, who was born at Naval Hospital in Norco, and sons, Travis, age four-and-a-half, and Bobby, age three.

In selecting the photographs we had to work with what was available. For this reason, the photos don't always match the text, and there are several stories that we are unable to illustrate. The photos may have been lost through time, destroyed, or even taken in the first place. A good example would be the mock wedding held at the grand opening of the Corona Country Club in 1913. We would have loved to have had some photos of those fellows dressed up as the bride and the wedding party. Both the Heritage Room and the Norco Historical Society would like very much to have any historical photos that you may have of their community.

From the Ancient Temescal Road to the new houses on the hilltops, the history of Corona is unique and exciting. I have really enjoyed writing about a city of which my husband and I have such fond memories. In addition, the book gave us an opportunity to renew valuable friendships and participate in a community that is truly special.

Diann Marsh

Chapter 1

The Ancient Road

THE SUN-KISSED LAND

For almost 50 years after Columbus discovered the east coast of our country, the west coast slumbered in undisturbed splendor. The only inhabitants were the Indians who roamed freely over the plains, foothills and mountains, gathering the seeds of wild grasses and fishing in the rivers, lakes and sea.

California — the musical word brings to mind pleasant, exotic, and somewhat romantic scenes. Discovered by Juan Rodríquez Cabrillo in 1542, California first appeared on the maps of geographers and the charts of navigators as an island. A good example was the map drawn by R. W. Seale in 1744, titled "A Map of North America with the European Settlements and whatever else is remarkable in ye West Indies from the latest and best observations." It shows California as a fairly large-sized island that stretches from Mexico to Alaska, 50 to 100 miles out to sea. Robert Cowan, in *Ranchos of California*, puts forth the theory that the name California comes from a novel, *Las Sergas De Esplandian*, authored by Garcia Ordonez de Montalvo and published in 1510 in Seville, Spain. Montalvo described a place he called California as being close to the imaginary Terrestrial Paradize, "to the right of the Indies." He described the mythical land as being inhabited by powerful black amazons and griffiths and ruled by Queen Calafia and rich in precious stones and gold.

For several years after Cabrillo's exploratory mission in 1542, little interest was shown in further exploration or development of Upper California. However, the threat of Russian occupation and settlement from the north forced the issue, and in 1769 a land expedition was ordered by the Spanish Visitador General Don José de Gálvez. Arriving in Lower California, he made plans for the exploration and occupation of the land, through the establishment of a system of missions, in Alta (Upper) California. Four expeditions were planned, two by sea and two by land, with San Diego as their destination. The mission at San Diego was dedicated on July 16, 1769.

Earlier in July, a reorganized party of 62 men, headed by Gaspar de Portolá , began its trek northward, in search of the Bay of Monterey. Although the expedition skirted the foothills on the west side of the Santa Ana Mountains and did not come far enough east to cross the land that was to become the future site of Corona, Portolá's expedition signaled the beginning of the vast changes that would soon begin to take place in the unspoiled and untamed land of California.

The party camped near the site of the town of Olive, located at the western end of a wide canyon. The soldiers had already named the mountains from which the canyon flowed after Saint Ann (Santa Ana Mountains). On Friday, July 28, 1769, the expedition experienced a strong earthquake while camped along the river. Undoubtedly they were quite frightened because they christened the river "El Rio del Dulcisimo Nombre de Jesús de los Temblors," which translates to "the river of the sweetest name of Jesus of the earthquakes." However, because the river seemed to flow from the mountains they had named in honor of Saint Ann, the soldiers gradually changed the name of the meandering stream the Santa Ana River. In those days the wide shallow river had water in it all year round. Even in the dry summer season the water averaged 12 to 16 inches in depth.

THE ALLUVIAL FAN

Corona was born on a gently sloping alluvial fan, encircled on the south side by the foothills of the Santa Ana Mountains. The Temescal Wash, which ran along the east side of the fan, had a shallow but permanent stream. When it rained, water poured from the canyons in the foothills, and sank into the gravelly soil below. It was this topography, along with the availability of water, that made the Corona site the ideal location for growing citrus. Twice during ancient times, during two different archeological periods, the land was covered with the lapping waves of the ocean. Evidence of this was found in the existence of two separate layers of petrified shellfish and a variety of ancient shells.

Many kinds of animals abounded in the foothills, mesa's and plains leading from the Santa Ana Mountains. Rabbits, coyotes, hawks, wild pigs, and a bumper crop of rattlesnakes occupied the lower elevations, while bears, cougars and mountain lions ranged in the foothills. Cactus and mustard grass covered the mesa and

plains. The creek beds were lined with a variety of trees and thick underbrush.

THE OLD TEMESCAL ROAD AND POMONA-RINCON ROADS

In the beginning, the Old Temescal Road was of a mere footpath, used by the Luiseno and Gabrieleno Indians. In the early 1800s the wooden wheels of the Mexican carretas and the sound of horse's hoofs began to traverse the dirt road. The mid-1880s brought the tramp of marching feet as some of California's early explorers brought their expeditions along the road. The fast-moving wheels of the Overland and Butterfield, along with wagons and buggies, were next. Finally, the roar of automobile engines could be heard along the now paved Old Temescal Road and Pomona-Rincon Road.

The Temescal Canyon and the ancient road were so named because of the many Indian sweat houses in the region. Located in proximity of the hot springs, the sweat houses were popular with the Indians who felt that the hot spring water had many health benefits. With the hot water available, the Indians of the region bathed almost every day.

Tradition says that Leandro Serrano, who established Rancho Temescal along the road in 1820, was the first white settler in Riverside County. He built at least three adobe's in the valley and grazed his sheep and cattle in the surrounding hills.

Some of California's earliest explorers traversed the road as it led from the east to the Mission San Gabriel and Los Angeles. In 1774, Captain Jean Bautista de Anza and his party marched along the road, coming from Tubec, New Mexico. Pioneers Jackson and Warner (1831), and Frémont (1849), traveled the road. Later, it became a much-traveled military road between the mission and presidio at San Diego and the Mission San Gabriel. It was part of the Southern Emigrant Road, which brought gold seekers to California in 1849-1851. Between 1858 and 1861, stages from the Overland and Butterfield mail routes raised clouds of dust as they rushed hurriedly through the countryside, trying to keep to their schedules.

When Lake Elsinore and Glen Ivy were established as resorts in the late 1800s, they set the stage for the automobile traffic that began to appear soon after the turn of the century. At the

Around 1,500 years ago, members of the Shoshonean (also spelled Shoshonian) linguistic group drifted across the Great Basin and through the mountain passes and settled here. Their language was related to the Indian tribes of the western desert such the Hopis, Comanches, and Utes. Although the Shoshoneans moved around to find available food sources, they had some semi-permanent villages throughout the region. Musical-sounding names such as Paxavxanga, Pashinonga, Wapijanga and Pamajam were given to these villages.

When the Spanish padres founded the missions, they gave their Indian subjects tribal names reflecting the connections with each mission district. For example, the Indians attached to the San Gabriel Mission were called Gabrielenos (sometimes spelled Gabrielino). Those who lived on the lands given to the Mission San Juan Capistrano were called Juaneños. Mission San Luis Rey was the home of the Luiseños. The Gabrielenos were spread over a large area stretching from the Prado Dam area, up through the Chino Hills. The Juaneños occupied a large area which

northwest edge of town the old Pomona-Rincon Road lead across the river approximately where Prado Dam is now located. It made its way past the Yorba-Slaughter adobe, once a stage stop, and headed for Los Angeles through Pomona.

You can still follow the Old Temescal Road as it winds its way through the Temescal Canyon, coming south from Lake Elsinore. The road makes an arc toward the west, crossing the alluvial plain on which Corona is now located, following Ontario Street. The trail picks up again where Yorba Street angles northwest from West Sixth Street. However, the street deadends at the 91 Freeway. The old Pomona-Rincon Road ran along the north side of the 91 and turned north on Highway 71, which roughly parallels the Pomona-Rincon Road. Some sections of the old road, particularly near the Yorba-Slaughter Adobe, is still in existence.

THE INDIANS INHABIT THE LAND

The stone age tribes who first occupied the hills and valleys of Southern California could have been here as early as 6000 B.C. Archeologists continue to search for physical evidence of these early aborigines.

The Indians had their own names for some of the more permanent villages. The community called Paxavxanga was located on the east side of the Temescal Wash, while the village of Pamajam was nestled high in a mountain valley above the future site of Corona (noted by a star *). Pashinonga was a major settlement in the Prado Dam area. The Indians used Temescal Canyon as a major thoroughfare, and bathed in the hot springs on a daily basis.

A noble member of the Luiseño community sits beside a thatched hut that was typical of those constructed by Shoshonean tribes. A frame of poles was erected, the outside thatched with tules or palm leaves, and poles made of branches tied to the frame on the outside. The photo was taken about 1905 by George Wharton James for his book *In and Out of the Old Missions of California. Courtesy History Room, Santa Ana Public Library.*

included the Temescal Valley and ran up to the south side of the Santa Ana River. It is not known whether the Indians identified themselves by these names. The Gabrielenos, Luisenos, and Juanenos having no written language, passing the knowledge and traditions of the past down through song, dance, ceremonies, storytelling, petroglyphs, and pictographs.

RELIGION, CHINIGCHINICH, AND PUBERTY RITES

Only a few early scholars made significant efforts to describe the life of the Indians living in southern California. One of the earliest and most detailed descriptions was written by Father Geronimo Boscana. He served at the Mission San Juan Capistrano from 1814 to 1846. When he died at the Mission San Gabriel in 1831, his observations, written in Spanish, were found. It was not until 1846 that it was translated into English by Alfred Robinson, who realized its value. In modern times the manuscript has been printed under the name of *Chinigchinich*.

Chinigchinch was the name of one of the major gods worshiped by the Shoshonean tribes. Chinigchinch was one of the key figures in the religion practiced by the Indians. Religious beliefs, customs, and superstitions played a strong role in the everyday life of the average Indian. According to Father Boscana, Chinigchinich was not particular whom he protected. He could shield the evildoer as well as the believer who worshiped him.

Each tribe made a Chinigchinich figure out of a coyote skin, with the hair, feet, and head still attached. It was stuffed with feathers of specific kinds of birds, deer horns, mountain lion claws, bird beaks, talons, and crow parts. When finished, the deity looked like a coyote with arrows projecting from its mouth and a skirt of special hawk feathers. Ritual sand paintings in deep colors were spread on the ground in front of the special temple, called a *vanquech*, used to house Chinigchinich. Constructed of bent poles covered with rushes,

the temple was oval, with a circumference of four or five yards, and topped with an open roof. The same method of construction was used for the homes which made up the village. A fence was erected around the temple compound.

LIVING AMONG THE GABRIELINOS, LUISEÑOS AND THE JUANEÑOS

Father Boscana said of the Indians, "they neither cultivated the ground nor planted any kind of grain, but lived upon the abundance of the game." In ancient times, rabbits, quail, deer, squirrel's, bears, and other animals were plentiful in the foothills and valleys. This activity not only helped with the food requirements, but also helped with their clothing needs. The people put to good use any kind of animal obtained. In addition, there were fish, water birds, and frogs in the river, and, if they wanted to journey to the ocean, shellfish and ocean creatures.

As with many Indian cultures, the puberty ceremony represented a significant rite of passage. A young girl was allowed to marry only if she had completed her ritual. Lying on a bed of hot coals in a shallow pit, she was the center of attention as the women of the tribe danced around her and prayed to Chinigchinich to make her the mother of many children. Both males and females were required to fast for three days as part of this important ceremony. In hopes of making the young male fierce in battle, he was branded on the upper arm, whipped with nettles, and covered with ants. After he had survived these events he surely felt worthy to take his place among the men of the tribe.

According to Father Zephyrin Englehardt, the women wore skirts or cloaks made of rabbit skins. They wore their hair long and loved to wear jewelry made from shells or feathers. The children usually wore nothing. The men sometimes wore one or more animal pelts about their shoulders, and, in cold weather they sometimes plastered themselves with mud.

Acorns provided the major food for the Indian's sustenance. They were gathered from oak trees in the hills, dried, and stored in large baskets. In order to make them edible, the acorns had to be leached with hot water to remove the strong tannin. In addition, they picked many kinds of berries and fruits. Wild grapes, manzanita berries, wild plums, gooseberries, and cactus fruits added various vitamins to their diet.

Each community had its share of small semi-circular sweathouses, used primarily by men, either for hygiene or ritual purposes. These sweathouses had roofs of wooden poles and were-set into the ground and covered with soil. A fire, built near the doorway, was used to heat the interior to high temperatures. A nearby pool was used for rinsing.

By the turn of the century the Indians were building houses of adobe bricks with roofs clad in rushes. They made beautiful baskets and pottery. Hugo Reid wrote that the Gabrieleno baskets were so well known as to require no description. (Both coiled and twisted baskets were made). The acorn harvests were brought into the village in cone-shaped baskets carried by the women. Woven water bottles with necks and flat bottoms were coated with asphalt on the inside to

make them watertight. Among the most beautiful baskets were the ceremonial baskets, usually made by the most skilled of village artisans.

"Nothing is forever," is certainly an appropriate saying in regard to the massive changes that were to take place in the future of the Indians. As the small band of Spanish padres and their accompanying soldiers marched into Alta California, heading resolutely toward the future site of the mission at San Diego, the Indians had no clue that the only way of life that they had known was about to disappear forever.

THE CALIFORNIA MISSIONS

The land of Alta California, under the Spanish flag from 1542 until 1822, received little attention from the Spanish government for the majority of that time. It was the threat of Russian activities in the Pacific area that alarmed the Spanish to the extent that they founded the

Indian basket-makers at Palatingua are captured on film in 1905 by George Wharton James for his book *In and out of the Old Missions of California*. Such baskets, beautifully made and highly prized by Victorian collectors, are considered priceless today. *Courtesy History Room, Santa Ana Public Library*

The Mission San Gabriel, as it appeared in 1913, in the book *The Old Franciscan Missions of California* by George Wharton James. Founded on September 8, 1771, by Father Junipero Serra, it was the fourth California mission. The lands belonging to San Gabriel covered hundreds of thousands of acres, stretching to the Corona area. *Courtesy History Room, Santa Ana Public Library*

Father Junípero Serra, the founder of the Mission San Gabriel de Arcangel, is shown here in a portrait from *The Old Franciscan Missions* by George Wharton James. It is labeled Founder and First Presidente of the Francisan Missions of California; From the Schumaker canyon. Corona area. *Courtesy History Room, Santa Ana Public Library*

Three young children wait at the bottom of the steps to the choir entrance of the Mission San Gabriel. Taken in 1920 by Trowbridge Hall, the photograph appeared in his book *California Trails: An Intimate Guide to the Old Missions. Courtesy History Room, Santa Ana Public Library*

first mission and presidio in San Diego in 1769 presidio was a fort with headquarters for the army).

The focus of the mission system was to bring Christianity to the natives and turn them away from their "heathen practices," and into productive citizens and good Catholics. To what degree this was accomplished is open for speculation. However, scholars do agree that the mission system changed the lives of the Indians dramatically and led them on an irreversible path to a mission-centered peasant society.

The determined and dedicated Franciscan padres, given the job of founding the missions, accomplished a remarkable deed when they established the 21 missions in Alta California. The best known of the founding padres was Father Junípero Serra, who provided a dynamic leadership despite his many physical problems. Among the missions he established were San Juan Capistrano (1776) and San Gabriel Arcangel (1771). A much-loved historical figure, he died at Carmel in 1784.

Father Fermin Lasuen, who served as president of the mission chain from 1785 until 1803, performed the remarkable feat of founding nine missions during his tenure. Mission San Luis Rey de Francía was established in 1798 in an area in which was known for its cooperative and even-tempered Indians.

There were approximately 100,000 Indians in California when the padres arrived on the scene in 1769. The tribes were renamed according to the missions on which lands they lived. Thus the people given the name Luiseño lived within the territory of the Mission San Luis Rey de Francía. They inhabited the Temescal Valley and the plain on which Corona was later established. The Gabrieleno Indians, so named because they lived on the several hundred thousand acres belonging to the San Gabriel Mission, had a village in the Prado Basin, where the Prado Dam now stands. Tribal members traveled eastward from San Gabriel or northward through the Temescal Valley. The Santa Ana Mountains formed a natural barrier between the Mission San Juan Capistrano and the Temescal Valley, although the Juaneno Indians attached to that mission did cross the mountains occasionally. All three tribes were from the Shoshoean language group.

MISSION SAN GABRIEL ARCANGEL

Founded on September 8, 1771, by Father Junípero Serra, the Mission San Gabriel Arcangel was called the *"Queen of the Missions."* San Gabriel lands covered several hundred thousand acres,

stretching from the sea to the mountains. It led all California missions in the agricultural production, with its output accounting for almost one-fourth of the total wealth of the Alta California missions. Over 25,000 cattle grazed on the rich grass-covered hills. During the years of mission activity, the vast farmlands had produced more than 12 million pounds of wheat.

Named for the Arcangel Gabriel, the Divine Herald who announced to the Virgin Mary that she was to become the mother of Jesus, the existence of the mission led to the founding of the great city of Los Angeles. On September 4, 1781, 11 families trekked nine miles to establish the Pueblo of Los Angeles.

Father Jose Zalvidea, known as the "Great Padre," was the driving force behind the building of the Mission San Gabriel. Known for his constant hard work, Father Zalvidea was constantly in the process of adding new quarters to the complex. After the earthquake of 1812 destroyed the original bell tower, Father Zalvidea redesigned the campanario to include frames for six bells.

The Securalization Act of 1833 brought disaster and doom to the San Gabriel Mission, just as it had the others. The main focus of the legislation was supposed to be the turning over of the mission lands to the Indians. The churches were to be transferred from the control of the missionaries and given over to the care of resident priests. The plan did not work because graft and corruption led to the giving of the lands to friends and relatives of those in political power.

President Buchanan restored 190 acres and the vandalized and ruined buildings in 1859. This was the largest parcel of land given to any of the missions during the restoration period.

One of the best preserved of all of the mission churches, the Mission San Gabriel Arcangel was restored and refurbished by the Claretian fathers, who began the project in 1908.

MISSION SAN LUIS REY DE FRANCIA

From its very start on June 13, 1798, the Mission San Luis Rey de Francia was prosperous and successful. The last mission to be founded in the eighteenth century, the last of President Fermin Lasuen's administration, and the last of those built south of Santa Barbara, San Luis Rey was founded approximately 23 years after the Mission San Juan Capistrano on the other side of

An ancient statue of the Arcangel Gabriel from the Mission San Gabriel. The photo was taken in 1905 and appears in the book *In and Out of the Old Missions of California* by George Wharton James. *Courtesy History Room, Santa Ana Public Library*

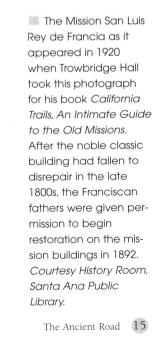

The Mission San Luis Rey de Francia as it appeared in 1920 when Trowbridge Hall took this photograph for his book *California Trails, An Intimate Guide to the Old Missions.* After the noble classic building had fallen to disrepair in the late 1800s, the Franciscan fathers were given permission to begin restoration on the mission buildings in 1892. *Courtesy History Room, Santa Ana Public Library.*

The Ancient Road 15

the Santa Ana Mountains. It was named for King Louis IX, a canonized Crusader who lived from 1226 to 1270.

Father Lasuen himself explored the region, looking for a site among a group of Indians that he had been told were industrious and peace loving. After deciding on the location, he petitioned the Governor of California for the lands. After receiving permission on February 27, 1798, he proceeded immediately from San Diego with a guard attachment to help erect the necessary buildings for the new mission. With Captain Grajéra and his men, a few San Juan neophytes, and several Indians, President Lasuen performed the dedication ceremonies, assisted by Padres Peyri and Santiago. Fifty-four children were baptized that day.

Father Peyri ran the mission with a sensible, zealous, and energetic hand. He knew what he wanted and was adept at persuading the neophytes to help him accomplish his goals. By July 1st the Indians had made over 6,000 adobe bricks

for the new church. By the end of 1800 there were 23 neophytes, 617 horses and cattle, and 1,600 head of cattle.

The beautiful and noble new mission church was completed in 1801-02. A whole group of other new buildings was erected, and by 1810 the population had reached 1,519 loyal souls. Father Peyri, assisted by a talented architect from Santa Barbara, designed the church, which is crowned by an elaborate shaped parapet, a dramatic three-tiered tower, and an arcade. Sunken gardens and a lavanderia (used for laundry and bathing) were located outside the front of the building.

Called "King of the Missions" because, under Father Peyri's direction, the mission prospered to nearly 6,000 Indians, the largest number of neophytes living at any California mission. The mission complex grew to cover six acres. Father Peyri established rancherias out in the countryside to care for the more than 26,000 sheep, 27,000 cattle, and 2,000 horses.

After the Secularization Act of 1833, San Luis Rey took a dramatic downturn. The Franciscan missionaries were forced out and the property sold by Governor Pio Pico. Once considered to be worth $300,000, the property was sold to Pico's relatives for the paltry sum of $2,437. Vandalism and looting soon took place and the buildings were reduced to mere shells. U.S. military forces moved in to protect what was left of the complex, President Abraham Lincoln, in 1865, returned the missions to the Catholic Church.

However, 32 years of neglect and abuse had taken its toll. For the next 27 years the buildings sat vacant, falling further into a state of disrepair. Restoration efforts were begun by the Franciscan fathers in 1892, when the mission buildings were made into a training school for the Franciscan Order. The Mission San Luis Rey de Francia stands today, in

its restored splendor, on State Highway 76, approximately four miles east of Oceanside.

THE END OF THE MISSION PERIOD

The beginning of the end for the Missions came in 1822, when Mexico assumed control of Alta California. The succession of Mexican governors who followed were said to have spent the majority of their time and energy on various rivalries, jealousies, and infighting. These were unsettling times for Southern California. Unfortunately, after the Mexicans took over in 1822 the missions were no longer a priority. The magnificent mission buildings, courtyards, and arcades fell into decay. Much of the credit for the final end of the Mission Period can be attributed to Governor José Murua Echeandia. Serving from 1825 to 1831 and 1832 to 1833, he ordered the secularization of the mission system during his final year in office. This act effectively ended the control by the missions of vast areas of Southern California. The granting of the ranchos ushered in a new period of economic and social growth. The Mexican secularization laws of August and November of 1833 provided the setting for the establishment of the large land-grant ranchos that would control Southern

California until the late 1868, a period of 35 years.

What happened to the Indians? Most of them settled down to farming or living in one of the small towns beginning to appear as settlers moved to Southern California. Some intermarried with the new arrivals. Within the last two decades many of their descendants are rediscovering their roots and taking pride in their heritage.

THE DAYS OF THE GREAT RANCHOS

We picture life on the early California ranchos as colorful and festive, with the typical senorita wearing a tight red gown with a flared skirt below the calf, a black lace mantilla with Spanish comb, a rose between her teeth, and, of course, the eternally waving lace fan. The men wore tight black pants, bolero-style jackets, and string ties. They are thought to have spent a lot of time dancing the fandango. Life was very romantic!

Of course, this vision is not accurate. The early rancho families had varied lifestyles, habits and attitudes, just as we do today. Some of the dons were hard-working, while others gambled constantly, focused on horse racing, rodeos, drinking, and living the high life. Most had large families, but some did not. Celebrations such as fiestas, rodeos, and family rite-of-passage ceremonies were more important to some families and less important to others. A commonality was that almost every family considered that gracious hospitality was an important part of daily life.

In *On the Old West Coast*, Major Horace Bell says of the early Californians: "...*many of the families lived in comfort, some in sumptuous elegance; that is to say, they lived in fine houses, had good furniture, good kitchens, and good cooks and wore fine clothing. These Californians were dignified people, and it is the desire of this truthful historian, so far as is able, to give them their proper standing in the history of the state they founded.*

Precious illuminated choir missals stand on a leather-covered table in the Mission San Luis Rey de Francia. This 1913 photograph is from the book *Old Franciscan Mission of California* by George Wharton James. *Courtesy History Room, Santa Ana Public Library*

They were rich, powerful, and happy in ante-gringo times. They were not lazy, neither were they shiftless, dissolute nor dishonest. On the contrary, they were a dashing and enterprising people. Their very manner of up-bringing... developed a vigorous physical manhood and womanhood."

In 1929 a member of one of Californians "first families," Mrs. Florence Dodson-Schoneman, presented a paper giving her observations about life on the ranchos. She had been born in the Diego Sepulveda Adobe in Palos Verdes,

the daughter of Rudicinda Florencia Sepulveda Dodson, and the granddaughter of Jose Diego Sepulveda, the grantee of the Rancho Palos Verdes in 1820.

"Spanish women created the most hospitable homes California has ever known. Most of the 60 or so first families came from Spain and followed the traditions of that country," she said. She felt that there were many false assumptions about life on the typical rancho that needed to be corrected, and she wanted to share her first-hand knowledge. Mrs. Dodson-Schoneman pointed out that there were two standards by which the typical family lived—the men lived one life and the women lived another.

The senora, who was in charge of family life, was required to be a superwoman when it came to managing the household. Most families had 10, 12, or more children, so she spent a lot of time being pregnant, as well as caring for babies, toddlers, and young children. Along with running a home containing 30 or more rooms, the senora was also in charge of 30 or 40 Indian retainers and an extended family of widowed sons and daughters and their families. The first schools were in the larger ranch homes and the school master, as well as some of the pupils, usually lived with the family.

Between the fiestas and celebrations, there were long months of serious living for the senora.

The head housekeeper assisted her in managing the household, the preparation of huge meals, and the care of the family's clothing. The housekeeper would go to the senora's room every morning to discuss the day's activities and menus.

Mrs. Dodson-Schoneman observed that the Spanish people loved beautiful things, and brought intricate laces, shawls, fans, and satin slippers to the new world. The women treasured these heirlooms from Spain, just as we do the family silver and our mother's dishes. It was her opinion that because the families usually came by ship rather than overland, their possessions arrived intact, instead of being left behind along the prairie trail.

Mrs. Dodson-Schoneman, who died in 1967, was very proud of her Spanish heritage. The paper she prepared on the subject has been preserved in the *1929 Orange County History Series*, published by the Orange County Historical Society.

THE FAMILIES OF THE RANCHOS

The names of Serrano, Yorba, Sepulveda, Cota, Bandini and Botillier are among those of the old Spanish families who settled on the large ranchos established during the 1820s to the 1840s in the Corona area. Many of the families were interrelated. In *Saddleback Ancestors*, published by the Orange County Genealogical

Society, actor Leo Carrillo is quoted as saying, "Even as a small child, I remember being everybody's cousin." The ancestors of Mr. Carrillo and his cousins could be traced back to American, English, Peruvian, Portuguese, German, French, Spanish, and Mexican ancestry. Each rancho family had its own unique story.

after, because of his exemplary work record and ability to organize and communicate with the Indian work force, he was assigned to explore the still-wild Temescal Valley as a prospective site for cattle raising and agriculture. In 1818, Leandro and his Luiseño helpers began clearing the land for settlement. Experts claim that the tanning vats

DON JOSE LEANDRO SERRANO, PRESENTACÍON YORBA, AND JOSEPHA MONTALVA

The first non-Indian settlers in what is now Riverside County were Jose Leandro and Presentacíon Yorba Serrano. They built an adobe home in Temescal in about 1820, raising cattle and farming the land.

Don Leandro's father, Francisco, was a soldier who traveled with Portola as part of his trail-blazing expedition in 1769. He settled in San Diego, where he married María Balbaneda Silvas. They had eight children, of whom Leandro Jose was the oldest. He was baptized on February 27, 1875 in Old Town San Diego and spent his younger years there.

After serving as a soldier at the presidio at San Diego, Don Leandro Serrano became the mayordomo (foreman) at the Asistencia at Pala. This rancheria and chapel at the foot of Mt. Palomar was established by Father Peyri in 1816. Soon

used by the Serranos were in place by 1819 and the first adobe by 1820. Leandro, Presentacíon, and their large family moved into the adobe, located about a mile north of the site of Glen Ivy Hot Springs, on a full time basis in May of 1824. In addition to the cattle raising enterprise, the Serranos raised peaches, grapes, wheat, corn, and other crops. The site of this first Serrano Adobe is marked by a large rock, called the Serrano Boulder.

Presentacíon Serrano died about 1835. Two years later he married the young and spirited Josepha Montalva from Mission San Gabriel. Erlinda Serrano remembered her great uncle Leandro's second wife as a "beautiful, but loud" person who had a special surprise for guests at her wedding. After the vows had been said and the blessings given, Josepha reached for the bullets carefully hidden in her wedding gown, loaded a gun, and shot several rounds into the air.

Don Leandro and Josepha became the parents of Leonora (born 1837), Ramona (1838), Maria

Eustaquida (1839), María de Los Angeles (1843), Leandro (1846), and Delores Bernardo (1848).

Unfortunately, when Leandro tried to obtain clear title to the vast Rancho Temescal from the government, the only proof of ownership he was able to produce was the original grazing permit. So, after lawsuits and disappointments, Leandro and his family moved to a site near present-day Olive (then called Santa Ana Vieja) on the Rancho Santiago de Santa Ana. Because this was the ancestral home of his first wife, Presentación Yorba, he thought that he and his children would have the right of inheritance. Sadly, Don Leandro died in early October of 1852, never to return to his beloved Rancho Temescal.

Josepha moved back to the Temescal Valley and petitioned the U. S. government, on October 26, 1852, for ownership, but her claim was denied by the U. S. Land Commission. She continued to live in the adobe (known as the second adobe) that Don Leandro had built for her when they married. In 1865, when the region was opened for settlement, Josepha was given 160 acres of homestead land fronting on the old Temescal Road. She occupied the "third Serrano Adobe," located on her new property, until she died in 1898. She was buried in the Catholic Cemetery in Agua Mesa. Her two daughters, Dolores and María lived with her until she died. A family friend, well-known attorney and author Horace Bell, gave the sisters a home on East Sixteenth Street in Los Angeles. The property, which was mortgaged to the South Riverside Land and Water Company, passed from the Serrano family's hands.

DON BERNARDO ANTONIO YORBA

The spacious two-story adobe of Don Bernardo Antonio Yorba, said to have been one of the finest adobe homes in Southern California, stood above the banks of the Santa Ana River on the north side of Santa Ana Canyon. Bernardo, the third son of Jose Antonio Yorba I, was born August 4, 1801. As a young man he helped develop the very large Rancho Santiago de Santa Ana owned by his family; however, in 1834 he requested and received the rights to a new rancho, christened the Rancho Cañon de Santa Ana. He built his home on the bluff and called it San Antonio, after his favorite saint. When traveling the Riverside Freeway through Santa Ana Canyon, look to the north to see the meandering Santa Ana River, the trees and verdant underbrush along the valley floor, and the hills and canyons that rise to the north. This was once Don Bernardo's land.

Don Bernardo married Mariá de Jesús Alvarado, the daughter of Xavier Alvarado of San Diego, on April 16, 1823, while still living in an adobe on the Rancho Santiago de Santa Ana. In the five years between her marriage and her death, Maria gave birth to one son and three daughters.

A year after María's death, in 1829, Bernardo married 15-year-old Felipa Domínquez, the daughter of Juana and Mariano Dominquez. About five years later the Yorbas moved into their new adobe on the Rancho Cañon de Santa Ana. As the rancho thrived and his household expanded, the family grew by 12 more children. Sadly, Felipa died after giving birth to her twelfth child, Felipe, on September 8, 1851.

The next year Don Bernardo took Andrea Elizalde as his third wife. The marriage was conducted by proxy and the 22-year-old bride, who was 29 years younger than her new husband, was brought to the ranch after the wedding vows were

In 1834, Don Bernardo Yorba, son of Jose Antonio Yorba I, applied for and received a grant of 13,328 acres in the Santa Ana Canyon. He named it the Rancho Cañon de Santa Ana and built one of the finest adobe houses in Southern California.
Courtesy First American Title Insurance Company

said at the Plaza Church in Los Angeles. Andrea was the daughter of Juana and Nicolás Elizalde. She and Don Bernardo had four sons: Francis, Bernardo, Xavier, and Gregorio. The commodious two-story adobe housed not only the large Yorba family, but also many retainers. Estimates of the house's size range from 50 to 100 rooms. Approximately 20 of these rooms were occupied by artisans and tradesmen who worked at the rancho. Included at one time were a large house staff, a mayordomo, four woolcombers, two tanners, a harness maker, two shoemakers, a jeweler, a plasterer, a carpenter, a harness maker, two errand boys, a sheepherder, a cook, a baker, two washer women, four seamstresses, a woman to do the ironing, a dressmaker, two gardeners, a schoolmaster, a winemaker, and a butter/ chesseman who supervised the milking of 50 to 60 cows each day. Providing the food and clothing for the many workers was a tremendous task. Approximately 100 Indian workers living in a nearby village of their own were supported by the rancho.

The rancho was able to supply almost everything needed to feed and house all of the inhabitants. There were two orchards and plots for corn, wheat, and beans. It took an average of 10 steers a month to supply the needs of the people who lived on the ranch. The vineyards and crops were irrigated by water from ditches connected to the Santa Ana River. Don Bernardo was known as a hard–working, intelligent, and moral man. His rancho grew more and more prosperous as the years went by. In 1846, he petitioned for the lands that would become the Rancho La Sierra. He claimed that he and his father, Antonio Yorba, had occupied the land for more than 20 years. Governor Pio Pico, upon receiving his petition, granted the ranch on June 15, 1846. However, the U. S. Land Commission refused to ratify the petition because the boundaries were not well defined between the portion intended for Don Bernardo and that of his brother Tomas' widow, Vincenta Sepulveda. Finally, in 1877, the upper part of the La Sierra Rancho was divided between

the heirs of Don Bernardo, who had passed away in 1858, at the age of 57.

When Don Bernardo died, he left a large and prosperous rancho, including about 37,000 acres of land and over $100,000 in assets. Of the 20 children (some historians say he had 25) born to Don Bernardo and his three wives, most survived to adulthood, married and had families of their own. Eighteen years after he died his widow sold the square league she and her children had inherited to John Bixby, for $3 an acre.

THE YORBA-SLAUGHTER ADOBE

Raimundo Yorba, son of Don Bernardo Yorba and Maria de Jesus Alvarado, built the adobe home now known as the Yorba-Slaughter Adobe sometime between 1850 and 1853. He had as his helpers several Indians from the Gabrielino tribe. He chose a rounded hill, with a beautiful view of the Santa Ana River, surrounded by lush greenery, as the ideal spot for his new home. He named the house "Buena Vista" (beautiful view).

Raimundo, the first of 20 to 25 children of Don Bernardo Yorba, was born November 25, 1825. He married Francisca Domínguez at the mission church at San Juan Capistrano. Francisca died in 1850, at the age of 21, and did not have any children. Raimundo married his second wife, Conceptíon Serrano, the daughter of José Serrano, on May 11 1856. He brought her home to the new adobe compound on the

The Raimundo Yorba-Slaughter Adobe on the Rancho Rincón, was built about 1850-53 by Raimundo, the oldest son of Bernardo Yorba. Located on the historic major north-south inland route, the adobe was a stopping place for the Butterfield Stage Co. and other overland stages. It was purchased by Fenton Slaughter in 1868. It was his daughter, Julia Slaughter Fuqua, who in honor of her father, restored the adobe. It is now part of the San Bernardino County Museum system, and is open to the public. *Courtesy Heritage Room, Corona Public Library*

hill above the Santa Ana River plain. Raimundo and Conception had seven children, Raimundo II, Zenaida, Floriza, Celeste, Victor, Constancia, and Betsaida.

When the adobe was built, the property was thought to have been part of the El Rincón Rancho. There was some confusion as to which rancho the lands legally belonged. Much to Raimundo's dismay, the U. S. government, after surveying the land in the early 1850s, concluded that the property was on public land. Raimundo managed to keep his rancho by homesteading the 300 acres surrounding the ranch buildings. In 1859 he was able to record a clear title.

The Yorbas built their property into a successful 1,000-acre ranch they called the Rancho El Rincón. The ranch house and headquarters, built along the major north-south inland route between San Diego and Los Angeles, was a stage stop for the Butterfield Stage lines between 1858 and 1861, and continued to be a major stopping place for stagecoaches for many years.

In 1868, Fenton Mercer Slaughter and his wife, Maria Delores, purchased the ranch from Raimundo and Conception Yorba. María Delores was the daughter of the mayordomo of the San Bernardino Mission Rancho. The Slaughters bought an additional 2,000 acres and called the spread the Buena Vista Ranch. The Slaughters had 10 children, nine of which survived to adulthood. Fenton Slaughter was a prominent civic leader in San Bernardino County, serving as a member of the San Bernardino Board of Supervisors for several years in the 1880s and 90s. He was elected to the state legislature in 1871-72. In addition to raising grapes, sheep, and cattle, he established the Old Country Store and post office in the set-

tlement in Rincon. He operated a successful winery on the grounds near the adobe. In 1885 he sold off 2,000 of the more than 3,000 acres.

After Fenton Slaughter died in 1898, his wife lived in the adobe until her death on June 30, 1916. Julia Fuqua Slaughter, realizing the importance of the adobe, acquired the property from the other heirs in 1928. By then, the adobe was in ruins. Julia began the restoration process in honor of her family. She was able to find many of the original furnishings and returned them to the adobe. Julia lived to the great age of 91, dying in 1957. Louise Fryer, Julia's daughter, inherited the property. When she died, in 1960, her husband, Walter, became the owner. Eleven years later, the adobe and remaining buildings became the property of the San Bernardino County Museum system.

THE BANDINIS AND THE COTAS

Juan Bandini, who built his first adobe in 1839 on the Rancho Jurupa, was described thusly by author Henry Dana, in his book *Two Years Before the Mast.*:

A great deal has been said about our friend, Don Juan Bandini, and when he did appear, which was toward the close of the evening, he certainly gave us the most graceful dancing I had ever seen. He was dressed in white pantaloons, native made, a short jacket of dark silk gaily figured, white stockings, and thin morocco slippers upon his very small feet. He moved with the grace and daintiness of a young faun. An occasional touch of the toe to the ground seemed all that was necessary to give him a long interval of motion in the air.

Bandini, in spite of his remarkable dancing abilities, was known as a powerful and intelligent public figure. He was elected to the California legislature, a deputy to the Mexican Congress, and administrator of the secularized Mission San Gabriel. Born in Peru in 1800, he moved with his family to San Diego in about 1820. In 1838, he was granted the 32,259-acre Rancho Jurupa due to his influential connections. The first adobe home built by Bandini was built on a high bluff on the west side of what is now Hamner Avenue, overlooking the Santa Ana River. From their vantage point on the bluff, the Bandinis had a spectacular view across the plain, as far as Rancho Cucamonga.

However, due to flooding problems on that site, Don Bandini applied for and was granted the 4,431 — acre Rancho El Rincón (1839). The family lived in the adobe for two years before moving to a new two-story adobe at Rancho El Rincón. The family servants continued to live on in the house until about 1880. At that time the roof was removed for use on another building. Exposed to the weather, the adobe bricks immediately melted back to to earth.

In 1849, the two story adobe at rancho El Rincón was sold to Don Bernardo Yorba. He gave the rancho as a wedding gift to his daughter Marie Ynez, and her new husband, Leonardo Cota. Among the civic offices Don Leonardo held in Los Angeles, were alferex de defensores, regidor, comisionado, and alcalde. At the battle of San Pasqual he was captain of the lancers under General Flores and Pico. The Cotas, who became the parents of six children, were known for their hospitality and charm.

THE YORBAS AND THE BOTILLERS

Anastacio Botiller, a descendant of French nobility, married María de Jesús Yorba, daughter of Don Bernardo and Felipa Yorba, at the Mission San Juan Capistrano, in 1846. They built an adobe in the Santa Ana canyon, near what is now the Green River Golf Course, and lived there happily with their four children, José Jesús, Adolfo, Frederico, and Eloisa. In the 1960s the adobe was still standing, but had been so vandalized that there was little hope of saving it.

Frederico Botiller married Zenaida Yorba and they became parents of six children. Their son, Fred, who was born in the adobe on January 20, 1885, lived out on the River Road for most of his adult life. He was involved in the development of the roads in the Corona area. He was supervisor for the building of Hamner Avenue as well as other roads in Riverside County.

THE BEGINNING OF THE END

Major Horace Bell said of the rancho families in *On the Old West Coast* "With but a few notable exceptions they all became the meat of the Shylocks (crooks), after the American occupation." Major Bell went on to say:

"The Californians were so rich, potentially, that they never suspected that they could, by any possibility, become poor. But they had one

On April 12, 1876, the lands of the Rancho La Sierra were officially divided among the heirs of Don Bernardo Yorba. The rancho was bordered on the west by the Rancho El Cañon de Santa Ana, on the north by the Rancho El Rincón, on the east by the El Sobrante de San Jacinto, and on the south by the Santa Ana mountains.

weakness common to all Spanish-Americans. When they wanted cash, they wanted it immediately. The Californian couldn't wait, nor would he; and with his ample security he could get all the money he wanted. But how he paid for it! He would pay interest as high as 12 and a half percent per day on each dollar borrowed, compounded daily! That was for small amounts. For large amounts he would pay the low (!) rate of five percent per month on the dollar, compounded monthly. These rancheros were encouraged to run bills."

A series of disasters started with an unprecedented rain in 1861-62. The storms started shortly before Christmas and continued for a month. In his book, *The Cattle on a Thousand Hills*, Robert Gless Cleland reported that the tropical rain fell so continuously that the editor of the *Los Angeles Star* remarked, "On Tuesday last the sun made its appearance. The phenomenon lasted several minutes and was witnessed by a great number of persons." The ranchers lost thousands of heads of cattle to drowning, and staggering amounts of property and crops were destroyed. The great flood of 1861-62 was followed by two years of unparalleled drought. Between the spring of 1862 and fall of 1865, there was so little rain that all of the grass died and there was so little food that an estimated 200,000 cattle died in Southern California. A traveler remarked on the eeriness of the sound of dried bleached cattle bones as his wagon drove over them on the road.

It was into this dramatic and depressing situation that the Americans began to arrive. After purchasing property, they set about building houses and corrals, clearing land, and planting crops. The cattle and wild horses that had freely roamed the open rancho land were destroying the farmer's crops. The new settlers sometimes had to guard their crops at night in order to prevent the new seedlings from being trampled and ruined. Tempers flared as two distinctly different lifestyles clashed. Soon, the Americans would arrive, looking for rich farm land on which to settle, and a new era would begin.

THE BUTTERFIELD CROSSES THE MESA

Clouds of dust accompanied the Butterfield Stage as it made its way across the Corona plain, coming from Temescal Canyon, and heading toward Los Angeles. There was a stage stop at the old Temescal Rancho in the canyon. After crossing the Santa Ana River approximately where the Prado Dam is now located, the stage would next stop at the Yorba-Slaughter Adobe. The rock-strewn road followed the path of what is now Route 71.

The Butterfield Stage came into being when the Post Office Appropriation bill was signed on March 3, 1857. John Butterfield was given a six-year contract, along with a government subsidy, and set about plotting the fastest route possible in order to bring the mail speedily to California.

Leaving from two different termini, the first two stages set off at a fast clip. The inaugural stage came through Temescal Canyon, crossed the mesa, and arrived in Los Angeles on October 7, 1858. For three years the stage ran twice a week, bringing mail, passengers and supplies to the California pioneers. The stages traveled 24 hours a day, stopping only to leave the mail, change horses, or make repairs. The horses they changed every 12 to 20 miles.

Each stagecoach carried six sacks, with each weighing approximately 170 pounds. You can imagine the sense of anticipation with which the stages were met by the settlers, anticipating news

from "back home." Built by the firm of Abbot-Downing, the coaches were well-made and sturdily endured the mud of the rainy season, the sands of the desert, the steep snow-covered mountain passes, and long stretches of wild land.

Along the route approximately 500 mules and 1,000 horses were kept in readiness. The stage lines employed as many as 800 people at the various stations, including farriers (horseshoers), drivers, blacksmiths, harness makers, stable boys, and stagestop personnel.

The stages weathered storms, Indian attacks, and the harsh desert landscape as they met the challenge of getting the mail and passengers to their destination on time. If you close your eyes, you can almost imagine the coaches, as they exited Temescal Canyon about where Ontario Street is now, charged across the rock-strewn, weed-covered mesa, and headed toward the crossing at the Santa Ana River.

THE TIN MINES

Even before Robert Taylor purchased the land for the new town of South Riverside, the area was the focus of investors from England who were excited about the prospect of opening a tin mine in the hills northwest of Lake Matthews.

The Luiseño Indians had kept the secret of the location of the tin ore in the San Jacinto Sobranté well. Tradition says that it was not until about 1858 that they revealed the location to Daniel Sexton. Test samples revealed that the ore was 97.9 pure tin. In the early 1860s, land baron Abel Stearns was the first to become interested.

Edward F. Beale, the U.S. Surveyor General for California and others were next to become connected to the mines. The potential mine site was considered as being on public lands. However, the San Francisco syndicate which brought the rancho known as Sobranté de San Jacinto contended that when Governor Pío Píco, in 1846, had granted the land to Mariá del Rosario Estudillo de Aguirré, the mining land was included. They conceived the U.S. Land Commission to approve boundaries.

In 1888 the title was finally clear, and the San Francisco syndicate immediately sold the site to a company of prominent Englishmen headed by Sir John Stokes and Sir James Belfour, representatives of the California Mining and Smelting Co. A sum of $2 million was spent to install a battery of high grade machinery and dig shafts and tunnels before the mining operations could begin in 1890.

However, the richness of the vein had been overestimated and the mine failed to live up to expectations. It has been suggested that the mining engineer apparently misled the potential investors. During the two years of operation the mine shipped 136 tons of tin bars to England. The last shipment of tin bars was sent east in 1892. Today, only a few foundations and tunnels survive, at the old location near Lake Matthews, as evidence of Corona's once blossoming tin mine.

Hundreds of Wells Fargo Overland Stages traversed the country in the years before the railroads arrived in the late 1870s. They helped immeasurably in the settlement of the West. *Courtesy History Room, Corona Public Library*

PIONEERS OF THE CANYONS

While the future site of Corona was lying in wait with only the rough road crossing its brush-covered surface, the canyons to the south (Temescal Valley) and the Chino Hills and Santa Ana River banks to the north were home to several early pioneers. Some kept bees, while others tried their hand at mining or sold wood.

Watt Bonfoey, who wrote a series of valuable articles in the *Corona Daily Independent* in 1939, declared that the Temescal Valley or Canyon was one of the most picturesque valleys in Southern California. He thought it resembled a Swiss Alpine scene, with the high Santa Ana Mountains in the background and its numerous canyons running down to the valley. The Temescal Wash meandered through the center of the valley, which was approximately seven miles long and one and a half miles wide ate the widest point. The old Butterfield and Overland Stage route traveled the ancient trail created by the Luiseño Indians Mr. Bonfoey remembered many of the pioneers who lived in the hills, canyons and valleys. Some of the pioneers who lived in Temescal Valley were named Herkelrath, Mayhew, Rolph, Mccarty, Craw, Damron, Moody, Lee, Riley, Manning, Brown, Woods, Hoag.

Lee Lake gets its name from Barney Lee, who lived on its shores for many years. Barney, like many of the canyon dwellers, did some farming, some beekeeping, and sold wood. Mr. Bonfoey recalled that Barney was a great storyteller and loved to be called "Colonel" after his ancestor, Col. Lighthouse Harry Lee of Revolutionary War fame. Abraham Hoag, for whom Hoag Canyon was named, was a mining man who came to the area to work the Gavilan Gold Mine located in the eastern part of the

Tin Mine Grant. Later he built a house and barn, put down a well, and settled near the soon-to-be developed site of Corona. He raised grain and set out olive and pepper trees on the hills by Temescal Road. Mr. Hoag often rode into town with his double-barreled shotgun by his side. He was one of a handful of pioneers killed in runaway accidents during the pioneer settlement years.

In 1885 John Hart built a lime kiln in Hagador Canyon. The lime, which was a good quality, was used in the foundations of some of Corona's first houses. After about a year, Hart abandoned the lime kiln and took up coal mining. However, the coal deposit in Hagador Canyon was of poor quality. Later he found a deposit of antimony, but the pocket soon ran out. (Antimony is a metalloid element used in alloys and semiconductors.) George Lord (a.k.a. George Barber) came to Rincón or Prado in the earlier 1880s, working for some of the ranchers in that area. He finally moved to what was at one time called Lord Canyon, but is now called Main Street Canyon. After the Water Company acquired the

Originally built by a Mr. Hagador in Hagador Canyon before South Riverside was founded, the cabin shown was occupied by A.F.B. Lawson and his family when this photo was taken in 1887. The cabin was typical of those that dotted the hills and canyons surrounding the future site of Corona. *Courtesy Heritage Room. Corona Public Library*

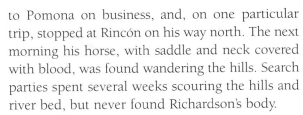

canyon, he moved to Dry Canyon, immediately to the west. He developed some clay beds and planted an apple orchard. He lived out his years in the canyon. Havens Canyon was named for John Havens, who lived there for many years. He made his living by cutting wood and selling it in Riverside. He could remember seeing the mesa covered with waist-high wild oats.

LIFE COULD BE TOUGH IN THE CANYONS

Of course, not all of the memories are happy. Major Horace Bell, in *Reminiscences of a Ranger* identified the section of road at Glen Ivy Hot Springs, located at the mouth of Cold Water Canyon, as the scene of a fight between rangers and horse thieves. Tradition says that a certain tree in Temescal canyon was named for the many horse thieves that used it as a spot to rendezvous. The feud over water rights between the Wall and Walters families took place in Horsethief Canyon. Both families lost a son in the gun battle, and Mrs. Wall was wounded by flying buckshot.

Watt Bonfoey remembered Henry Kline, who lived north of Santa Ana River. Kline had at one time been the hangman for Los Angeles and San Bernardino counties, having sent several bad men from these counties to their untimely end. Kline was proud of his past occupation. He was heard to brag about his ability to do a very neat job of neckbreaking. He was killed in a runaway accident.

Then there was the mystery of Richardson Canyon, now called Hidden Canyon. John Richardson lived there in the early 1880s and employed several men as woodchoppers. He often went to Pomona on business, and, on one particular trip, stopped at Rincón on his way north. The next morning his horse, with saddle and neck covered with blood, was found wandering the hills. Search parties spent several weeks scouring the hills and river bed, but never found Richardson's body.

Meanwhile, over in Hagador Canyon, a man named Miller was found lying in his cabin. He had been shot by someone outside his window. He was taken to San Bernardino Hospital, where he recovered after a long convalescence. The ruins of his dugout were visible for several years.

Hagador Canyon was named for a mysterious man who was considered by the townspeople to be a gunman. Living in an old shack at the opening to the canyon, he made a living cutting and selling wood. When Robert Taylor bought the site for Corona in 1886, he also bought Hagador Canyon for the water rights. After Hagador left, A.F.B. Lawson lived in the cabin, followed by John Priest.

Pat Harrington planted the first orange grove about a mile and a half southwest of town. He started a brick yard in that location in 1886, and hauled the first load of lumber from Riverside to build a house on his property: however, he did not build the house for several months and Robert Taylor's office became the first building in the new town. Harrington met an unfortunate end when his team ran away and threw him against the tree on the Pomona Road near the Yorba-Slaughter Adobe. The hills and canyons of the Corona area were very appealing to that particular type of individual who enjoyed adventure, solitude and an independent lifestyle.

The adobe ranch houses of the old Spanish families were melting back into the earth. Most of the heirs to the ranchos had sold their property, had married the new settlers, and had moved into town. Most of the cattle were gone from the hills and canyons. The scene was set for a new act in the drama that was to become Corona and Norco.

Chapter 2

The Birth of South Riverside

THE SETTING

Walt Bonfoey, in a 1939 column in the *Corona Daily Independent*, remembers seeing the town of Corona being laid out. Coming from Arlington to the east, he topped a hill and saw a team of horses grading the huge circular boulevard and the cross streets at what would become Sixth and Main.

The small red flags which marked the corners of the lots could be seen waving all over the townsite. Mr. Bonfoey must have been impressed with what he saw, because he bought lots 10, 11, and 12 of Block 26 at the northeast corner of Seventh and Ramona Streets, on the spot. By the time he had built his new house and moved from the ranch at Arlington, in February of 1887, there were quite a few houses and places of business in town.

All over Southern California the time was ripe for the establishment of the "Boom of the Eighties" towns. However, many of the platted villages did not have a future, and did not get beyond being anything but a dream on paper. Vernondale, Gladvstra, Walteria, Lugonia, Meadow Park, Acosta, Hyde Park, Greendale, Oro Grande, Irvington, and Randolph are but a few of these towns. Auburndale, north of Corona near the Santa Ana River, also platted by H. Clay Kellogg, did not survive to the turn of the century. Some of the houses were moved to Corona.

Why did Corona succeed while other fledgling communities did not? The gently sloping alluvial fan, encircled on the south side by the foothills of the Santa Ana Mountains, and on the east by the Temescal Wash, appeared to be ideal for raising crops and citrus. A Professor Hilgard predicted that the air currents caused by the angles of the canyons would result in a comparatively frostless mesa immediately to the south of South Riverside. This would be particularly advantageous in the raising of citrus crops.

Perhaps most important was the potential for an adequate source of life-giving water. A marshy basin, fed by the waters of Cold Water, Mayhew, and adjacent canyons, covered much of the Temescal Valley. Underneath the marsh was a large artesian basin, thought to be capable of providing enough water for the future agricultural and residential needs of a future settlement.

KELLOGG'S HUNTING TRIP

Hiram Kellogg loved to go to the Lake Elsinore area to hunt. As early as 1877 he traversed the mesa between the Santa Ana Canyon and the Temescal Canyon, on his way to and from his home in Anaheim. Realizing the potential for a promising development, he mentioned the mesa to two friends from Anaheim, Adolph Rimpau and Mr. Witte. They soon secured an option on parts of Rancho La Sierra and El Rincon from Vincente Yorba and Ynez Yorba de Cota, the heirs of Don Bernardo Yorba.

THE BOOM OF THE EIGHTIES

The great "Boom of the Eighties" is considered by some historians to have been one of the most outstanding events of Southern California's history. A whole new population of Americans from other sections of the country moved to the state, forcing the region to go one step further from the old rancho system. The break up of the ranches completed the transition from cattle ranching to an agricultural economy. Tracts of land that had been considered worthless desert were purchased and divided into lots for commercial buildings and residences.

Historically, the credit for the "Boom of the Eighties" is given to the railroads. The completion of the Southern Pacific to Los Angeles and its subsequent extension through Yuma to Texas increased migration to California and created the winter tourist season. When the Santa Fe was completed, during the mid-1880s, passenger fares dropped quickly and a rate war escalated. The migration reached a peak in 1887, when the railroad fares from Kansas to Los Angeles dipped to an unprecedented low of $1 per person.

As Southern California became more prosperous, promoters moved to California in droves, founding new towns as fast as they could. In June, July, and August of 1887 a buying frenzy took place which outpaced the state's usual rapid rate of property acquisitions. During that time $38 million changed hands in real estate transactions in Los Angeles County alone. The amount of property sold in all of 1887 was almost $100 million.

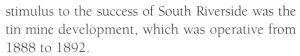

Excitement escalated to a fever pitch. Even though the excitement persisted through the winter of 1888, the boom collapsed as suddenly as it had begun. Although a few speculators lost their shirts, the number was comparatively small because the banks had been fairly conservative while making loans. Even though there were towns that were never developed, others flourished and became established settlements. South Riverside was one of these.

In his book, *The Boom of the Eighties in Southern California*, Glen S. Dumke called South Riverside (later named Corona) "the most important boom town in the vicinity." He goes on to tell of Robert B. Taylor's 1886 purchase of 12,000 acres of Yorba Ranch property. The fledgling settlement was named the "Queen Colony."

Dumke noted that the settlement of South Riverside was aided by the tendency of speculators to move southward as the lands closer to Los Angeles were developed. Most inland boom towns were glad to see neighboring communities founded in their region, while along the Coast the competition was less welcome, and land more scarce. He felt that another

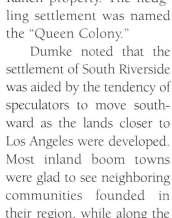

stimulus to the success of South Riverside was the tin mine development, which was operative from 1888 to 1892.

As we move forward to the mid-1880s, we find the heyday of the great ranches is gone and the seed of development of these vast lands beginning to sprout.

ROBERT B. TAYLOR
THE FATHER OF SOUTH RIVERSIDE

Robert B. Taylor, land speculator and promoter, was excited about the prospect of establishing a town somewhere in Southern California. When his father, who lived in Anaheim, urged him to come west to see the property owned by the Yorbas, Robert immediately came west to see the property for himself.

Mr. Taylor, born in Millbrook, Wayne County, Ohio on October 26, 1849, attended schools in Shreve, Ohio. When the Civil War broke out, he tried to enlist in the army as a flag bearer. Fortunately for him, he was rejected. The boy who took his place was killed. Taylor, went to college to become a teacher. After teaching school for six months, he bought out his father's store in Columbia City, Indiana, for $1,000, and became a merchant. Involved in the shipping of cattle, horses, butter, eggs and other farm products, he often traveled to other states where he bought several pieces of property and subdivided them.

Early in 1886 he and his wife, Emma, whom he married in 1873, and his family, came with him to Anaheim. Taylor immediately bought 105 acres in the center of that town, selling it at a profit a year later. After meeting and talking to Adolph Rimpau and Mr.

Witte, he took over their option on the El Rincon and La Sierra properties of Vincente Yorba and Ynez de Cota, He was encouraged by the interest of H. Clay Kellogg, a civil engineer with an expertise in water rights. He went immediately back to Iowa to raise money to begin the community of South Riverside.

We are fortunate to have two letters written by Robert B. Taylor, the father of South Riverside. The first, written on April 14, 1913, did not reveal itself until 1961.

THE HIDDEN LETTER

When the old Corona City Hall was being torn down, a painting of R.B. Taylor, along with an old amp, was sent to Rudy Ramos to be cleaned and reframed. To Ramos' surprise, as he removed the old backing he discovered a letter written by town founder Robert B. Taylor on April 14, 1913, 26 years after he founded the city. In the letter, Mr. Taylor describes his visit to Corona on Easter Sunday of that year. It had been 12 years since he had last come from his home in Los Angeles to the Corona area. The letter, which was printed in full in the May 4, 1961 edition of the *Corona Daily Independent* outlines the history of the beginnings of South Riverside.

Taylor notes: *"I was agreeably surprised but not disappointed with my visit to your city on Easter Sunday, after an absence of about 12 years, and viewed with much pleasure the great improvements made in both public and private buildings and streets in the short space of 12 years."*

He goes on to tell how, in May of 1886, he secured an option from Vincente Yorba for 5,050 acres of land at $10 an acre; from the Pulaski and Goodwin 5,500 acres of land at $10 an acre; from the Cota 960 acres of land at $5 an acre; making 11,510 acres of land on the mesa, being the same lands now occupied by the city of Corona. He also secured option on the Pat Harrington ranch, $30,000; on the Barney Lee ranch, which included the laguna, $3,000; and several other pieces of

less importance. Five thousand acres of land were in the Temescal Canyon and constituted the water-bearing lands. With these options in hand he went to Iowa to find investors for his prospective colony.

Taylor was appointed superintendent with full power to act in all matters of the company and proceeded at once to take up the options and secure title to all lands held under option, paying cash for all of the holdings. His first act was to hire H. Clay Kellogg to survey and plan the town and William Sweeney of Santa Monica as engineer to lay out and do the field work on the water lines.

When the surveys were completed, camps were established at the Pat Harrington ranch and at Gregory Canyon. Some smaller camps were built to accommodate the 300 or so men employed to lay out the roads and water lines. They laid out the circle that was to be the Grand Boulevard first. Taylor remembered that the founders had predicted that the boulevard would "some day be used as a great race track and bring to the town good residents and make South Riverside now called Corona, famous, but we did not know, nor did we understand that it might be used for a speedway for machines instead of horses."

Taylor went on to say: *"Don't think it was all clear sailing at the start. It required many wakeful nights to study out a line of argument to meet the objections of enemies to our enterprise. Some claimed we could not get the water on the mesa, others claimed our soil would not grow citrus fruits, and still others claimed that we had too much frost, etc., and with no water yet on the mesa, and no trees growing, these claims were hard to refute or answer, but we had a good friend and an able writer in L. M. Holt, then editor of the Riverside Press, who had faith in our enterprise and who was more than a match for all of them. The old saying is still true. 'A prophet is not without honor save in his own country.' "*

In the second letter from Robert B. Taylor, received in 1936, by the *Corona Daily Independent* on the occasion of the fiftieth anniversary of Corona, Mr. Taylor tells us of the first time he saw the land: "*On going to visit the land I was captivated by, the beauty of the site, the rich soil, and the prospects of obtaining water for the tract from the Temescal Valley, a few miles southward.*"

After viewing the property that the Yorbas had for sale, Robert B. Taylor was filled with enthusiasm about the future of his new town. He traveled immediately from Anaheim to Iowa. There he met with several old friends and convinced George L. Joy, A. S. Garretson, and ex-governor Merrill to help finance his venture. When the final incorporation papers were signed, Adolph Rimpau of Anaheim became the fifth partner. Most of the official transactions, as well as the naming of the streets, took place in Rimpau's Anaheim office. Robert Taylor tells us, in the letter he wrote in 1913, that Joy, Merrill, and Garretson did not visit the new community until it had been established, about one year after they had provided the funds. It is important to note that, without Joy, Garretson, and Merrill, the city of South Riverside (Corona) might never have become a reality. Each of them worked very hard to become successful and each one has a unique story:

GEORGE L. JOY

A vice-president of the Sioux City (Iowa) National Bank, George L. Joy was born into a wealthy family in Vermont in 1832. After attending private schools, he graduated from Montpelier College. He worked in the mercantile business for several years, moving from community to community. This was surprisingly typical of the average merchant. As more towns were founded and new regions were opened up for settlement, new stores were one of the first services needed. Many merchants were willing to move to a new town and open a general store. Eventually, George Joy set-

tled in Pomeroy, Ohio, where he engaged in the wholesale salt business. As his business expanded, he moved to the larger city of St. Louis, settling there for 20 years. His salt business evolved into meat packing and other related fields. He frequently traveled to Europe on business, which was no easy feat in the 1870s and 80s. Eventually he moved to Sioux City, Iowa, where he founded the bank. It was in Iowa that he met Robert Taylor, and they became good friends.

In 1887, George Joy and his family left Sioux City and moved to South Riverside. He served as an officer in the Riverside Land and Water Company and the Temescal Water Company. He brought with him his daughter, Hetty, her husband William Henry Jameson, and their one-year-old son, Joy G. Jameson. Ella and George Joy were active in the community's early growth and civic life.

A. S. GARRETSON

One of Taylor's oldest friends, A. S. Garretson was, in 1886, the cashier of the Sioux City National Bank. He was the first person Taylor approached with the idea of buying the Yorba property and founding the town of South Riverside. The term "cashier" in old banking circles meant the same as bank manager means today.

After moving to Iowa, he became a bank teller. After a few years he organized the Sioux City National Bank, managing that institution until 1890. The owner of the largest ranch in Iowa, he also was a successful builder of hotels. Among those was the finest hostelry in Des Moines. He also had interests in Coronado, California, and is said to have been involved in the hotel in that beach city. To Corona residents, however, his biggest accomplishment was the donation of the land for the Hotel Temescal, the centerpiece of the new town of South Riverside. He built the three-story Victorian hotel for Orlando A. Smith, who owned and managed it for the first 11 years of its existence.

ADOLPH RIMPAU

A resident of Anaheim, Adolph Rimpau was born in his mother's family home, an adobe on Olvera Street in Los Angeles. His parents, Theodore Rimpau and Francisca Avila, divided their time between the Los Angeles and the Avila Rancho at Santa Anita. When Theodore heard about the founding of the Mother Colony of Anaheim, he and his family joined the 50 German families of the Los Angeles Vineyard Society in establishing the community.

After becoming established in Anaheim, the Rimpau family cultivated 900 acres of grapes, raised sheep, and operated the general store. Adolph Rimpau and his partner, Mr. Witte, were the first to have an option on the land that was to become South Riverside. Rimpau was the person who set the wheels in motion when he told Robert Taylor's father, a resident of Anaheim, about the good prospects for founding a town on the mesa. Mr. Taylor immediately urged Robert to come from Iowa to buy the property of Vincente Yorba and Ynez Yorba de Cota for a future townsite.

EX-GOVERNOR SAMUEL MERRILL

During his trip back to Iowa to raise the money to buy the land for the new community, Robert Taylor contacted Ex-Governor Samuel Merrill, an old friend who had participated in other ventures led by Taylor. After serving as Governor of Iowa for two terms, Merrill went into the banking and investment business. As one of the participants in the Gage Canal project in Riverside, Merrill was already involved in California. His decision to become a member of the proposed South Riverside Land and Water Company helped to make the project a reality.

Robert Taylor returned to California with the funds he needed to pick up the options on the property, and, on May 4, 1886, the South Riverside Land and Water Company was incorporated, with ownership of 12,000 acres.

HIRAM CLAY KELLOGG

As has already been mentioned, H. Clay Kellogg appears to have been the first of the men involved in creating the colony to recognize the potential sites. In 1884 he laid out the city of Elsinore, and in 1886 was hired to do the same for South Riverside. In his own words, in an article reprinted in the *Corona Daily Independent* (May 4, 1961), he tells us about his experiences:

"...With R. B. Taylor as manager, I commenced the survey of the colony and townsite in July of 1886, pitching my tent in 'Pat' Harrington's orange orchard on July 6th. This tent, which I made myself, was a novel affair, circular, with eight equal points and arms and center pole the same as an umbrella; the arms were above the head which proved very handy. It was a small matter to teach my wife the art of cooking by camp fire and doing baking with a Dutch oven, and we lived here comfortably as the clans and knights of the dark ages until November 6, 1886.

"...The Circle of Boulevard was the first thing laid out, after the boundary lines. I remember Mr. Dunlap, the hydraulic engineer, said that on such sloping ground, it would take three months to lay it out, and then it would not be true. It took four days, and we set a stake every 21 feet, painted white, and we closed on a stake three inches square. Mr. Taylor took the hydraulic

It was in Adolph Rimpau's Anaheim office that the final paper work for the platting of the town was completed and the streets of South Riverside were named. He was the fifth partner in the South Riverside Land and Water Company. *Courtesy Elizabeth Schultz History Room, Anaheim Public Library*

Hiram Clay Kellogg, a prominent civil engineer, platted the town of South Riverside in 1886, giving it its unique circular pattern. *Courtesy Heritage Room, Corona Public Library*

engineer out and showed it to him the next day. That was the last time I ever saw him."

Soon after Mr. Kellogg finished his job laying out South Riverside, he bought a lot on East Sixth Street and built a home (opposite what is now the location of the theater building). Mrs. Kellogg was the first woman to live in South Riverside. However, the family sold out to the Tabers within a few years and moved back to Anaheim. Kellogg laid out the town of Auburndale in 1888. It was located south of what is now Norco, near the Santa Ana River. He continued to do survey and engineering work in Corona for several years.

The founders of the fledgling town set about making it a place people would want to live. The Indians and the ranches were gone, and the missions had lost their influence. It was time for a new group of settlers to create the towns that would provide opportunities for pioneers from the Midwest and tap Southern California's rich agricultural resources.

NAMING THE STREETS

After Kellogg surveyed and platted the circular plan for South Riverside and laid out the pattern, it was time to name the streets. As Walt

Bonfoey has told us, after the grading equipment had accomplished its goal of forming the streets, little red flags were used to mark the boundaries of the individual lots.

The meeting to name the streets was held in Adolph Rimpau's office. Present were Rimpau, Kellogg, and Taylor. It only took an hour to name all of the streets within the Circle. Grand Boulevard had already been named, and the founders of the community already had visions of horse and buggy races around the new boulevard.

The streets running east and west were numbered from First to Eleventh, with Sixth Street being at the center of the Circle. The streets running north and south were:

Crawford Street —
named after a man from Anaheim
Merrill Street —
named after Ex-Governor Merrill of Iowa, a city founder
Sheridan Street —
named for General Sheridan
Belle Avenue —
named for Belle Garretson, the wife of founder A.S. Garretson
Washburn Avenue —
named after Mrs. R. B. Taylor's grandfather
Main Street —
the center of town
Ramona Avenue —
named for Helen Hunt Jackson's story, *Ramona*
Victoria Avenue —
named after Queen Victoria
Howard Street —
named after Howard Robinson
Joy Street —
named after city founder George L. Joy
Fuller Street —
named for O.B. Fuller

While driving around the city, the names of several of the pioneers can be seen on street signs:

Taylor Avenue —
named after the "Father of South Riverside," runs south from Ontario, west of Main Street

Garretson —
named for founder A.S. Garretson, extends south from Joy Street, outside the Circle

Rimpau Street —
named for Adolph Rimpau, a city founder, angles southeast from Circle City Drive

Smith Street —
named for Orlando A. Smith, the owner of the Hotel Temescal Hotel, angles north from Tenth and Sherman

Hudson Street —
named for N.C. Hudson, secretary of the South Riverside Land and Water Company, runs north from Chase Drive

Kellogg Street —
named for H. Clay Kellogg, who laid out the city of South Riverside, angles south from Garretson Avenue

Hoag Street —
after Abraham Hoag and Hoag Canyon, winds southwest from Chase Drive

There are also several streets named for the owners of the Spanish ranching families who built their adobe homes in the canyons surrounding the site of Corona. Cota, Yorba, Serrano, El Sobrante, and Rinion are among the families and ranches honored with street names.

PLANTING TREES ON THE MESA

According to an article in *The Bee,* tree planting along the streets of South Riverside commenced soon after the town was platted. It was felt that "beautiful shaded streets and ornamental grounds surrounding the houses add much to the value of the property." The article goes on to point out that South Riverside could become one of the most attractive towns in Southern California within a few years, because of the rich soil, plentiful water, and surroundings that "could grow almost anything".

P.M. Coburn claimed to have had the honor of planting the first tree on the mesa, within the townsite. He brought a pepper tree from Riverside and planted it on his lot at the northwest corner of Ramona Street early in the winter of 1886-87.

The first orange grove had already been set out by Pat Harrington on his ranch about a mile southwest of town. The Wyeth and Shepherd Nursery Company, of Ontario and San Bernardino, advertised that it had 300,000 one-year-old orange seedlings for sale at its nursery. R.B. Taylor, in his letter, gives credit to William Dyer for the planting of the first citrus grove. It appears that his grove was the first within the city limits; it was on the southeast corner of Main Street and Grand Boulevard.

A TOWN WITHOUT WATER CAN BE NO TOWN AT ALL

The founders of South Riverside realized that water was an essential ingredient for the development of the proposed townsite. The South Riverside Land and Water Company had discovered marshlands, fed by water from Cold Water, Mayhew, and adjoining canyons, about 10 miles from town in Temescal

One of the region's earliest citrus and walnut groves, Pat Harrington's ranch was located on the north side of Temescal wash, north and west of the future site of South Riverside. (The trees on the left are walnut trees). Harrington also established the first brickyard in the area and made the bricks for South Riverside's early brick buildings. *Courtesy Heritage Room, Corona Public Library*

(Below) A flume carries water from Cold Water Canyon to South Riverside in 1887. The Temescal Water Company, incorporated in 1887, built a 30-inch pipeline from Temescal Canyon at a cost of $45,000. *Courtesy Heritage Room, Corona Public Library*

Canyon. Early settlers in the canyons remembered a large lake on the site, densely covered with a jungle of tules and brush. Plans were made to build a pipeline from the lake to South Riverside, a distance of about 10 miles.

The first well was dug near the center of town by the Company. A natural artesian basin was discovered which would provide water for the new town.

L.L. Andrews, who shared his remembrances of that first well in April 27, 1936 issue of the *Corona Daily Independent*, tells us that the earth was brought to the surface in buckets by manpower. The water was more than 100 feet below the surface. After the well was established, a constant line of people waited their turn to get a pail of water. This well furnished all the water for both the residents and their animals until the first pipeline from Temescal Canyon was completed.

The irrigation of crops was new and experimental for the Americans, although the Spanish Dons had used irrigation systems to water their crops on a limited basis. The new property owners of South Riverside decided that they wanted to take over the ownership and management of the water supply and distribution system of the S.R.L. And W. Co. The Temescal Water Company was organized for that purpose. The Company spent $45,000 to build a 30-inch pipe line from Temescal Canyon. In 1887, when the pipeline had become a reality, a daily flow of 600 miners inches was being brought from the Temescal Canyon.

As more and more property was developed, the need for water grew. More wells were drilled into the basin below South Riverside. A series of dry years caused the Temescal Canyon source to become inadequate. In 1895 Lake Elsinore was purchased for emergency use, and a canal built from

Elsinore to Temescal. However, the water from the lake was alkaline and could not be used for the irrigation of citrus groves for a long period of time. For this reason, the Lake Elsinore system was abandoned within two years.

THE FIRST BUILDING; THE SOUTH RIVERSIDE LAND AND WATER COMPANY OFFICE

The redwood lumber used to build Robert Taylor's single-storied office had to be hauled from Riverside. The 16 x 24 - foot building, was located behind the future location of the Citizens Bank. Robert Taylor's family still lived in Anaheim, so Mr. Taylor used the office as a place to stay when he was at the townsite. After the brick Citizens Bank Building was completed, the South Riverside Land and Water Company moved into an office on the first floor. Conrad Shearer bought the old wooden office building, moved it onto his lot on Main Street between Seventh and Eighth, and used it as his home for a number of years. The Taylor family had lived at the Hotel Temescal for about a year when the bank building was completed. They then moved to an apartment on the second floor.

WILLIAM HENRY JAMESON II ARRIVES

One of the people most responsible for the success of the new colony was William Henry Jameson II, the son-in-law of one of the town's original founders, George L. Joy. Mr. Jameson arrived from St. Louis in 1887, when the town was several months old, with his wife, Hetty, and their one–year–old son, Joy G. Jameson. The Jamesons quickly became active in the community, making numerous contributions in the agricultural,

Arriving in South Riverside in early 1888, William Jameson and his associates purchased the Temescal Water Company, along with 2,000 acres of land north of the Temescal Wash. The Jamesons came to South Riverside because of the urging of her father, George L. Joy. Both families became very prominent in the community. *Courtesy Heritage Room, Corona Public Library*

agrarian, civic, development and organizational history of South Riverside.

Robert Taylor notes that Mr. Jameson was the person who replaced him as superintendent of the South Riverside Land and Water Company when he resigned from that position. Mr. Jameson, who instantly recognized the need for an adequate supply of water for multiple purposes, became active in the Temescal Water Company and its domestic subsidiary, The Corona Water Company.

In addition to developing the Jameson Ranch Company, he built and operated the Jameson Packing House, preparing and packing citrus fruit for shipment. Selected to serve on a committee made up of influential citizens from Temecula, Elsinore, Riverside, Banning and Hemet, Jameson helped orchestrate the action to petition the Governor to form Riverside County out of the giant San Bernardino County.

When, in 1896, South Riverside residents discussed the idea of incorporating, William Jameson was one of those who served on the committee and brought the plan into reality.

The Jamesons, who had great faith in their new community, purchased property about town. William and Hetty Jameson not only served South Riverside/Corona well, but also taught their children and grandchildren the importance of being an integral part of the community.

THE TEMESCAL HOTEL: SOUTH RIVERSIDE'S GRAND QUEEN ANNE VICTORIAN CENTERPIECE

Visitors and prospective settlers coming to South Riverside would arrive in the fledgling city by horse and buggy, along dirt roads, or by train from San Bernardino. As the town came into view, its magnificent centerpiece, the Hotel Temescal, rose from the mesa like a figure on the top of a wedding cake. It was built in 1887, one year after the town was founded.

A. S. Garretson donated the land for the hotel. Surrounded by spacious and beautifully landscaped grounds, the building occupied a square block in the center of town, to the west and south of Sixth and Main streets. In the 1880s almost every speculator town had a large roomy Victorian-era hotel in which to lodge potential property owners. The Hotel Temescal cost $38,000 to build and the owners, Mr. and Mrs. Orlando Smith, reported that they had spent more than $9,000 for deluxe furnishings, carpets, bedding, dishes, silverware, and table linens. The skilled workmen who built the hotel received $3.50 to $5 per day, while the common laborers were paid $2.50 a day. The materials were costly because they had to be hauled from Riverside. The grand opening was held on September 19, 1887, with the Smiths presiding over the festivities.

Mabel Miller, in a letter written in 1942, remembered clearly her family's arrival in South Riverside in May of 1892. Mr. And Mrs. A. C. Miller, Mabel, Charles (who was later to become Corona's Mayor), and Bert came by train from San Bernardino to South Riverside's Santa Fe Railroad station. From there they were taken by "an ancient bus drawn by two shaggy old horses" to the hotel, entering the property by the wide circular drive that curved around to the main

The grand opening of the Hotel Temescal was held on September 19, 1887 with the owners, Mr. and Mrs. Orlando Smith, presiding. Located west of Main and south of Sixth, the hotel was built to house prospective buyers who had come to look at the town and needed overnight lodging. R. B. Taylor, the founder of South Riverside is seen on the left. *Courtesy Heritage Room, Corona Public Library*

entrance of the building. Mr. and Mrs. Smith often personally welcomed guests when they arrived at the front steps. The Smiths owned and managed the hotel for approximately 10 years after they built it.

Rising three stories above the plain, the Temescal Hotel contained 40 rooms, spacious parlors, dining rooms, a large kitchen and back porches. An assortment of wicker rockers and chairs provided lounging space on the two large front verandas. Facing north, the hotel had a breath-taking view of the open land and surrounding hills. In June of 1905, Dr. J. C. Gleason wrote that "those who had the pleasure of being entertained in its spacious parlors or tasted the viands (food) spread in its dining halls or slumbered on its pillows, or had been led by its thoughtful and generous owner about the elaborate grounds where no expense was spared cannot forget the Hotel Temescal. It was indeed the one thing to which every public spirited citizen pointed to with ecstasy and pride."

Ocie Taylor recalls, "Mrs. Smith consistently dressed in tailored suits and was always either smiling or whistling. She was familiarly called 'Pete' and her constant companion was a pug dog." Mr. Smith preferred his famous trotter "Dandy" for whom he built a special barn on the

corner of Seventh and Main. The loft in those early days was much in demand for sleeping (hay beds) when there was no room anywhere else.

When the Taylors first came to live in South Riverside in 1887, they moved into the Hotel Temescal for approximately one year. The children were quite young and Mrs. Smith let them use the room above the kitchen for a play room. Ocie Taylor recalls that they invited their new friends over and had tea parties. Mr. Hough, the cook, had an eight–year–old son, Harry, who was always invited to the parties because the children had quickly discovered that when Harry was invited his father would send along cakes and cookies.

Ocie goes on to tell us, "I caught some horned toads on the mesa one day, and Mrs. Smith let me keep them in boxes on the back porch. Before long, we had a regular colony of them. And since they were tame, we let them run loose.

"About that time (1888) we moved to the second floor living quarters in the new bank building. Mrs. Smith came to see me one day and begged me to help her get rid of the toads, as they were frightening the guests away. Whenever they sat on the porch steps, the toads would jump in their laps. So we caught them and took them back to the mesa south of town." Ocie remembers a monkey who lived on the grounds and was a delight to the children.

Orlando A. Smith died in 1898. The Hotel was sold to J. T. Burton in September of that year. Wanting to develop the block-sized parcel, he spent $4,000 to move the hotel to the northwest corner of the block and to prepare the building for occupancy. The hotel again became an active center for travelers.

On a November morning in 1899 smoke was seen pouring from the roof. Every available person pitched in to help save the belongings of those living on the first two floors, but everything was lost on the third floor. The majestic hotel burned to the ground. The loss was estimated at $14,000 above the $5,000 insurance coverage carried by Mr. Burton.

A circular driveway led to the main entrance of the three-story Victorian Hotel Temescal, which occupied a full square block. In 1898, when the hotel was 11 years old, the Burtons purchased the building and moved it to the corner, planning to develop the rest of the large lot. Sadly, a year later the refurbished hotel burned to the ground. This drawing was traced from a Sanborn Insurance Map dated 1890.

The Hotel Temescal was the temporary home of many of the families that came to South Riverside to buy land, build a house, and become permanent members of the new community.

THE RAILROAD COMES — THE FIRST TRAIN IS THREE DAYS LATE

Early in the spring of 1887, Santa Fe Railroad extended its line from the town of Arlington, between Riverside and South Riverside, through the Santa Ana Canyon to Orange. A box car served as a temporary station for railroad agent, E. H. Taylor. A Victorian-style depot was planned for the south side of the tracks, to the west of Main Street.

The first train was due to pull into South Riverside on June 27, 1887, at 8:20 p.m., but failed to appear, according to the fourth issue of the *Riverside Bee*. On that evening of the historic occasion, the town of South Riverside bubbled over with excitement. Coburn and Thomas, owners of the local livery stable, ran a free bus to the corner of Main Street and the railroad tracks. As the large crowd gathered, someone, in honor of the occasion, made clanging sounds on an anvil. Wood was gathered to build bonfires, to be set ablaze when the large headlight of the train appeared. As the evening wore on and the train did not appear, the crowd gradually dispersed.

The steam driven engine finally made its historic visit on June 30th, much to the approval of the crowd. The train was scheduled to stop in South Riverside twice a day, leaving for Riverside at 6:10 a.m. and returning at 8:30 p.m. The train was a boon to business, as well as very convenient for passengers wanting to visit the new townsite.

At first, the Taylors lived in the office boxcar; however when the new depot was finished they moved into the baggage room to live for two years. It was while the family was living there that one of their children died. It was the first death in South Riverside.

After the train service was established, Orlando A. Smith, owner of the Hotel Temescal, would send a horse and buggy to pick up passengers coming to his hotel, six blocks to the south.

SOUTH RIVERSIDE'S FIRST BUSINESSES

New! New! New!
Everything New! New Town!
New Store! New Stock of Drugs!

Druggist's Sundries, Patent Medicines, Paints, Oils, Gasoline, Coal Oil Lamps, Lamp Chimneys, Stationary, Tobacco and Cigars, Choice Wines and Liquors, Etc. Just Opened up in the New Brick Block-Plate Glass Front-Opposite Hotel Temescal, South Riverside, California.

B. C. Turner, Proprietor

Built in 1887, the Victorian-style Santa Fe Depot was a welcoming site to those coming from San Bernardino or Riverside to visit the new town. It was located north of Grand and west of Main Street, on the site of the present 1937 depot. *Courtesy Heritage Room, Corona Public Library*

Grace Shepherd Tuthill poses gracefully for this portrait, taken about 1886. *Courtesy Heritage Room, Corona Public Library*

Soon after the townsite had been laid out, merchants began arriving. They bought property and built the first commercial buildings in the vicinity of the intersection of Sixth and Main

streets. The ad on page 13 appeared in the *South Riverside Bee* in 1887. Mr. Turner and his son, Byron, were the proprietors of the first drug store to open in the new town.

South Riverside's first business was operated by John Matson, whose first location for his dry goods venture was a tent on Ramona Street, near Sixth Street. Sadly, Mr. Matson died of "consumption" (an early name for tuberculosis) shortly after he came to town. He was the first person to pass away in the new town and the first to be buried in the old cemetery on the north bank of the wash. Shortly after Mr. Matson's demise, Abe Hineman and E. N. Davison moved to South Riverside and opened a clothing store in part of Mr. Turner's Drug Store. When Robert Taylor completed the two-story brick Citizens Bank Building in 1887, they moved into the store next to the bank. A few years later, they were bought out by Ambrose Compton.

James Taylor, the brother of Robert Taylor, opened the first hardware store at 422 S. Main Street. One of the first requirements of a new town was a hardware store, which sold the equipment and supplies for the construction of the much-needed early buildings. An old cracker box in James Taylor's store served as the very first post office. The mail was deposited there and residents would come to the store to get their mail out of the box. At that time, the mail was brought from Riverside via a stagecoach operated by the owners of the City Livery Stable — P. M. Coburn and Jack Myers. Billy Castelman was the driver of the stagecoach, which ran three times a week. The first official postmaster was Orlando A. Smith, the owner of the Hotel Temescal. After the Santa Fe train service began, on June 30, 1887, the mail was brought by the daily trains.

The first grocery store was founded by Adolph Hesler and was built just north of the bank building. It was not long, however, that he sold his grocery business to John Stege, who launched the first meat market, and added Mr. Hensler's grocery supply to his meat business, located in a store he built on the northeast corner of Fifth and Main streets. In connection with the meat market, he built a slaughterhouse northeast of town, near the Temescal Wash.

A two-story brick building, built in 1888, served as the headquarters for the Citizens Bank, the offices of the South Riverside Land and Water Company, and the second floor home of the Robert B. Taylor family.

The officers of the bank were George L. Joy, president; Robert Taylor, vice president; and Harry Woodall, cashier. After Mr. Woodall had been with the bank for several years, he returned to his old home in the East and his position was taken over by Herbert Wood. Mr. Wood also served as City Clerk of Corona for several years.

The majority of South Riverside's first commercial buildings were constructed of redwood and clad in wide shiplap siding. Western storefronts, which featured a wide space for a sign above the roof line, were a simple and often-used form of construction. In 1887, Robert Taylor built the first brick building, a large two story bank with storefronts on the first floor and an apartment on the second floor. It was located on the northwest corner of Sixth and Main streets. Quite elaborate, the building featured arched windows on the second floor and a turret and a diagonally-placed entrance on the corner.

The name of Leo Kroonen appears frequently in the records of South Riverside's early construction industry. He built the Auburndale Hotel in the new townsite of Auburndale on the bluffs of the Santa Ana River, north of South Riverside.

William Dyer, a pioneer in the building of concrete houses, built his residence in 1888 at the corner of South Main and Grand Boulevard out of concrete (plaster). His concrete was made mostly of lime, and his local critics called the structures "mud houses," and were sure they would fall apart or wash away during the rainy season. However, one of the houses is still standing on Grand Boulevard.

THE SOCIAL LIFE OF SOUTH RIVERSIDE

By the time the 1880s had grown to a close, South Riverside was a successful town with a commercial center along South Main and Sixth streets, many fine Victorian homes and successful citrus groves and ranches surrounding its borders. The community was ready to develop a social life. In those days, people had to invent ways to entertain themselves and develop a social life.

The Hotel Temescal, with its lovely walks and gardens, was the social center of South Riverside for the first several years of the villages existence. Many a young couple courted while strolling along its paths. Parties and major events were held in the parlors and dining rooms. Picnics were popular weekend activities, and the shady trees and swimming hole at Coldwater Canyon were frequently used by both families and young adults. They were transported to the idyllic picnic area by family buggies or an early bus pulled by horses. Hayrides in huge wagons pulled by four horses were enjoyed by the younger crowd. A Sunday afternoon drive to Bear Valley or Lake Elsinore was an activity enjoyed by many.

The Fourth of July became a traditional holiday, with fireworks and picnics, and a horse race that brought excitement to the day. Foot races and one-legged races were usually part of the celebration. Birthday parties, girls' afternoon parties, weddings, and whist parties, usually held in people's homes, brought people together to socialize. At such events a game called "Page of Confessions", portrait drawing and Hearts, a card game, were all played with lots of enthusiasm.

Bicycling was a popular pastime, according to Norma England, who reported in the *Corona Daily Independent* that Art Tabor won all of these races. She cited a story which appeared in the *South Riverside Bee* in 1898. It concerned some young ladies who were bicycling down Main Street in their bloomers. How shocking!

As the town became settled, cultural groups began to form — the Choral Society, the Town and Band Music Club, and the Mandolin Club all provided musical enjoyment. The Myrtle Dancing Club held formal dances at the Opera House. The St. Cecelia Club, Priscilla Club and Town

A hunting party poses for a photograph while sitting on a huge limb in Temescal Canyon. *Courtesy Heritage Room, Corona Public Library*

Improvement Club were volunteer civic groups for women, and the Paradise Club, fraternal lodges, and hunting/fishing clubs provided a social outlet for the men.

WEDDINGS, BIRTHS AND DEATHS

Since 1887, the *South Riverside Bee* and its descendants have continuously provided news and articles of interest to the residents of the community.

On June 21, 1888, Alma Kate Dwyer became South Riverside's first bride. Alma, the daughter of William Dyer, married Herb C. Foster, the new owner of the *South Riverside Bee*.

Miss Tamar Robinson, born on September 15, 1887, was the first child born within the city limits of South Riverside. A short time later, the community's first boy baby was born. His name was Cecil Bainbridge, and he was the son of Mr. And Mrs. John Bainbridge.

Mr. John Matson, the drygoods store owner, was the first person to die in South Riverside. He had been ill with tuberculosis for a long time. The second to die was John Baimbridge, the father of the new baby, Cecil.

COWS, CITRUS, AND NURSERY STOCK

George A. Scoville, shown here playing the violin, was the first graduate, in 1895, of the new high school section of the school system. At that time, all grades were housed in a large impressive two-story brick building constructed in 1888.
Courtesy Heritage Room, Corona Public Library

South Riverside, renamed Corona in 1896, was supported by agriculture for more than 80 years. The growth of the citrus industry allowed the settlement to survive beyond the first few years and through the lean years the nation experienced in the 1890s.

The need for a citrus packing house arose when the oranges and lemons began to bear fruit. George Brown, Frank Scoville, and D. P. Drinkwater built the first packing house on the

north side of the railroad at Sheridan Street.

D. W. Walkinshaw and Joe Cechin were the first to operate a commercial dairy in the early spring of 1887. Walkinshaw delivered milk from the Roberd's Ranch near the bluff of the Santa Ana River, and Chechim from his ranch at the head of Santa Ana Canyon, on the north side of the river. Roberds eventually moved his house to town after the community of Auburndale failed.

These early pioneers had demonstrated their faith in the future success of South Riverside. As more merchants, tradespeople, ranchers, and services moved into the new town, that promise of success was solidified.

THE FIRST SCHOOL

By the summer of 1887 there were 10 or 12 children in South Riverside, and the city fathers were anxious to establish a school. By fall the new wooden building, located on the southwest corner of Eighth and Howard streets on land owned by the South Riverside Land and Water Company, was ready for the new students. Howard Robinson and Mat Craig were the builders.

Miss Gertie McEwen, stepdaughter of Judge Riche and the first teacher, not only had to teach the students, but also had to ask each of the families for their portion of her salary. Times were hard after the end of the Boom of the Eighties, and the families often did not

have the money to pay her. She finally went to Robert Taylor, and through his efforts, she was given a monthly salary of $50 by the S. R. L. And W. Co.

Only two years later, an impressive nine-room two-story brick building, accented with ornate gables and an elaborate cupola, was built on the west side of South Main Street, immediately south of the circle. The community, recognizing the importance of a good school system, approved the $20,000 bonds needed for its construction. In 1905 a three-room annex was added to the back of the school. Throughout the years Corona would continue to be known for its commitment to education and its schools. The abandoned wooden school house was moved down to Rincon where it served that community. Eventually, it became a pool hall in the Mexican workers camp.

Mr. George Scoville, who, in 1895 was the first graduate of the new high school section, lived in the spacious Victorian at the corner of Main and Ontario. In a letter replying to the High School Alumnus staff, he wrote:

May 5, 1914, Miss Ethelyn Hampton, Editor, High School Annual, Corona, Cal.

Dear Miss Hampton:
Replying to your notice of April 27th, enclosed please find my subscription of 50 cents. I surely want the High School Annual.

The only information that I can give about myself is that I am married; without a family; am not bald; have not even grown in good looks. Am living here in Elyrai, which is a dandy town, but not so nice as "God's Country," Southern California.

One thing that I always pride myself on is the fact that I was the first graduate from Corona High School and was valedictorian of my class — class Historian — in fact, the whole works, inasmuch as I was the only graduate from that class.

In one way it was a goal to work for, wasn't it? I regret not being able to be on hand at the Alumni meeting. Trusting that I will shortly receive the Annual, I am,

Very truly yours,
GARFORD MANUFACTURING CO.,
Geo. A. Scoville, Sales Manager

CRIME AND PUNISHMENT IN SOUTH RIVERSIDE

In the lawless days of the Old West, it does not appear that South Riverside received its fair share of criminal activity during those early years. However, the issues of law and order were bound to appear, and soon after the founding of the village it was decided that a Justice of the Peace and Constable were needed. Early in the spring of 1887 South Riverside's Justice of the Peace, a painter named Le Fon, was appointed. Tom Blade, a water company foreman, became

SOUTH RIVERSIDE

THE

Queen Colony of Southern California

Offers the best conditions for Citrus
Fruit Culture in the State

Orange Growing a Great Success. No better lands. Adapted to the Raising of all the Products Common to Southern California

---

2000 Acres already planted to citrus fruits. Beautiful location.
Abundance of Water. Unsurpassed Irrigation System.

The

Best of

Lemon

Land

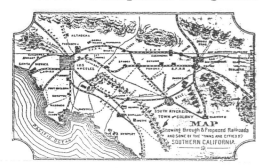

The

Best of

Orange

Land

The Beautiful **HOTEL TEMESCAL** built at a cost of $40,000 is one of the best kept
Hostleries in Southern California and is kept open the year round.

AMONG THE PERMANENT IMPROVEMENTS

Are a $25,000 Bank block. Other Brick Buildings and Stores, also
Blacksmith, Wagon Carpenter, and Harness Shops. Numerous Residences
with Improved Grounds. Two Fine Commodious Churches and
a Handsome $20,000 brick School House.

Extensive manufacturing establishments are located here, namely, the Pacific Clay
Manufacturing Co., for the manufacture of sewer pipe, terra cotta, etc. The Porphyry Paving
Co. The Standard Fertilizing Co. using vast quantities of gypsum. Two small potteries. The
material for all these manufactures being found in abundance here. The famous Temescal Tin
Mines are near town, where extensive works are in operation and already large quantities of
metalic tin are being placed in market.

**The Town is on the Southern California Division of the Santa Fe System
and proposed P. S. R. & E R'y. is graded through town.**

WATER FOR IRRIGATING PURPOSES

From numerous Artesian Wells cienegas, etc. is furnished
in great abundance the sources being inexhaustible. The
domestic water system is compete, furnishing pure water
under heavy pressure.

LIBERAL TERMS TO ALL PURCHASERS AND
ESPECIALLY TO THOSE WHO INTEND IMPROVING.

the first Constable. However, Le Fon left town soon after being appointed and R. D. Riche took his place. In 1890 Howard Robinson was appointed Marshal, mainly to keep law and order among the visitors and residents on Saturday night.

THE FIRST JAIL

The first jail was a wooden shack, measuring approximately 10 by 10 feet, and located behind the water company office at 707 S. Main Street. According to Watt Bonfoey, in his column in the *Corona Daily Independent*, after several years the jail became so dilapidated that the drunks could break out. A new jail was needed.

The new jail was constructed on a lot on the east side of S. Main, between Fourth and Fifth streets. At first, there were no occupants in the new jail. The town joke was that "the people of Corona were so good and law-abiding that it seemed the city had no use for the jail."

Bonfoey, in his October 7, 1939 column, tells us about the time a prisoner tried to burn his way out of the sturdy structure by setting fire to an old mattress. Unfortunately, the mattress gave off more smoke than fire and he was nearly suffocated to death. When he realized the situation, he yelled "fire" at the top of his lungs. Because it was about midnight, Marshal Robinson was awakened to unlock the jail. He rescued the prisoner from the death trap in the nick of time.

The majority of prisoners were local men jailed because of drunkenness. They were usually put in jail overnight to sober them up and then sent home the next morning. The first real prisoner in the jail was a rough individual from out of town who proceeded to get howling drunk and breached the peace and quiet of the town. According to Bonfoey, the Marshal rushed from his carpenter shop, grabbed the culprit, jerked him to his feet, gave him a few vigorous shakes, then rushed him down the street to Judge Phillips' office. Because he was so obviously drunk, the judge gave him a stiff sentence in the new jail.

Mrs. George Allensworth poses next to the porch post of her home. Her sister is shown below, at left. The Allensworths were a prominent family in town and their daughter, Jewel Allensworth Hutchinson, was a teacher at Rugby School in 1919. *Courtesy Heritage Room, Corona Public Library*

Ocie Taylor Songer, the daughter of South Riverside founder, Robert Taylor, poses with her small daughter, Lucille, in front of their home at 714 Washburn. *Courtesy Heritage Room, Corona Public Library*

THE FIRST MURDER

It was not until January 14, 1896, a full 10 years after the founding of South Riverside, that the first murder occurred. Fred Hazen shot and killed S. E. Cooke during a drunken fight at the Hazen home on North Ramona Street. After he was shot with a large caliber rifle bullet which entered his chest, exited his back and lodged in a post on the back porch, Cooke grabbed a revolver away from Hazen and tried to shoot him. The gun refused to go off. Cooke staggered out the back door and fell to the ground, mortally wounded. Hazen went to trial in Riverside and was acquitted.

FIRE!

Corona did not have a formal fire department for nearly 12 years after the city was founded. If the yell "Fire! Fire!" went up, volunteers pulled a hose cart to the job as fast as they could. Obviously, in a city with so many wooden store buildings and houses a fire department was needed. The first volunteer groups was organized on January 14, 1898. B. E. Savery was elected chief; Frank Connell, first assistant; William Riddell, second assistant; and W. A. Wheeler, secretary.

THE PLAGUE OF GRASSHOPPERS

In the years 1888 and 1889, grasshoppers invaded South Riverside by the millions. The insects were everywhere and there seemed to be no way to get rid of them. Local residents were hired to go into the orchards and knock them off of the trees.

Some orchardist covered their trees with white muslin, covering row after row of citrus trees completely. This provided a strange sight — rows of white lumps standing in the sunshine. Another method of extermination involved bringing flocks of turkeys and ducks into the orchards. History does not tell us how they finally got rid of the pests, but the groves and the crops survived the onslaught.

THE FIRST JURY TRIAL

The first jury trial, which took place in the spring of 1887, involved two employees of the South Riverside Land and Water Company. Charles Adams, also known as "Frenchy" and a man who called himself "Gilhooley", but known in town as "Whiskey Dick" had gotten into a fight.

According to Watt Bonfoey, in an article in the September 29 *Corona Daily Independent*, Frenchy, who considered himself quite a good fighter, hit Gilhooley. Gilhooley responded by pounding Frenchy's face raw with a brick. Consequently, Frenchy had him arrested for assault and battery and Gilhooley demanded a trial by jury. Tom Blade, the constable, found nine men who would agree to be on the jury and Justice Le Fon was called upon to preside over the event. It was held in the residence of James Wilson (Corona's first black resident) at 102 S. Main Street a large unfinished two-story house was braced on the south side by long 6 x 6 timbers to keep the fierce Santa Ana winds from blowing it over. Gilhooley was judged not guilty by the jury.

Located on a prominent corner at Ontario and S. Main Street, this fine example of American Foursquare/Colonial Revival architecture was built in 1893-94 by Mr. and Mrs. Frank Scoville. One of the first houses erected outside the circle, it was surrounded by 8.14 acres of orange and lemon trees planted by R.D. Barber, an earlier owner of the property. The Scovilles planted a border of palm and pine trees along Ontario and Main. *Courtesy Heritage Room, Corona Public Library*

These men are gathering honey in an open field near Corona. The boxes at the right are hive boxes. *Courtesy Heritage Room, Corona Public Library*

Chapter 3

The Queen Colony

The 1890s brought important changes to South Riverside. Victorian homes and urban cottages appeared not only on the streets within the circle, but also on the surrounding ranches. A solid commercial center at Sixth and Main was growing rapidly and, by 1890, featured almost every kind of business needed to sustain the town. In addition, there was the economic support of the surrounding ranches, including citrus, olive, and walnut groves, as well as row crops, milk cows, and poultry operations. The tin mine was in its heyday, producing ingots of tin until the vein ran out in 1892. A more enduring industry, clay mining and manufacturing, was begun in 1887 when the Pacific Clay Manufacturing Company was established to make sewer and water pipe for the new community. The constant need to keep an adequate water supply flowing was successfully met by the Temescal Water Company. South Riverside had taken its place among the list of stable, successful boom towns which survived the national economic depression of the early 1890s, and continued to grow throughout the last decade of the 19th century.

CORONA IS VISITED BY A PRESIDENT AND A PRESIDENTIAL CANDIDATE

In April of 1891, an excited crowd gathered at the Santa Fe Depot to greet President Benjamin Harrison. Touring the country aboard the Santa Fe, he paused in South Riverside for all of 20 minutes. Elaborate preparations were made in the small park at the corner of Main Street, across from the depot. A citizen's committee, headed by Colonel Robinson who was superintendent at the tin mine, erected a special raised platform. According to Watt Bonfoey, in his *Corona Daily Independent* column of October 5, 1939, a pyramid of shiny tin bars was assembled in the center of the platform. A large sign read, "The first tin smelted in the U. S." President Harrison made his speech standing beside the tin bars. At the conclusion, he was escorted back to the train, leaving town amid the enthusiastic cheers of the crowd.

William Jennings Bryan came through town on the whistlestop trail during his second presidential campaign. He stood on the platform of the last car and gave a five-minute talk. According to Bonfoey, Bryan said, "Well, ladies and gentlemen, if you can never say that you shook hands with a President, you can say that you shook hands with a man that once thought for fifteen minutes he was going to be President."

A BITTER BATTLE GIVES BIRTH TO THE NEW COUNTY OF RIVERSIDE

During the first seven years of its existence, South Riverside was located in San Bernardino County. A bitter fight, raging for more than three years, resulted in the creation of the new county of Riverside.

When San Bernardino County was created in 1853, 590 square miles were taken from Los Angeles County and 7,300 square miles from San Diego County to create the new entity. By 1883, when the City of Riverside was incorporated, there was already ill feelings between the cities of San Bernardino and Riverside. The Riverside residents considered themselves more refined and genteel than those in San Bernardino. Riverside has always been particularly proud of its orange groves, which had by that time become tourist attractions. The rivalry escalated when San Bernardino received laudits for its successful citrus exhibits in New Orleans and Chicago. In addition, a dispute existed over the share of San Bernardino County money each city received.

The straw that broke the camel's back, however, was the issue of the new county court house. First, the town of Colton tried to secure a change of county seat location. A mass meeting of disgruntled citizens was held in Riverside on January 2, 1891. The purpose of the meeting was the planning of a campaign to establish a new county. After several impassioned speeches, the decision was put forth to establish a new county which would include the communities of Riverside, South Riverside, Jurupa, Rincon, Beaumont, Banning, Alessandro, and Perris. H. M. Streeter, state senator representing Riverside,

President Benjamin Harrison, standing to the left of the giant stack of tin ingots, visited Corona on April 26, 1891. *Courtesy Heritage Room, Corona Public Library*

(Opening Photo) Mason and Daisy Clayton Terpening built this lovely Queen Anne Victorian home in 1899, at the corner of Romona Avenue and Grand Boulevard. Terpening was a bank cashier and served as City Clerk in the 1910s. *Courtesy Heritage Room, Corona Public Library*

(Right Photo) A crowd has gathered to listen to William Jennings Bryan during a whistlestop campaign tour through California in 1891. *Courtesy Heritage Room, Corona Public Library*

had agreed to support the plan when it went before the legislature. A plan calling for a new Pomona County was also presented, but failed.

Naturally, the citizens of San Bernardino County opposed the plan. They headed for Sacramento in large numbers, lobbying the legislators to vote against a new county. On March 5, 1891, the Riverside and Pomona County measures were defeated.

Although the San Bernardino Board of Supervisors had already been faced with two failed bond issues regarding the court house, they went ahead and called for a third such issue on June 13, 1891. Adding fuel to the fire, they raised the total amount to $350,000 for the proposed new court house addition and accompanying jail. Although there was a simple majority in favor, the law required a two-thirds majority in order to authorize the bond issue. The bond proposal lost. The Supervisors were not deterred by this vote and advertised for bids to build the county jail and extensions anyway. The action was extremely unpopular in Riverside. Two members of the board, Supervisors Glass and Garcelon, resigned because they considered themselves useless against the majority of three.

The remaining three Supervisors were still determined to have their way. In 1892, the funds were advanced from the general fund to begin the construction.

The city of Colton called a convention where vigorous protests were heard, and a resolution was adopted against the building of the jail and court house additions. Again, on June 18, 1892, the Board of Supervisors held an election which asked for $250,000 in bonds. The voters defeated the measure resoundingly, and began to think seriously about a proposed new county.

There were other ideas about where the new county should be, however San Bernardino County was then the largest in California, and was larger than many of the New England states. There was a proposal for a San Jacinto County, with that town or Perris as county seat. The idea of an Ontario County, with Ontario, Chino and Pomona, was brought forward. However, the strongest group was the one that favored the new county of Riverside.

Amid angry recriminations, political pressure was brought to bear upon the members of the

(Above) The Serrano family, shown here in the 1890s, all dressed up, ready for a trip to town. *Courtesy Heritage Room, Corona Public Library*

This elaborate Stick-style Victorian house was situated on a bluff over-looking the Temescal Valley about four miles from South Riverside. It was built in the late 1880s by Captain Townsend. *Courtesy Heritage Room, Corona Public Library*

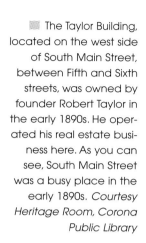

legislature. One of the most prominent of the divisionists was Banning rancher, C. O. Barker. He made his way around Sacramento with a six-gun strapped to his hip.

Riverside supporters won the fight, and on February 25, 1893, the bill to establish the new Riverside County was passed. The City of Riverside, with 2,140 votes, was selected as county seat.

After Governor Markham signed the bill on March 11, 1893 to form Riverside County, he appointed a commission of five to organize the new county. Representing South Riverside was Orlando Smith, the owner of the famed Hotel Temescal.

WILLIAM G. MCVICAR
SOUTH RIVERSIDE'S FIRST COUNTY SUPERVISOR

William Mc Vicar was the first county supervisor from South Riverside to be elected to the new five-member Riverside County Board of Supervisors. He and his brothers had owned land in McVicker Canyon, which, although incorrectly spelled, was named for his family. After operating a dry goods store in Lake Elsinore for a few years, he moved to South Riverside in 1891, becoming a lumber merchant. He was also an officer in the Consolidated Bank of Elsinore. McVicar was defeated in his bid for

re-election as Supervisor of the First District by Ambrose Compton in November of 1894. In addition to his county office, he served as a member of the Corona City Council from April 1900 to June 1906.

Ambrose Compton represented the First District from January 5, 1895 to January 5, 1899. Born in England, Mr. Compton came to California, and settled first in Temescal Canyon, where he owned a store and served as Postmaster. After moving to Corona, where he owned a large orange grove, he operated a dry goods store. He also served as a member of the Corona City Council from 1900 to 1905, and as Mayor from April 1902 to October 1905.

COXEY'S ARMY ARRIVES IN SOUTH RIVERSIDE

In April of 1894, the news that Coxey's Army was heading toward South Riverside, alarmed many of the area's citizens. The marchers, under the command of Colonel Vinnette, were sited in Prado, heading toward town. Some of South Riverside's citizens began to worry about the security of their homes and hen houses. The Marshal deputized several local men, expecting to have trouble at the saloons. The community braced for trouble.

Coxey's Army, about 200 strong, began marching from Massillion in late March of 1894, heading toward Washington, D. C. Coxey's plan was to produce a large public demonstration that would bring the plight of the poor to national attention. By amassing a throng of 400,000 jobless men, women, and children in front of the Capitol steps. To protest the disastrous economic state of the nation.

On that afternoon, April 3, 1894, it was reported that the members of Coxey's army would be in town by nightfall. Shortly before 5 p.m. they appeared on West Sixth Street, heading in the direction of Sixth and Main. A restless throng of townfolk was waiting for them there. The "army" marched right through Corona and camped on the south side of Riverside Road, under the banks of the Temescal Wash. Because the excitement was too much to ignore for some people, a large group went to the camp site to observe the "troops". Some, who were in sympathy, took blankets and provisions for the men. To the relief of the local residents, none of the 60 or 70 men left their camp that night.

Watt Bonfoey, who reaccounts the visit in his column in the October 5, 1939 of the *Corona Daily Independent*, notes that Coxey's Army did Corona one good turn, "they took with them a town character who used to loudly proclaim himself as 'Shorty the Stiff' when drinking and that was most of the time. He was the only recruit they got from this place."

SOUTH RIVERSIDE BECOMES CORONA

The Incorporation of South Riverside was becoming an increasingly important topic of conversation, and many residents wanted to change the name of South Riverside to something uniquely its own. In the beginning, it was Robert Taylor's idea to name the fledgling town after the bustling small city of Riverside, 10 miles to the east. His intent was to trade upon that community's success and name identification. Once South

Riverside had become an established village, its citizens were eager to gain a separate identity for their town.

Choosing a new name proved to be difficult because almost everyone had a strong opinion. According to the May 4, 1936 edition of the *Corona Daily Independent*, the first vote was taken in 1894. The name "Montebello" won the majority. However, a mass meeting of residents in the same month voted for the name "Reyna." Another name that was considered was "Superior" .Baron James Hickey of El Cerrito Ranch was given the credit for the first mention of the name. He wrote to Robert Taylor from Tucson with the suggestion of "Corona", which meant "crown" or "garland".

Baron Hickey, an international adventurer, duelist, self-made king, and novelist was certainly one of the most colorful characters to ever make his home in the Corona area. Married to Anna, the daughter of J. H. Flagler, a Standard Oil and steel magnate, Baron Hickey was born a commoner in California and went on to become an international playboy. Sadly, the Baron committed suicide in El Paso, Texas, in 1898, at the age of 43. Although it was revealed that one of the reasons for the Baron's suicide was in dire need of money, the words he left in a suicide

■ The George and Ella Joy House, located at 1127 E. Grand was an outstanding version of the Shingle-style Victorian home. The Joys, who were married in 1853 in Windsor, Vermont, were among the most prominent pioneers of south Riverside/ Corona. *Courtesy Heritage Room, Corona Public Library*

■ W.C. Barth, a partner in the firm of Barth and MacGilvary Hardware, served as Corona's first temporary Mayor. *Courtesy Heritage Room, Corona Public Library*

note to Anna said, in part, "I prefer being a dead gentleman to a living blackguard like your father."

In the election of May 1, 1896, the name "Corona" was selected over "Circle City" by a vote of 120 to 13. Baron Hickey undoubtedly left an important mark on the city.

CORONA BECOMES AN INCORPORATED CITY

During the election held on June 22, 1896, the citizens of South Riverside voted to become an incorporated city and change the name to Corona. On July 20th they selected the first members of their official family. The first Board of Trustees consisted of W. C. Barth, J. T. Burton, F. M. Coburn, Ellwood Lilly and H. F. Sykes. The City Clerk was J. L. Merriam and the Marshal was F. H. Robinson. V. O. Harter became City Treasurer.

W. C. Barth served as temporary chairman of the board (Mayor), but the first permanent chairman was J. T. Burton. The members of the board drew lots to determine who would serve for two years and who for four-year terms. Burton, Lilly, and Coburn drew two-year tickets, while Barth

and Sykes became the four-year members. William Corkhill was selected by the Board to become the City Recorder.

CORONA CELEBRATES ITS TENTH BIRTHDAY

An aura of excitement was felt throughout the village as the 10th birthday of its founding approached. A gala celebration was planned for August 5, 1896. In the short span of 10 years, Corona had progressed from a bare uninhabited plain to a flowering orange and lemon-bearing colony of approximately 1,500 people.

The headquarters of the August 5, 1896 birthday celebration was the Hotel Temescal, newly landscaped and festooned with red, white and blue banners and flags. Japanese lanterns bordered the walks and the hotel was ablaze with light from top to bottom. Inside, long rows of banquet tables were decorated with flowers, in preparation for the guests. Large fan palm leaves covered the walls.

Robert B. Taylor, founding father of Corona, and his wife received the guests as they arrived. The menu consisted of Eastern oysters, chicken salad a la mayonnaise, Westphalia ham, olives, radishes, chow-chow, salted almonds, pressed chicken, Parker house rolls, Algerian punch, Manhattan ice cream, angel cake, lady fingers, macaroons, Spanish kisses,

peaches, bananas, plums, strawberries, assorted nuts and candies, tea and coffee.

In his speech Mr. Taylor remembered the beginnings of the settlement. He noted that all he had to do to get everyone in town out was to beat on a tin pan and the residents would line up   all six or seven of them. Numerous toasts were enthusiastically given in honor of the newly incorporated town and its new name of Corona.

CORONA GREETS THE TURN OF THE CENTURY

"Southern California is no longer a land of primitive ways. The roughness of the pioneer times has given way before the tide of immigration which has steadily swept into it, bringing a far larger percentage of the wealthy and refined than new States generally receive."

From *Corona, California, The Queen Colony.*
Written in 1902, the brochure, *"Corona, California, The Queen Colony,"* promised that Corona featured the "many advantages of city life along with the quiet and comfort of the country." It pointed out that those who came as visitors decided to stay and become permanent citizens. A familiar story heard throughout Southern California told of persons who came to the area because of ill health, recovered among the sunshine and balmy breezes,

and stayed to become permanent and healthy citizens. Additionally, the opportunity to participate in outdoor sports and horticulture the year round made Corona the ideal place in which to live.

In 1849, adventurous Americans, as well as men from Europe and Asia, began coming to California to seek gold, and while they

may not have realized their dream of easy wealth. They found a spacious country with many opportunities. The new residents often sent glowing reports back to the Atlantic Coast and Midwest regarding the climate and scenery of the new land.

Meanwhile, Corona, as it approached the turn of the century, was becoming an attractive and inviting community. The wide circular drive named Grand Boulevard, the town's unusual location on a sloping alluvial plain of 15,000 acres, and the surrounding groves gave the town a unique beauty. By 1900, the many fruit trees planted in orchards in the 1880s and 90s had matured and were producing bountiful yields. The completion of the railroad system linking Corona with the transcontinental railway system, and the new methods for cooling perishable citrus and vineyard crops allowed the farmer to reach new markets in the Midwest and East. Raisins, prunes, olives, lemons, oranges and walnuts were among the successful crops being harvested on Corona ranches.

Within a few years of the 1886 founding of Corona (South Riverside) more than 3,500 acres of citrus were planted, as well as deciduous fruit orchards and alfalfa. The liberal use of irrigation systems was made possible by the continuing efforts to develop a plentiful water supply.

(Above) The Davis House, built in 1905 by Edward Davis, is a typical example of the American Foursquare/ Colonial revival style of architecture. Davis was a former Corona mayor and owned a citrus grove at 1934 S. Main St. *Courtesy Heritage Room, Corona Public Library*

(Left) The home of W.C. Barth, Corona's first mayor, and member of the first Board of Trustees. He was a partner in the pioneer hardware firm of Barth and McGillivary. This delicate Victorian is located at 818 S. Howard St. *Courtesy Heritage Room, Corona Public Library*

There were approximately 1500 residents living in the community at the turn of the century. Within two years, another 500 citizens moved to the growing town. Brick buildings were replacing the early wooden storefronts along South Main and Sixth streets. Several churches were founded and, by the turn of the century, already had their own places of worship. Students attended a large two-story brick school, soon to be joined by an impressive new Neo-classical high school on the southwest corner of South Main and Grand Street.

Except for the weather, the daily life of the average Coronan at the turn of the century was much like that of the average Midwesterner. Shopping at the stores along Main and Sixth Streets, attending church on Sunday, raising a family, and doing volunteer work occupied the time of the women of Corona. The men worked at their trades and professions. A sizable percentage were engaged in agriculture or worked at a packing plant.

The members of the Corona Christian Catholic Church Endeavor group pose under a tree in 1904. *Courtesy Heritage Room, Corona Public*

AN ACTIVE BOARD OF TRADE

In 1901, Corona formed an enterprising and progressive Board of Trade, the forerunner of the Chamber of Commerce. The group immediately began working hard to promote the interests of the city. *Corona, California; The Queen Colony*, quoted earlier, extolling the virtues of the community.

In 1902 W. J. Pentelow was president of the Board of Trade; W. H. Jameson, vice-president; H. A. Prizer, secretary; C. A. Kinney, treasurer; Board members were A. C. Wood, W. C. Barth, Dr. S. S. Willard, John Triolo, and G. R. Freeman. In one of its publications, the Board described California thusly:

"...an earthly paradise, a geographic poem set to atmospheric music. Here are to be found the charm of southern France, the quaint beauty of Spain and the climate of the Mediterranean.

"The lure of the land is not to be resisted. The tourist, the invalid, the homeseeker should come and join the ranks of enthusiasts. Oranges and roses in December, under sunny skies, make it hard to realize that the traffic of half of the continent is suspended by ice and snow."

In addition to the glowing phrases of the brochure, the people living in the Midwest and East were being bombarded by colorful postcards featuring attractive homes surrounded by blooming gardens. The cards often bore the inscription, "California Gardens in Winter." Another popular style of card, called "Oranges and Snow," displayed orange groves or clumps of fruit with a snowy mountain in the background. This romanticized view of Southern California drew many new visitors and residents to settle in the "land of perpetual sunshine".

PIONEER CHURCHES OF SOUTH RIVERSIDE-CORONA

South Riverside founders, Taylor, Joy, and Merrill, eager to help establish churches and schools in the new community, offered $900 and a large lot to the first religious organization to agree to build a church in the new village. According to Joe Bridges, the very first church service was held in 1886, in front of the partially built Hotel Temescal. Piles of lumber served as pulpit and pews. Horace Houlding of Riverside preached the first sermon. This first group went by the name of the First Church of Christ of South Riverside. They met wherever they could find a space.

By 1902 Corona had seven churches. Among the pioneer churches were:

FIRST CONGREGATIONAL CHURCH

The first prayer meeting of the Congregationalists, led by Reverend Houlding, was held in P. O. Coburn's kitchen. After being given a large lot on the corner of Eighth and Ramona, they were the first, in May of 1887, to build a church. The wooden gable-roofed building cost $2,200, with most of the work done by the 12 founding members of the church. The first service was held in the unfinished building, with nail kegs as seats.

Mary Savage remembered that the church also served as the town's first meeting place, with all kinds of community gatherings held there. She was there when the town auctioned off lots and the women of the church would fix a nice lunch for the people who came to town to attend the auction.

FIRST UNITED METHODIST EPISCOPAL

The Methodists were the second church organization to form, with the first eight members transferring from the Congregational Church. In September of 1887, Rev. S. P. Snowden was appointed to the Rincon Circuit, and, on Christmas Day of that year organized The Fletcher Methodist Episcopal Church, named for a man from Boston who had sent a gift of $250 to help build the church. The 16 founding members included the Pratt family, William and Mary Dyer, P. O. and Minnie Coburn, and Ocie Songer, the daughter of Robert Taylor. For nearly two years the group met at the Rincon Hotel, where Prado Dam is now located. A parsonage was the first building built on the property given to them at Tenth and Main, just south of South Riverside's commercial center.

In 1889, 35 members were reported and a church building that cost $2,500 was erected at Tenth and Main. The year before, the name of the church was changed to the First Methodist Episcopal Church. The first organization to be formed in the new congregation was the Ladies Aid Society, in December of 1888. By 1904, the church, then under the direction of Rev. Carl Ross, had grown so much that a 32' by 40' addition, costing $2,400, was built.

In 1909 the present church school building, with its prominent three-story tower and Tudor architecture was erected. The Ladies Aid and Missionary Societies had been organized and the Epworth League, a young people's group, was growing rapidly in membership.

THE FIRST BAPTIST CHURCH

The First Baptist Church, organized on April 3, 1891 at the home of N. C. Hudson, at 1052 East Grand Boulevard, got off to a rousing start with 25 charter members. J. C. Gleason was elected the first clerk, W. H. Jameson as treasurer, and N. C. Hudson and S. W. Lockett as deacons.

The congregation met for the first two years in a room on the second floor of the old brick Lincoln School. In 1894-95 they built a striking new church on the northwest corner of Main and Eighth streets. Costing $4,000 to build, the church featured an elaborate bell tower, clad in fish-scale shingles, and intricate stained glass windows.

The church grew rapidly, and by 1908, it needed to expand its building to allow for the increased Sunday School attendance. The Young People's Society, Dorcas Society, and Missionary Society were all flourishing groups within the congregation.

THE CHRISTIAN CHURCH

The Christian Church had its beginnings in Corona in January of 1893. By 1908 the membership was about 80 persons, and the congregation prepared to build a new building on their property at Main and 9th streets. By this time, there were 90 in the Bible School and several active groups including the Ladies' Aid Society (aided the local church), a Woman's Missionary Society (for mission outreach), a Christian Endeavor Society (high school age group), and a Junior Society (for older children).

EPISCOPAL CHURCH
(ST. JOHN THE BAPTIST MISSION)

Reverend Alfred Fletcher, came to South Riverside in 1892 to start a mission church for the Episcopalians. Services were held in an unoccupied room at the school. The small wooden church and parsonage were ready for occupancy on March 18, 1894. Rev. Fletcher was replaced by Rev. Erastus De-Wolfe, who became the first full-time pastor. In 1906, Rev. John Brann, a part-time missionary priest, was assigned to the congregation. A very active Woman's Guild, which met each week, held twice yearly bazaars to raise money to pay off the church debt.

ST. JOHN THE BAPTIST CATHOLIC CHURCH
(ST. EDWARDS CATHOLIC CHURCH)

The first Masses in the Corona area were said in the Cota adobe in the Rincon (Prado) area. In 1896 Mr. and Mrs. Arthur Lawson offered their home at Eighth and Howard as a place to hold the first Corona services.

Father McCarthy came twice a month from St. Francis de Sales Church in Riverside to conduct mass and administer to the people. Father McCarthy obtained three lots on the corner of Sixth and Merrill streets, and built a small wooden church there. St. John the Baptist was the patron saint.

The Church was dedicated on October 13, 1898 by Bishop Montgomery of Los Angeles. The church continued to be considered a mission of the Riverside church until 1909. At that time Father Powers became the first resident pastor of the Corona church.

By the late 1910s, Father Clarence Kimmons realized that a much larger building was needed. He put forth a plan to build a fine fieldstone church, with the stones gathered by the parishioners — the task took three years. Finally, on July 13, 1919, Monsignor Fitzgerald dedicated the new building, christening it St. Edwards Church, in honor of Mr. Edward Alf, whose widow made a substantial donation to the new building through the Catholic Church Extension Society of Chicago.

FIRST CHURCH OF CHRIST SCIENTIST

The First Church of Christ Scientist was organized January 12, 1902, with the first services being held at the Masonic Temple on Main Street. By 1909 the society had approximately 50 members and was making plans to build a church building at 122 W. 7th Street, on the southeast corner of 7th and Washburn streets.

(Below Left) St. John the Baptist Catholic Church in Corona. The name was changed to St. Edwards Catholic Church in 1920. *Courtesy Heritage Room, Corona Public Library*

(Below Right) The First Christian Church. *Courtesy Heritage Room, Corona Public Library*

In 1920 the First Congregational Church built this magnificent Gothic Revival building. It still stands today on the corner of 8th and Romona streets. *Courtesy Heritage Room, Corona Public Library*

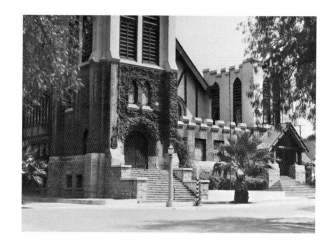

STORIES OF THE PIONEERS

Most of the pioneer families who settled in South Riverside/Corona lived adventuresome lives in the past. Coming across the prairie by wagon or train, they struck out for the unknown, leaving their home and loved ones behind, to make a new home in the West. It is surprising how many times they went back and forth across the country and how often they pulled up stakes and moved to a newly established territory. Unfortunately, many of the stories will remain untold because they have been lost through time.

Ocie Taylor Songer, the daughter of founder Robert Taylor, compiled a scrapbook of newspaper clippings in the late 1890s through the 1910s.

The members of the Boy's Sunday School Class of the First Christian Church are shown at a birthday party at the Sargent home at 101 E. Grand Blvd. *Courtesy Heritage Room, Corona Public Library*

She gathered the reports of her friends and relatives, pasting them in the scrapbook so that they would be saved forever. Fortunately, she had the foresight to give her manuscripts, artifacts, pamphlets, photographs, tapes, and a family scrapbook to the Heritage Room at the Corona Public Library.

Here are a few of the stories from her scrapbook:

A SURPRISE BIRTHDAY PARTY (1888)

"The young folks gave Grace Robinson a surprise party Monday evening, it being her eleventh birthday. The young lady was utterly unconscious that anything unusual was on the program for the evening until her mother sent her to the parlor for something. When she opened the door she was much astonished to find all her playmates there and at first could scarcely believe her senses. The assembled guests were delighted at the success of their plans for surprising Grace, and soon all were engaged in having a good time."

THE BENTON LINCOLN SHEPHERD FAMILY

From Mr. Benton's obituary we learn that:

Mr. and Mrs. Benton L. Shepherd were two of South Riverside's earliest settlers, arriving in June of 1888, a year after the town was platted. Mr. Shepherd, as was often the case with the pioneers, moved frequently until he came to South Riverside. Born in Lincolnville, Maine in 1836, Shepherd made his first trip to California while in his 'teens, following the rush for gold. After returning to his home in Maine, he decided to move to Minnesota, where he engaged in wheat farming. It was there that he and Florilla Heal, also from Lincolnville, were married. While in Minnesota they had eight children, five of whom died in early childhood.

In 1883 the family moved to Cathlamet, Washington, living there for five years before coming to South Riverside. Mr. Shepherd died in 1921, and was survived by Florilla, two daughters: Mrs. Winnie Riddell and Grace Shepherd Tuthill, and several grandchildren.

THE R. F. BILLINGS FAMILY

One of those coming to South Riverside because of failing health was R. F. Billings, who moved to the colony shortly after it was founded. Recovering his health, he became a prominent member of Corona's business community for over twenty years. His obituary in the *Corona Daily Independent* tells of his establishment in town:

"...he passed through all the struggles of the formation of a new colony and knew better than most of the old residents here what vicissitudes meant...When the town was very small and the business houses might have been counted on one hand, Mr. Billings engaged in the drug business."

Billings, born in Rutland, Vermont in March of 1854, spent his early years in Kingston, Wisconsin. After he and Virginia were married they moved to Cedar Rapids, Iowa, where he went into the pharmaceutical business. They soon moved to Mankato, Minnesota, where he opened a new drug store. It was at this point that the doctor recommended that he move to the healthier climate of Southern California. After arriving in South Riverside, Billings opened a drug store with a partner, William F. Lilly. After Mr. Lilly died, Billings maintained the firm by himself for 20 years, passing it to his son, Sumner. Billings died 1907 from a heart attack while on a hunting trip in Temescal Canyon at the age of 53 years, 10 months, and five days.

(Above) L. H. Ware's crew from the Corona Lumber Company poses for a photograph in 1902. *Courtesy Heritage Room, Corona Public Library*

(Left) The Corona Lumber Company. *Courtesy Heritage Room, Corona Public Library*

GENERAL AND MRS. DERIUS ABNER ALDEN

An account of the fiftieth wedding anniversary of:

General Derius Abner and Emilie Alden, who retired in Corona after spending many years traveling with various circuses. They claimed to be the world's smallest perfectly formed couple. He was four feet tall and she was three feet, ten inches. The couple could be seen regularly about town in their miniature buggy, pulled by a Shetland pony. Tradition says that, while they lived in a regular house (212 W. Tenth St.), the furniture inside was miniature in size.

Born in 1842 in Medina, Ohio, Alden spent his childhood in Binghampton, New York. The *Corona Courier* reported that when Alden left Binghampton to meet P. T. Barnum, his friends had a special suit and stove pipe hat made for him. When he got to New York, Barnum was waiting for him on the station platform. Alden was only 18 inches tall at the time. When Barnum saw him, he picked him up and carried him out of the station. It was clear that Alden had been given a job with P.T. Barmun's circus. While he

was with the circus he also learned and performed the art of glass blowing.

Besides traveling with the circus for many years, General Alden is said to have served in the secret service during the Civil War. He reported directly to President Lincoln regarding the supplies being shipped to the Confederacy from Europe. He considered Lincoln a good friend and was severely saddened by his death.

The Aldens, who were married in Millport, New York. in 1871, moved to Corona soon after the turn of the century. He died at the age of 84 in 1926, and Emilie, who was born in Redwing, Minnesota,

in 1853, died in 1928 at the age of 75. They had no children, but had many friends in town.

―――――――――――――――――

HARRY V. UNWIN LOST AT SEA

From his obituary:

The trip by steamer from the West Coast to the East Coast through the Panama Canal was often fraught with danger. Harry V. Unwin, on his way from the port at San Francisco to New York, boarded the *Colima* in the early 1890s. The ill-fated ship was wrecked on a reef and went to the bottom of the ocean in over 400 fathoms of water, some 50 miles southeast of Manzanillo, Mexico. Twenty-six passengers

survived while 188 were lost. Unwin's body was never found.

SURPRISE TENDERED TWO POPULAR YOUNG PEOPLE

This newspaper clipping describes a surprise party:

"One Thursday night about two dozen of the young people of our town took it into their heads to have a little bit of fun by giving Mr. Vernie and Miss Ocie Taylor a surprise party by the assistance of Mrs. Taylor and Mrs. Charles Lord. Ollie Baer was selected as chief engineer to invite the guests. At just eight o'clock the door bell rang while Master Harry was making a little fun for the old folks in the parlor and Miss Ocie was fixing to retire for the night, and Vernie was down town, ignorant of what was going on at home.

"Mrs. Taylor answered the summons of the bell, when Miss Ocie said, 'Oh, it is only Vernie.' When Mrs. Taylor opened the door, in marched a score of more of young ladies and gentlemen, and you would have laughed to see Miss Ocie throw up her bands and say, 'my, did you ever!'

"Vernie found out when he was downtown that all of his friends had gone to his house. When he came home, he sneaked up the back stairway so he could change his clothes, then rushed downstairs to welcome his guests. The young people played games, visited, and had refreshments."

JUDGE BENJAMIN J. RICHE

From his obituary we learn about:

"Judge Riche, South Riverside's first elected Justice of the Peace. He was born in Harrison County, Ohio in 1934. When he was 17 he struck out for the California gold country. In 1873, he married Maggie McEwen in Merced. They moved to South Riverside in 1886, becoming two of the first settlers. Judge Riche served as Justice of the Peace until his death in 1894, and was known for his wise and practical opinions. His obituary

notes that he was "a staunch democrat, a good citizen, honorable in his dealings, a devoted husband, and a warm friend."

W. G. WALL

Mr. W. G. Wall according to his obituary, was one of those pioneers who moved back and forth across the country frequently. He first came to California in 1849, at the start of the gold rush. He returned to Missouri the following year and again came to the West Coast in 1852. He then spent 15 years in Colorado before coming back to California moving to South Riverside in 1886, when the town was only a few months old. He died of an enlarged liver at the age of 67 years, two months and 8 days.

Some of the stories in Ocie's Treasures are sad, while others reflect joyful events. For more stories 1book lovinglty preserved in the Heritage Room.

The inviting gateway to Lemonia Grove, developed by Oscar Thieme in 1893, led to a cornucopia of rare trees, plants, and flowers planned to mimic the gardens of his European homeland. He built a two-story Victorian carriage house and a packing house. *Courtesy Heritage Room, Corona Public Library*

CORONA BECOMES THE LEMON CAPITAL OF THE WORLD

The lemon, a sour oval-shaped yellow citrus fruit, was a major factor in the survival and success of Corona. By the turn of the century, more than 3,500 acres of lemon and orange trees

killed in a train wreck, his estate included 350 acres and packing house.

The Corona Foothill Lemon Company, founded by S. B. Hampton in 1911, was one of the largest locally owned citrus ranches in the area. The original plantings covered 900 acres. After Hampton died during the terrible influenza epidemic of 1918, his son, Lester, ran the company. Robert Willits, the brother of Nora Hampton, eventually became the president of the Foothill Lemon Company. His son, Ned Willits, after graduating from the University of Colorado, spending time in the U. S. Navy, and working in Boston, returned to Corona to help his ailing father in the citrus business. Under his leadership, the Corona Foothill Lemon Company expanded by developing ranches in the Eagle and Coachella Valleys. He, along with his partner,

stretched to the south of the circle. Sixty-two percent of the citrus trees in Riverside County were in the Corona area. Corona, in 1913, was the largest shipping point for lemons in the United States.

Of the several varieties of lemons tried, three stood out as the most profitable locally — the Lisbon, the Eureka, and the Villa Franka. Sixty-five percent of the trees in the 1910s were Lisbons. Lisbons could be picked year round and sent to the packing house for curing, storage, and packing. Where the standard orange grove in Orange County ran from 20 to 40 acres, many of Corona's orchards covered from 100 to 300 acres. One of the largest ranchs, 240 acres, was owned by A. F. Call and was located in the Orange Heights tract, in the hills above the city of Corona. The secret of the ranch's success was its location. Because warm air rises, the higher elevation was protected by the warm air currents from frost, fogs, and scale. Palms, cypress, and olive trees bordered the groves, creating a paradise of green, gold, and orange. The Call Ranch had its own packing house with lemon curing rooms, orange and lemon packing spaces, and a box factory. Formerly a lawyer, Call was often sent from Corona to Washington, D. C. to represent the local citrus industry. When A. F. Call was tragically

Reservoir in course of construction at Ben White's Foothill Corona Ranch, Corona, Cal.

Crawford Teague, developed the community of Canyon Lake near Elsinore and the 450-acre housing tract in West Corona called Village Grove.

The Wild Rose Ranch was located just beyond El Cerrito's Weirick Road. One of the earliest citrus ranches in the area, it included a beautiful oak grove called Wild Rose Park. In a July 4, 1889 newspaper article, Miss Alfaretta Wood described her plans for the planting of the Wild Rose Ranch:

"...about two weeks ago 2 finished planting 1,700 four-year-old orange trees at the ranch....and 150 deciduous trees. Upon the ranch 2 now have 1,000 strawberry plants growing and about the same number of blackberry and raspberry bushes, and was rooting 33,000 muscat grape vines on the South Riverside Ranch, to be planted next season at Wild Rose Park. The present season 2 raised and have now secured about 70 tons of bald barley hay. 2 have over 70 stands of bees, and the crop of honey is only half of what it was last year, which was then two tons....Miss Wood gave the entire work her personal supervision, and was assisted by her father, W. B. Wood and two laborers."

After being purchased by the Earl family, the ranch produced Valencia oranges, and packed its fruit under the Queen Bee label. The Earls also raised horses and mules. Eventually, the property was combined with the Dawson and Baldauf Ranches, making a total of 850 acres under the name of the Wild Rose Ranch.

The famed El Cerrito Ranch, founded by J. H. Flagler of New York City, had 125 acres planted to lemons and 30 acres planted to Navel oranges. The ranch was to become the future site of the community of El Cerrito.

Some ranchers, including Ben White, had a variety of crops on their ranches. Of the 138 acres owned by White, 22 acres were given to navel oranges, 38 acres to lemons, and the rest to grain and alfalfa. The Whites had a beautiful view from their home on a knoll at the top of Main Street. When Mr. White was considering the acquisition of the property, people discouraged him by telling him that there was not enough available water. However, he went ahead with the purchase and soon found water in abundance at 28 feet below the surface.

Alfalfa and dairying were the main crops of the C. E. Lillibridge Ranch. Lillibridge came to the South Riverside area in 1892 and immediately purchased land northwest of town. Most of his 42-acre ranch was devoted to the raising of alfalfa. An advantage to the planting of alfalfa in Southern

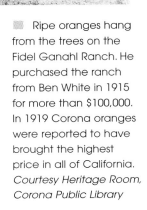

Ripe oranges hang from the trees on the Fidel Ganahl Ranch. He purchased the ranch from Ben White in 1915 for more than $100,000. In 1919 Corona oranges were reported to have brought the highest price in all of California. *Courtesy Heritage Room, Corona Public Library*

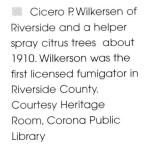

Cicero P. Wilkersen of Riverside and a helper spray citrus trees about 1910. Wilkerson was the first licensed fumigator in Riverside County. Courtesy Heritage Room, Corona Public Library

The Flagler Citrus Packing Company was one of many packing houses active in the Corona area. It was located where El Cerrito Ranch is now located and packed the fruit from Flagler's El Cerrito Ranch. *Courtesy Heritage Room, Corona Public Library*

California was the opportunity to harvest six or seven cuttings per growing season. In 1909, he sold his alfalfa for $14.50 a ton. Lillibridge also kept approximately 50 milk cows. He also sold fertilizer from an obvious source — the cows. Besides the cattle he had around 30 hogs and 25 to 50 calves.

Lemonia Grove, though not particularly large at 26 acres, provides a sad and romantic tale. Oscar Thieme, a native of Germany, purchased a sheep pasture on the corner of Rimpau and Chase in 1893. After planting in lemons, he built a large two-story Victorian carriage house in which to live after his new bride came from Germany. Lemonia Grove became famous for the beautiful gardens, ornamental shrubs, flowering vines, rare tree specimens, and flower beds planted by Thieme.

The 1906 San Francisco earthquake put an end to Thieme's hope of building a large house at Lemonia Grove. The earthquake wiped out all of the couple's investments there, ruining them financially. Additionally, their firstborn son died of accidental suffocation. In great sadness, they went back to Germany to stay forever.

William Henry Jameson bought the property, allowing then to leave as soon as possible. In the 1920s the packing house at Lemonia Grove was turned into a vacation home for Dr. Eloise Jameson. During World War II, her sister, Adelaide, became the first person to live full time in Lemonia Grove.

Mentioned above are only a few of the groves and ranches located in the rich agricultural lands surrounding Corona. It was the ranches that supported the town and caused it to grow and prosper from the 1890s into the 1980s.

The Queen Colony Packing House, one of Corona's early citrus packing facilities employed both men and women. This photo was taken about 1900. *Courtesy Heritage Room, Corona Public Library*

Chapter 4

The 1910s — Corona Comes Of Age

CORONA GETS A FINE NEO-CLASSICAL LIBRARY

As was typical of many fledgling California communities, South Riverside's first library began its life on a few shelves in a storefront building. Begun by the Woman's Christian Temperance Union (WCTU) in 1893, the library was funded by a hardworking group of women with a vision. To raise the money to buy the first books, they created handmade items and sold them at bazaars and fairs. For almost three years, the ladies of the WCTU ran the library successfully, with Dr. Flora Gleason serving as president and Miss Helen Jewell as secretary of the reading room committee.

In the early spring of 1895, a provisional YMCA was organized and agreed to take over the project. However, the men's enthusiasm did not last very long, and the reading room was almost abandoned. After a small Parmalee library was donated to the collection, William Corkhill, who felt that the library was very important to the community, volunteered to become the new manager. He succeeded in raising the number of books to 200.

On June 1, 1896, the library was first opened to the public. Mr. Corkhill was able to keep the room open two or three evenings a week. Approximately 1,200 books were lent out during that first year. However, by the end of 1897, budgetary problems made the outlook for the future of the library gloomy. Even after C. B. Webster, A. L. Taber and W. A. Wheeler joined Mr. Corkhill in an effort to keep the library open, the room had to be closed because of insufficient funding.

The Town Improvement Association, the library committee of the Corona Woman's Club, was the next organization to try its hand at maintaining library services for the public. The grand opening of the new library, located in a storefront on South Main Street, occurred on April 23, 1899. Bowers of roses decorated the room and ice cream was served. Guests were asked to donate a book or money as the price of admission. For the next couple of years, individual Woman's Improvement Club members helped pay for the costs of running the library and asked for outside subscriptions to provide the needed additional monies.

As the usage and number of volumes increased, the idea of the City taking over the library was discussed. In 1900 a petition asking that a public library be instituted was presented to the City Council by a group of concerned citizens. Placed on the ballot, the proposition was passed by the voters, and the first Board of Trustees elected. Serving on the first board were: S. S. Willard, T. C. Jameson, G. R. Freeman, F. M. Baldwin and F. F. Thompson. Miss Grace Taber was selected to serve as the librarian for the new library located in two rented rooms on the second floor of the bank building. Book circulation increased to 2,657 volumes in 1901. Miss Taber served as librarian until 1916, when she moved to San Diego.

The need for a permanent library building was identified officially in 1902 when the trustees applied to the Carnegie Foundation for a $10,000 grant to build a facility. The first request produced no results.

The story differs from this point as to the involvement of W. H. Jameson and J. H. Flagler. William Corkhill, in a posthumous article printed in the *Corona Daily Independent* (May 4, 1961), says that Jameson and Flagler were instrumental in obtaining the first $10,000 while other accounts say that Flagler, a close friend of Andrew Carnegie, was responsible for receiving the extra $1,500 needed to complete the project. However, there is no doubt that Jameson and Flagler were instrumental in seeing that the truly beautiful Neo-classical library building that was to serve the community for over sixty

As the automobile became more popular, Downtown Corona had its share of auto sales companies. *Courtesy Heritage Room, Corona Public Library*

(Opening Photo) The propietor of a cigar store on Sixth Street in Downtown Corona waits for the next customer. *Courtesy Heritage Room, Corona Public Library*

(Previous Page) Corona's grand Neo-classical Public Library, designed by architect Franklin Pierce Bunham of Los Angeles, was built with grant money from Andrew Carnegie. costing $11,500 to build and furnish, the library held its grand opening on July 2, 1906. *Courtesy Heritage Room, Corona Public Library*

years became a reality. After making the application in proper form, the library trustees received a letter stating the terms of the agreement. In exchange for the $10,000 grant, the city was to provide the lot and promise that 10 percent of the sum donated would be raised each year by taxation and used for maintenance of the property. The City quickly bought the quarter block on the southeast corner of Eighth and Main as the site for the new library.

The architect, Franklin Pierce Bunham of Los Angeles, designed a stately Neo-classical building with a grand entrance crowned by an ornate Romanesque pediment supported by pairs of round fluted Greek-inspired columns. Plans specified that cream-colored face brick made by the Corona Pressed Brick Company would cover most of the exterior. Red pressed brick, stone and concrete formed the contrast and decoration for the outside. S. L. Bloom of Corona submitted the lowest construction bid of $9,897. It soon was discovered that an additional $1,500 would be needed to complete the project. Jameson and Flagler are said to have prevailed upon Carnegie to grant the extra funding. The following letter was received by the board:

December 27, 1905
Dr. S. S. Willard, President
Public Library
Corona, California

Dear Sir:
Responding to your request of December 19, Mr. Carnegie will be glad to increase the allowance made for Library Building at Corona from ten thousand dollars to eleven thousand five hundred dollars, provided the City's Council makes a corresponding increase in the guaranteed fund for maintenance.

Respectfully yours,
Jas. Bertram, P. Secy.

On a balmy evening, July 2, 1906, the library celebrated its grand opening. The Woman's Improvement Club, responsible for the event, filled the rooms with flowers and served refreshments. The Corona City Band opened the evening's program with three selections played on the front steps. Next the rousing sound of a cornet quartet could be heard coming from the entry hall. Finally, a chorus from the Tuesday Musical Club sang a difficult composition by Sullivan entitled "The Long Day Closes". The group urged to

provide an encore, next sang "There Were Two Flies". At that point the doors were thrown open and the guests entered the building for the first time. The *Corona Courier* described the building as follows:

"It is a square massive building of Grecian type built of cream colored brick. Two massive doric columns guard either side of the entrance as sentinels protecting some great treasure. On entering the building one must pass through a small vestibule, the walls of which are concave and done in the most beautiful Vienna lake red, while the cabinet work is of Flemish stain as is the finish of the woodwork throughout the building."

William Corkhill is reported to have said, "I venture to say, that of all the buildings donated by Mr. Carnegie, few, if any can outshine the Corona Public Library."

A NEW NEO-CLASSICAL HIGH SCHOOL BUILDING

Corona Senior High School built in 1906-1908, at the cost of $35,000, represented Corona's strong commitment to education. The stately Neo-classical style of architecture so popular for public buildings during the first quarter of the 20th century was used to design the new three-story senior high school on South Main and Grand Boulevard. Important civic buildings and banks were often built in this style because it

represented strength, respect, culture, knowledge and solidarity. Frequently using the exact same patterns as the ancient Greeks and Romans did in the past, such buildings are impressive and have the appearance of having existed forever. Entered by wide steps centered below a prominent classically-designed, heavily-ornamented pediment, the building was similar in design to the Carnegie Library. Four years later, another Neo-classical building, the City Hall would be built across Eighth Street from the Carnegie Library. The students were dwarfed by the six huge two-story high Greek columns topped with Ionic capitals. Corona students must have been very proud of their new school.

CORONA'S MAGNIFICENT NEW CITY HALL

On Tuesday morning, October 28, 1912, City dignitaries gathered at a solemn ceremony to seal the copper box for posterity in the corner stone of the new city hall. Construction of the building had begun a few months earlier on August 26. The grand Neo-classical building was completed on March 18, 1913 and accepted by the City Trustees. Matching the architecture of the Carnegie Library and the High School, the building was two stories plus a basement, with a prominent pedimented gable and four two-story high classical columns forming the entrance. Ten broad steps flanked by wide piers and ornamental lights led to the double front doors. Norman F. Marsh of Los Angeles was the architect and F. M. Walton and Son were the contractors.

The need for a new city hall had been obvious to Corona for several years. In August of 1905, the *Corona Courier* reports that Councilman Corkhill

Built in 1906, Corona's impressive Senior High School, was one of the most beautiful Neo-classical school building in the Southland. Six massive columns, supporting a decorative pediment, guarded the entrance to the building. *Courtesy Heritage Room, Corona Public Library*

brought up the idea of purchasing four city lots next to the old city hall for the purpose of the "substitution of a grand and imposing structure for the little 'cooped up' rickety place now staggering under the dignifying appellation of 'City Hall'." Councilman Corkhill was appointed head of the committee to investigate the purchase of the lots.In October of the same year the Board of Trade (Chamber of Commerce) recommended the same action to the city fathers.

By adding the four 25 foot-wide lots to the two already owned by the City, the new city hall could occupy six lots on the corner of East Eighth and South Main Streets. Dr. Willard, the head of the Board of Trade City Hall Committee reported that the committee had secured agreements for the sale of all four lots. Daniel Lord owned one lot; Peter Provensal one lot; and W. H. Jameson two lots. Jameson was to receive $1,300, Provensal $500 and Lord $650. Each property owner received a $100 down payment. However, it was 1911 before any real action was taken to build the new city hall.

In the March 10, 1911 edition of the *Corona Courier*, the following was written:

"A few weeks ago the committee from the Corona Chamber of Commerce composed of C. H. Hoss, E. L. Sparr and R. D. Lamson, selected to investigate the building of a new city hall for Corona, began its labors and only yesterday was the committee rewarded in its initial work by receiving the plans for the new building which is bound to be built within the very near future."

These preliminary plans were in the form of a draft coming from the architect Norman F. Marsh of Los Angeles who noted:

"The building as shown in the draft will be two stories high, built of pressed brick and stone and will contain the offices of the city officers as well as the magnificent council rooms on the upper floor. On the ground floor in the rear of

the building there will be interior cells for offenders waiting trial."

In the fall of 1911 Corona residents voted for bonds amounting to $135,000. With this money the funding for the acquisition of land for the city park, a new fire truck, the extension of Sixth Street and the building of the City Hall were made possible.

There appears to have been plenty of enthusiasm for the long-awaited project because the City moved somewhat rapidly with the plans

Corona's grand Neo-classical City Hall, was completed on March 18, 1913, and located on the corner of East 8th and Main streets, across from the Carnegie Library. Norman F. Marsh was the architect. *Courtesy Heritage Room, Corona Public Library*

and was able to lay the cornerstone a little more than a year after the preliminary plans were presented.

Moving to the new building in March of 1913, were H. H. Homes, Mayor of the City (president of the trustees) F. J. Mueller, E. A. Stobbs, Edward Davis and A. H. Cross as trustees. Mason Terpening was city clerk, John L. Merriam, treasurer; G. C. Alexander, marshal; G. R. Freeman, attorney; O. P. Hull, recorder; A. B. Tuthill, superintendent of streets; Dr. W. H. Cahman, health officer; C. Gully, engineer; W. J.

Pentellow, tree warden and B. E. Savery, building inspector.

In the December 10, 1962 edition of the *Corona Daily Independent*, Dell Ridpath notes that "Their castles in the air had materialized into a magnificent building from which the city fathers for 50 years fended off the duels of dissent and dodging the stones of mistrust."

The Lord Building on the corner of 7th and Main streets was built by Daniel Lord in 1911.
Courtesy Heritage Room, Corona Public Library

THE VIEW FROM THE TURRET

Daniel Lord built the elegant building shown below in 1911. It had a dramatic turret that overlooked Downtown Corona. Leo Kroonen, who built many of the finest buildings in Corona, was the builder. A general store was located on the first floor and the second floor was occupied by rental rooms.

Can you imagine what a lovely view you would have had if you were lucky enough to have the room with the tower? In those days, buildings had character and individuality. As Corona grew, the first wooden business buildings were replaced by two and three story structures made of brick. Ornate classical details such as carved brackets, decorative banding, dentil trim, arched windows and round turrets added drama and character to the buildings.

A DAY OF SHOPPING IN DOWNTOWN CORONA

The typical Corona housewife had eight grocery and provision stores, two drug stores, three modern up-to-date dry goods stores, three meat markets, two bakeries, four fruit and confectionery stores, two furniture stores and three jewelry stores in which to shop. Her husband had his choice of five gentlemen's clothing stores and two well-stocked hardware and implement stores at his disposal. In addition, a combination photography studio and mortuary was located on the west side of South Main Street. For those needing building supplies, there were two large lumber yards, a planing mill and three plumbing shops. There were three livery stables, two harness shops and five blacksmith shops for those who had horses as well as a bicycle shop for those indulging in that popular activity.

The first automobile showrooms created a good deal of interest. When Mr. and Mrs. S. U. Graham moved to town in 1913, they opened a new dealership featuring the "Automobile of Mystery." It turned out to be a Dodge.

New brick buildings were replacing the wooden storefronts on a constant basis and the commercial center of Corona was expanding into the surrounding neighborhoods. Farmers, ranchers and canyon dwellers from miles around came to Corona to shop.

Livery stables and blacksmith shops played an important role in the lives of the turn-of-the-century citizen. Those living in town often depended upon the livery stable to keep their horse to rent them a horse and buggy when they needed it. Visitors coming to Corona by train would walk to the livery stable to rent a rig. Blacksmiths not only shoed horses, but also repaired wagons and buggies. *Courtesy Heritage Room, Corona Public Library*

DOWNTOWN CORONA, A GREAT PLACE TO SHOP

500 BLOCK SOUTH MAIN ST.
1. 508 - Laundry/office
2. 510 - Furniture Store
3. 512 - Meat Market
4. 514 - Barber
5. 514 1/2 - Brown and Granson
    Grain and Produce
6. 516 - Pool Hall and Bowling
7. 518 - Barber
8. 518 1/2 - Pool Hall
9. 520 - Grain and Fuel
10. 522 -Groceries
11. 524 - First National Bank

WEST SIXTH STREET
12. 111 E. Sixth - Harness Shop
13. 112 E. Sixth - Electric Plating

PHILLIPS BLOCK
(SOUTHERN HOTEL 2ND FLOOR)
14. 602 - Corona National Bank
15. 604 - Groceries
16. 606 - McGillvray Hardware, Paints, Oils
17. 608 - Gallery
18. 610 - Millinery (women's hats)
19. 612 - Pool Room
21 614 - Drug Store (1st)
22. 614 1/2 - Lodge Hall (2nd floor)
23. 618 - Corona Cash Store
24. 620 - Furniture Store
25. 622 - Millinery and Dry Goods
26. 624 - Groceries

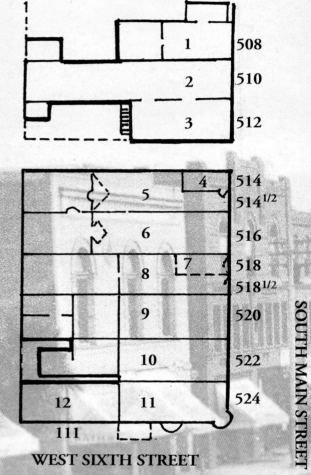

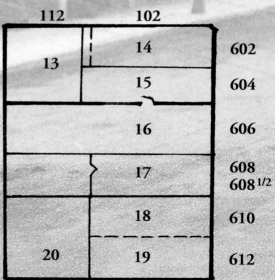

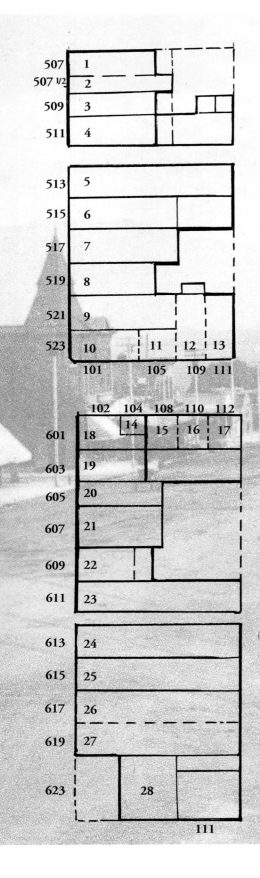

500 BLOCK SOUTH MAIN ST.
1. 507 - General Store
2. 507 1/2 - Bakery
3. 509 - Restaurant
4. 511 - Billiards
5. 513 - General Store
6. 515 - Harness Shop
7. 517 - General Store
8. 519 - General Store
9. 521 - Drug Store
10. 523 - Cigars and Confectionaries

EAST SIXTH ST.
11. 105 - Cigar factory
12. 109 - Barber and baths
13. 111 - Offices
14. 104 - Jewelry
15. 108 - Offices
16. 110 - Cigars
17. 112 - Restaurant

600 BLOCK SOUTH MAIN ST.
18. 601 - Corona Cash Market-meats
19. 603 - Billings Drug and Stationary
20. 605 - Cigars and Fruit
21. 607 - General Store
22. 609 - Groceries and Fruit
23. 611 - Corona Post Office
24. 613 - Corona City Bakery
25. 615 - Moving Pictures
26. 617 - General Store
27. 619 - Candy
28. 623 - Agricultural Implements

CORONA, A TOWN THAT GLOWS WITH HEALTH

The climate and abundance of healthful fresh food was given lots of credit for the health of its residents. An article in the *Corona Daily Independent* pointed out:

"It must be true that many people eat more in Corona than in their former place of residence because the climactic conditions are admittedly more healthful. We could name many who came to Corona sick and unable to eat and have become healthy and strong."

The stores opened early and stayed open late. Drummers sample trucks caused crowds to gather. The statement above gives the town credit for the residents' large appetites.

In 1915, fruits and vegetables in season were plentiful. Examples of some of the prices for fresh produce were listed in the *Corona Daily Independent* as:

Blackberries	4 cents a box
Strawberries	4 cents a box
Cabbage	5 cents a head
Celery	5 cents a bunch
Carrots	5 cents a bunch
Fresh figs	7 cents per pound
Apricots	3 cents per pound
Grapes	4 cents per pound
Pears	4 cents per pound
Summer squash	3 cents per pound
Lima beans	8 cents per pound
Tomatoes	3 cents per pound
String beans	5 cents per pound
Peaches	3 cents per pound
Cherries	10 cents per pound
Apples	4 cents per pound
Peas	5 cents per pound
Cantaloupes	5 cents each
Watermelons	15 cents each
Cauliflower	10 cents each
Lemons	10 cents a dozen
Oranges	15 cents a dozen
Grapefruit	50 cents a dozen
Sweet corn	25 cents a dozen
Artichokes	50 cents a dozen
Cucumbers	20 cents a dozen
Lettuce	25 cents a dozen

The wide variety of fruits and vegetables available must have helped those who came to Corona because of illness to recover their healthful glow quickly.

In addition, year round outdoor activities such as picnics and hayrides were popular forms of relaxation. The swimming pool and baths at Glen Ivy Hot Springs were pleasant gathering places in hot weather.

THE FASHIONABLE DEL REY HOTEL GAINS A THIRD STORY—FROM THE BOTTOM

In 1909, Corona was much in need of hotel accommodations. The Del Rey Hotel, located at 224 East Sixth Street, was the only one listed in

the 1913 City Directory. On April 13, 1909, Manager J. D. Sutherland announced in the *Corona Courier* that the hotel would be jacked up several feet to allow for a new first floor to be constructed. A new entrance, office, "commodious lobby", lavatory, and dining room were scheduled to occupy the new quarters. Also on the first floor would be a sample storage room for the convenience of traveling salesmen. The second and third floors were given over entirely to bedrooms. Each was fitted with a sink which featured both hot and cold running water and a new bell service. Five bedrooms would be provided with private baths.

F. G. Richmond of Riverside was in charge of raising the building. The Phillips Manufacturing Co. of Los Angeles installed a new and thoroughly modern heating system, guaranteeing a perfectly heated house throughout. The carpenter was H. Patrick and the Corona Hardware and Implement Co. was in charge of the new plumbing. The improvements cost approximately $5,000.

The Del Rey was also known for its good food and spacious dining room. Many special events, parties, and celebrations were held there.

CORONA'S PACKING HOUSES AND MANUFACTURING PLANTS

California lands for wealth
California fruit for health
    Sunset Magazine-Homeseeker's Bureau, 1913

By the turn of the century the orange and lemon trees planted in the late 1880s and early 1890s were mature enough to produce impressive crops of fruit. Eight packing houses were engaged in the processing and shipping of large amounts of Corona citrus. Over 120,000 square feet of packing house space was in use by 1909. A few years later in 1913, the number of packing houses had increased to 11 with over 300,000 square feet involved in the processing, curing and storing of citrus fruit. The largest packing house at that time was the Sunset Fruit Company, packers for the Queen Colony Fruit Exchange. Over 40,000 square feet of space on two floors was in use for the curing and sorting of lemons. Frank Scoville, secretary and general manager for the Exchange, also owned the building along with George Brown and T. P. Drinkwater.

W. H. Jameson, one of Corona's most influential pioneers, processed his own fruit at an 11,000 square-foot plant across the railroad track from the Sunset Fruit Company. His fruit was also marketed by the Queen Colony Fruit Exchange which had offices at 118 E. Sixth Street.

The Call fruit Company, owned by A. F. Call, one of Corona's most influential grove owners, erected a 10,500-square-foot plant to process the fruit harvested from the extensive groves owned by Mr. Call.

The Fay Fruit Company, owned by Frank Scoville, T. P. Drinkwater and Mason Terpenning, operated out of its two-story 16,000 square-foot plant. The packing house had a basement for fruit storage, an elevator and its own electric light and power plant.

George Turner managed the Boston and South Riverside Company's packing house with the assistance of J. Fred Howarth. The 10,500-square-foot plant was used exclusively to pack fruit from the groves owned by the Boston and South Riverside Company which had its headquarters in Boston and St. Louis, Missouri.

J. H. Flagler, who owned the El Cerrito Ranch a short distance south of town, built a 9,500-

(Previous Spread) Looking north on Main, Downtown Corona in 1908. The tower in the background is the Citizens National Bank building. Even further in the distance are the Norco Hills. *Courtesy Marsh Collection*

The Hotel Del Rey shown on this postcard in 1913, was originally two stories high. In early 1913 the manager, J. D. Sutherland, had the building jacked up and a third story built on the ground floor to provide for a large lobby, dining room, and entrance. *Courtesy Heritage Room, Corona Public Library*

square-foot packing house to handle his large lemon crop. The Corona Packing Company in its thoroughly equipped 10,000-square-foot plant, held lemons for curing and storage as well as processing. The manager, C. E. Collier, worked with the Spence Fruit Company of Los Angeles to market the high quality lemons.

In 1902, the Corona Lemon Company, owner of 150 acres of lemons, built a 11,000-square-foot packing house for the purpose of handling its own fruit. With a different floor plan than the other houses, the building contained several small curing and storage rooms instead of one or two large rooms. T. P. Drinkwater was the manager for both the grove and the packing house.

CLAY, GRANITE AND FERTILIZER

The Pacific Clay Manufacturing Company, established near Corona in 1887, grew to become one of Southern California's largest clay manufacturing companies. By 1909 it had 11 kilns producing over 1,000 tons of pipe at each setting. A specially built kiln produced pipe that was three feet in diameter — at that time the largest in the state. At the McKnight mine, also near Corona, the company mined the black flint clay that produced the best refractory fire brick on the coast. The bricks were used by the Southern Pacific and Santa Fe railway companies in their oil-burning

locomotives. Other products manufactured by the versatile company included vitrified salt-glazed sewer and water pipe, fire brick, hollow building blocks, terra cotta pipe, electric conduit and irrigation pipe, all produced with clay mined near Corona.

The Sierra Granite Company with headquarters in Corona and a quarry in Temescal Canyon, did a large business in the quarrying and cutting of granite slabs for building and monumental purposes. In the 1910s, street paving blocks and curbing provided much of their business. The Standard Fertilizing Company located near the Santa Fe tracks, to the west of Main Street, manufactured and shipped a large number of carloads of high quality fertilizer to all parts of Southern California.

The Alberhill Coal and Clay Company was organized in 1882 to work the coal beds located south of Corona, and continued to do so until 1895. At that time, the company converted to the mining of high grade clay, supplying clay to several companies. Among them was the Los Angeles Pressed Brick Company where Alexander Robertson, a well-known potter, created his works. In 1912, James Hill, the owner of Alberhill Coal, asked Robertson to experiment with Alberhill clays. Robertson produced many finely crafted examples of clay pottery and won the Gold Medal at the San Diego Exposition. Sadly, in 1914, a lawsuit involving the Alberhill Coal and Clay Company and the Los Angeles Pressed Brick Company versus the State of California became the company's focus. Plans for potter production was put on hold. The gifted Robertson left the company in late 1914. His beautifully crafted vases are very rare and today bring a very high price.

In 1916, the Temescal Rock Company built a huge rock crushing plant in Temescal Canyon to process porphyry — a rock used extensively for road construction. By 1920, the plant was owned by the Blue Diamond Plaster Company.

All of the above companies contributed a major boost to the early 20th century economy of Corona by providing jobs and paychecks to the people who shopped in the stores, bought the houses, paid taxes, invested in property and supported the growing city in many ways.

OIL

Were there ever oil wells in Corona? In July of 1913, Ben White of Corona and Los Angeles reportedly struck oil in Temescal Canyon about 12 miles south of Corona. The well was never brought into production, however, nine years later, the Rugby Oil Company drilled a well approximately two miles closer to town but nothing came of the project either. Even though there were people who thought there might be oil in the Temescal Canyon, it has never been developed.

There was some success with oil wells in the Chino Hills area, north of Corona. The Chino-Corona United Oil Well No. 1 was established on the Newman property.

WATER — THE KING OF SOUTHERN CALIFORNIA

Water is king in Southern California. Corona could not have survived if it had not been for the ample water supply. Still, it required constant ingenuity on the part of the town founders and ranchers to keep the water flowing.

At first, Corona had the valuable resources from the Temescal Valley and the town wells. When that source began to dwindle, the Temescal Water Company bought Lake Elsinore and built a dam at Lee Lake. Unfortunately, the water in the lake turned out to have too much alkaline for agricultural uses.

In 1901 the Temescal Water Company spent $500,000 to develop a source of water at Ethanac in Perris Valley. The company purchased 3,500 acres of water bearing lands and drilled 12 wells. Four pumping stations brought the water to the surface and sent it on its way toward Corona. From Ethanac, at an elevation of about 700 feet above the town, the cement conduit ran 31 miles through rough country, along the rocky bed of the San Jacinto River to the Temescal Valley. The pipeline cost $218,000. The water supply for both irrigation purposes and domestic water needs was greatly improved. The collecting lines in the Temescal Valley from Mayhew and Coldwater Canyons, Warm Springs and other

The Graham family ranch, shown here about 1910, raised alfalfa and other grains. It was one of several farms located northwest of Corona. The windmill in the background denotes the location of the well. *Courtesy Heritage Room, Corona Public Library*

streams amounted to several miles of steel and vitrified pile. After the water reached the groves along the mesa, there were 59 miles of distributing pipe lines. The total cost of all of the pipe lines, tunnels, ditches, headgates and other components of the system was $532,296.78. As a result of this elaborate system, many of the older groves began producing at a better rate and thousands of new citrus trees were planted.

The word "Ethanac" was a contraction of the name Ethan (Allen) C(hase), the owner of the Chase Nursery Company of Riverside and Corona. The purchase of the Perris water lands included the large holdings of the Chase Nursery Company with its modern electric plant. The power plant capacity was soon doubled and a power transmission line was extended 20 miles to Temescal in order to pump water from the wells there. This act enlarged the system to the capacity of irrigating 5,500 acres giving over 6,000 acres of citrus in the Corona area. The water carrying lines give life to the land around Corona, the Queen Colony of Southern California.

Olive orchards were once prevalent in the agriculture area northwest of Corona, in the area where Prado Dam now stands. This photograph was taken at harvest time in 1914. Courtesy Heritage Room, Corona Public Library

ELECTRICITY AND GAS COME TO CORONA

During 1901, electric power from the Ethanac Power Plant built by the Temescal Water Company was extended to Alberhill, Glen Ivy, the Chase plantation and a small portion of Corona.

In 1902, a petition was circulated by the citizens of Corona asking the Board of Trustees to approve bonds in the amount of $20,000 and proceed to construct a municipal electric light and power company. It was not until July of 1903 that a franchise was issued by the Trustees to a group of local citizens to build and maintain the gas and electric plant. Stockholders formed a company called the Corona Gas and Electric Light Company. With the available capital of $50,000, they built a one-story brick building, capped with a high smoke stack on the corner of Railroad and Cota streets. The directors of the company were A. C. Wood as president, W. H. Jameson, Leo Kroonen, G. F. Dean and I. N. Sears. A. C. Miller was the superintendent while Mrs. S. W. Lockett served as secretary.

As a result, on December 22, 1903, the streets of Corona were lit by electricity for the first time. Both gas and electric power were manufactured at the new plant by the use of crude oil brought from the Richfield Oil Company located in the lower Santa Ana Canyon. The eclectic generators were driven by a 125-horsepower Corliss Steam Engine.

TELEGRAPHS AND TELEPHONES

South Riverside's first telegraph system arrived in 1887 when the Santa Fe Railroad was completed from San Bernardino and Riverside. The telegraph office was located in the new depot and was probably operated by the station master.

Actual telephone service began in Corona in 1899, although a line from San Diego to Los Angeles by way of Elsinore and Corona was already in existence. The subsidiary of the Bell Telephone Company was called Pacific Bell Telephone Company. Miss Catherine Fraser operated the first exchange desk from her home and her assistant was thirteen-year-old Paul Palmer. The exchange had 43 subscribers.

By 1905 the Pacific States Telegraph and Telephone Company became the Sunset Telephone Company. That same year in 1905 the contract agency became the Corona Home Telegraph and Telephone Company — the first local independent service. The Bell system couldn't or wouldn't extend long distance service to the local company so a person had to have two phones to receive both local and long distance service. In 1906 Corona was able to connect

with the U. S. Long Distance Telephone Company. By 1909 the Corona Home Telegraph and Telephone Company had 528 subscribers and by 1913 the Corona Union Telephone Company at 116 East Sixth Street was handling both long distance and local calls. All in all, the community had been served by 12 telephone companies in its early years.

SEWERS AND DRAINS

Although a discussion of methods of sanitation, sewers and drains is not the most aesthetic topic to the residents of the community, it was a daily issue. When South Riverside-Corona was first founded and the population was small, outhouses, cesspools and leach lines took care of the problem. As the population grew, the need for an adequate sanitation system became an important matter. In addition, the rain water needed to be channeled so that it would not flood the town during heavy rain storms.

A $30,000 bond election allowing for the beginnings of a sanitation system passed in 1909. Neighborhood groups were required to form sewer assessment districts and pay a share of the costs for installation and maintenance. The drainage lines into the neighborhoods would then be connected to the main lines of the overall system. The bond election also provided for $91,000 to construct the first storm drains. City Ordinance 389 required the construction of a cesspool for any residence outside a sewer district. The property owner either had to join a sewer assessment district or build a cesspool.

It was not until 1922 that the sewer farm was built on land purchased from the Auburndale Colony Lands Company.

Six people examine a new car sitting on Grand Boulevard in 1909. An American flag decorates the front and banners saying 1909 are located on the struts. The man under the car appears to be making repairs. The ladies on the right are wearing hats designed to protect their heads from dust and wind during automobile travel. Courtesy Heritage Room, Corona Public Library

CORONA'S FIRST OFFICIAL FIRE DEPARTMENT

A hose cart, purchased for $130 by the City Trustees in 1898 was the first piece of equipment to be owned by the Fledgling Corona Fire Department. Sixteen volunteers were the backbone of the organization. B. E. Savery was the first fire chief with William Riddel and Fred Connell as assistants. W. A. Wheeler served as secretary. The volunteers were so happy with the purchase of the new equipment that they donated their services to build a fire house in which to keep the hose cart. A short time later, a two-wheeled steel ladder cart built by George Baer helped the firemen reach as high as the second story. A bell was placed on top of the firehouse to call the volunteers when a blaze broke out.

In the October 6, 1939 edition of the *Corona Daily Independent*, Watt Bonfoey explained the system:

"When the fire bell rang, Chief Savery would hop on his bicycle and pedal to the fire house as fast as he could. As soon as the others arrived, they all helped pull the hose cart and ladder carts to the fire. If the fire happened to be located in the downhill part of town, pulling the hose cart wasn't so bad. When it was in the uphill section, it took a deal of huffing and puffing to get to the scene of the fire."

The first big fire was the three-story wooden Hotel Temescal in November of 1899. To make

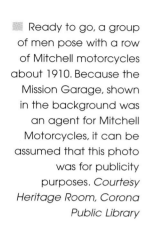

Ready to go, a group of men pose with a row of Mitchell motorcycles about 1910. Because the Mission Garage, shown in the background was an agent for Mitchell Motorcycles, it can be assumed that this photo was for publicity purposes. *Courtesy Heritage Room, Corona Public Library*

matters worse, someone drove over the fire hose, cutting it in half and completely shutting off the supply of water. The building was a total loss but the owners and occupants were able to get much of the furniture on the first two floors out before the fire reached those areas. The second big fire was the Fernandez livery stable

with the city livery stable following close behind. The hay and grain storage in these buildings made the stable fires hard to fight. In 1912 the City bought a Pope-Hartford hose wagon making fire fighting much easier for the volunteers.

1909 - THE PARK TRACT OPENS FOR DEVELOPMENT

In 1909 the headlines of the *Corona Courier* announced the development of the Park Tract, "a beautiful new home section...." 12 and one-half acres in the southeast section of Grand Boulevard, overlooking one of Corona's first parks. It adjoined the property of the Platt sisters to the east. The developers were listed as E. J. Genereaux, Dr. S. S. Willard, E. P. Kidder and George E. Snidecor. They paid $12,000 for the twelve and one-half acres. H. Clay Kellogg who had platted and designed the road system for Corona, was hired to lay out the new subdivision. The newspaper noted that "this quarter of the city is particularly picturesque" — not a tract in the sense of the word as it is used today. The new lots would be sold individually to persons who would then build or have built the home of their choice.

In January of 1909, an announcement regarding the new $12,000 building for the Glass Brothers Hardware Store appeared in the newspaper. The building was described as one of the

"handsomest and substantial structures of the coming business thoroughfare." The 40-foot by 150-foot building would be clad in pressed face brick on the front and feature two storefronts, increasing the size the floor space of the Brothers' hardware business. It was located at 120 East Sixth Street between the Queen Colony Fruit Exchange and the building of the Independent Publishing Company.

A CELEBRITY MOVES TO CORONA

In the January 23rd issue of the *Corona Courier,* the announcement was made that Edward Foley, a leading tenor with the Henry Savage Company of New York, had purchased property in the Stockwell tract on Main Street. After building a new house on two of the lots, he planned to teach music to local students. It was noted that Foley had recently starred in The *Price of Pulzen*, and was in Corona recovering from the strenuous concert work in New York City. He also announced plans to build on the third lot at a later time. By 1913 Mr. Foley is not listed in the City Directory and appears to have no longer lived in Corona.

THE GREAT FLOOD OF 1916

In January of 1916, one of the heaviest rain storms ever experienced in Orange and Riverside

counties sent a solid torrent water down upon the area. Five inches of rain in less than 20 hours, estimated at 30,000 inches of water, caused city streets to flood especially at the north end of town. The Temescal Wash which runs from Temescal Canyon to the south along the east side of town and across the flat land to the north of town became a raging river. The Santa Fe Tracks that ran across the north end of town just north of the Circle were all washed out. The Governor of California, Hiram Johnson, his party and 120 additional passengers were marooned in Corona for three days.

The Temescal Wash has since been tamed and is a mere concrete ditch that runs across town near River Road. Dams in the Temescal area aid greatly in the reduction of the flow of water into Corona.

THE GRAND SWEEPSTAKES PRIZE

In 1911 Corona won the Grand Sweepstakes Prize for the best display of lemons at the National Orange Show. W. J. Pentelow, president of the Chamber of Commerce was in charge of the creation of the display. 1911 was the year in which the Corona Post Office became a Postal Savings Depository allowing the residents to take advantage of the Postal Savings System. On June 15, 1914, Corona was granted free mail delivery with two deliveries per day.

CORONA'S NUMEROUS EARLY VOLUNTEER ORGANIZATIONS

For the first few years, the South Riverside pioneers were too busy establishing the town to think much about the clubs and volunteer organizations they had left behind in their former towns in the midwest and East. Soon they began to found new chapters of the existing organizations. Some of the new groups had a social

background, some a civic focus and some were fraternal aid societies.

THE WOMAN'S IMPROVEMENT CLUB

Since 1899, when the Woman's Improvement Club was founded with a membership of 21, the organization has continued to play an important roll in Corona history. Mrs. Helen Hudson was the first president. The club's motto, selected soon after it was formed is "The world is advancing; advance with it."

Over the years the Woman's Improvement Club has worked to improve many aspects of the city. First called the Town Improvement Association, the group worked to establish a reading room/library in a storefront on South Main Street. After it opened on April 23, 1899, the

The Woman's Improvement Club building, now listed on the National register of Historic Places, was built in 1913 and still serves as the clubhouse for this very civic minded group of women. *Courtesy Heritage Room, Corona Public Library*

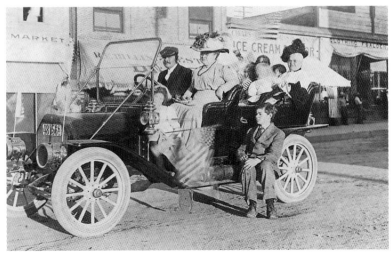

Proud of their new car, Mr. and Mrs. Fred Bairo pose in the front seat in about 1911. Mrs. C. A. Peeler and her grandchildren are in the back seat and Max Biaro is sitting on the running board. *Courtesy Heritage Room, Corona Public Library*

sometimes seen sweeping streets and cleaning up alleys. Teaching school children to sew, raising money to help poor families and lobbying for playground equipment for the local parks were a few of the activities sponsored by the group. In addition, the women worked to establish the preservation and protection of birds and animals.

A Progressive League was founded to provide a forum for political discussions with women's suffrage, one of the most important issues.

Clearly, a group as active as the Woman's Improvement Club needed a building to serve as headquarters for its many activities. With this in mind, Ella Joy donated a choice lot on the corner of South Main and Eleventh streets. With a strong desire to have a building of their own, the members in May of 1911 began collecting the funds for the construction of a clubhouse. After collecting a starting fund of $1,805, the group was able to collect pledges for the remaining $5,000 needed to build their building.

Los Angeles architect Thomas Preston was hired to draw up the plans and R. P. Mussetter was chosen as contractor. The cornerstone was laid on May 31, 1913 and the grand opening reception was held on October 19, 1913.

CORONA'S MANY FINE LODGE ORGANIZATIONS

By 1902 Corona had several active men's and women's group as well as fraternal insurance organizations. The groups are listed here in the order of their founding:

The first lodge to be formed in South Riverside was the Court Circle City, No. 831, Order of Foresters. Organized on June 18, 1891 with 25 members, it gained members rapidly because there were many who desired reliable fraternal insurance.

The International Order of Oddfellows founded its chapter in South Riverside on July 16,

women acted as volunteers in order to keep the library open. Individual members not only sought subscriptions to support the library but also donated their town funds. It was this group that spearheaded the drive to put the proposition to institute a public library system on the ballot.

These intelligent and civic minded women were very serious about improving their community. The newly-formed groups included Street and Sanitation, Finance, Children's Auxiliary, Parks, Humane and Library committees. Along civic lines, the organization worked to beautify the community by preserving and planting trees, maintaining parks and lobbying for such improvements as curfew laws. Members were

1892. Strong support for a lodge hall of their own brought several members to subscribe stock in the Oddfellows Hall Association of Corona. H. H. Holmes was president and J. J. Schliesman was vice president. Their building, with two storefronts on the first floor and a lodge hall and offices on the second floor was dedicated in January of 1903.

In October of 1892, 13 Corona men met for the purpose of founding a Masonic Lodge in Corona. At a session of the Grand Lodge of California one year later, a charter was granted to Temescal Lodge as F. and A. M. No. 314. Orlando Smith, the owner of the Hotel Temescal was the first Worshipful Master. Others who followed during the first few years were P. A. Bennett, 1894-95; C. H. Cornell, 1896; W. C. Barth 1897-99; A. H. Larabee, 1890 and M. Terpening 1901-01. By 1902 the lodge had 60 members.

Almost at the same time the Queen Council No. 100 was organized by Brother Fredericks, a state organizer. The date was April 3, 1893 and William Corkhill was the first president. By 1902 there were 114 beneficiary members and 39 social members.

The Carlton Post No. 168 of the Grand Army of the Republic was also a veteran's group. The chapter, founded in South Riverside about 1895, met monthly.

Next the Corona Lodge No. 33, a fraternal insurance brotherhood was founded in November of 1897. By 1902 there were 64 members carrying in all nearly $100,00 in insurance policies.

The Crown Chapter No. 162, Order of the Eastern Star was instituted in 1898 with 14 charter members. The first Worthy Matron was Laura Alice Currier and the Associate Matron was Kate Flora Scoville. Some of Corona's most prominent families and hardworking residents were members of the Eastern Star.

The Starlight Rebekah Lodge No. 231 was founded on March 5, 1898 and went on to become one of the most progressive lodges in the Seventeenth District. Ms. Lizzie Hendrickson was the first D. D. G. P. and the founding members numbered 13. By 1902 there were 91 members.

On December 12, 1898 the Corona Camp No. 478, Woodmen of the World was chartered. A few year later on February 21, 1901 the Corona Camp No. 9208, Modern Woodmen of America came into being. The first Venerable Council was Neighbor Charles Corkhill. A beneficiary insurance group, the membership met once a month.

The George A. Custer Camp No. 18, Sons of Veterans, was founded in 1900. The organization's mission was to maintain what their fathers had fought for, to preserve their memories forever, to aid the distressed comrades of the Civil War and to see that the graves of the nation's dead were properly decorated on Memorial Day.

Several other organizations were founded during the first 10 years of the 20th century. Included were the Narragansett Tribe No. 169, Internal Order of Red Men which was organized in January 1906 with 29 members. Also founded in 1906, the Corona Aerie No. 1310 had 96 charter members. The Sunnyside Camp No. 81 of the Royal Neighbors came into being on October 31, 1906.

Along with the many church activities including the Ladies Aid and Missionary Societies and groups for young adults, Corona was a busy place during the early days of this century.

In 1908 Corona had a prosperous Farmers Club of 50 members. The group met monthly to discuss ways and means of producing the best crops and marketing the same to the greatest advantage. Civic matters were also a frequent topic of discussion.

THE CORONA COUNTRY CLUB

Originally organized as the Corona Tennis Club, the Corona Country Club was organized in 1911 to find a way to provide tennis courts for the organization's many active players. The property at the corner of West Olive and Vicentia streets was purchased. A residence on the property was remodeled with an addition forming a large hall to be used for parties. A billiard table, piano and phonograph player were provided for use by the members. Three cement tennis courts were built in the yard. The official title of the organization was the Corona Country Club Holding Corporation, a group of over 100 Coronans who enjoyed the social life at the club. It's easy to picture a demure young lady, dressed in a proper shirtwaist, her long full skirts flying as she daintily chases the ball across the court.

The grand opening of the Country Club on August of 1913 was a gala event. The club room was decorated with plants, palm leaves, trailing greenery, beautiful cut flowers and a myriad of lights. The results, according to the *Corona Courier* "transformed the place into a veritable bower of beauty."

First on the program, giving several serious and humorous readings, was Goeffrey Morgan of Riverside. Next began the mock wedding, as soon as Lohengrin's Wedding March Legan, the ushers made their grand entrance. Mason Terpening, C. A. Holloway, Clarence White and Herbert Key were dressed in white Buster Brown suits, large pink ties, black belts, pink stockings under white half hose and black shoes. They were linked together with wide strands of pink ribbon. Next came the Judge (Charles Scoville) attired in a flowing black robe, white stole and mortarboard cap. Instead of a Bible he carried a tailor's sample book. T. C. Jameson, the best man, and the groom, Linus Andres, were dressed in white and green with bow ties.

The bridesmaids Fred Mueller and George Snidecor were bewitching in pink dresses covered with white lace curtains, short cotton picking gloves and necklaces of Christmas ornaments. They carried bouquets of lettuce with long pink streamers. The ring bearer Robert Ross entered wearing a white middy suit trimmed in pink. He carried a brass ring, eight or 10 inches in diameter, set with electrical insulators. Fred Snidecor playing the part of the sprightly flower girl, was dressed in a dainty white French dress with pink rosettes and sash.

At last came the bride, Robert Strain, on the arm of her (his?) father, George Blair. The proper dress was white with a bertha and train of hand-crocheted lace. The overskirt was draped in front with pink chrysanthemums and accessories included long white gloves, a pearl necklace, a large sunflower brouche and a wedding veil of lace with feathers, Christmas tinsel and bells. After the ceremony the wedding party adjourned to the refreshment table.

Mock weddings were one of the many forms of entertainment in the days before the radio, movies, television and Disneyland. Sometimes the sexual roles were revered, with the groom being played by a tiny woman and the bride by a large man. It was just as much fun to plan the ceremony, make the costumes and act the parts as it was to watch the performance. It is included here as an example of the type of entertainment people in Corona and other typical towns enjoyed in the 1890s, 1900s, 10s and 20s.

THE PACIFIC ELECTRIC RED CAR LINE REACHES CORONA

On February 13, 1915, the first Pacific Electric Red Car came cruising down the tracks from Riverside and San Bernardino arriving in Corona at 1:40 p.m. The Red Car was a tremendous link with the outside world

for Corona residents. It was the light rail system of 1910s.

The following article appeared in the *Corona Courier* on February 6, 1915.

"Before breakfast this morning the citizens residing in the vicinity of East Third Street were aroused by the shriek of the whistle of an electric engine coming down that thoroughfare. It was not the first appearance of the engine, however, for that came yesterday. Nevertheless, the engine made further progress up the street this morning and at noon-time had pushed a string of work cars up as far as Victoria Street. The engine crossed Main Street this afternoon. No official information as yet has reached this city stating just what date the line will be open for traffic."

The *Corona Courier* of February 18, 1915 further tells the story:

"To L. L. Andres and I. R. Nichols goes the distinction of being the first Coronans to make a regular trip from this city to Riverside and it happened yesterday after Mr. Nichols waited twenty years for the opportunity. He stated the running time of the first car between Corona and Riverside was 55 minutes and the time to San Bernardino was one hour and 50 minutes."

Grant Sunb...

Chapter 5

Road Races, Prosperity and Depression

RACE CARS ON THE CIRCLE

Even though it has been more than 82 years since the last road race around Corona's Grand Boulevard, many people still identify the city with the championship auto races held in the city in 1913, 1914 and 1916. Robert Taylor, when he made his plans for the new colony, dreamed of horse and buggy races around the wide circular boulevard. At that time, the reality of a car race, with motor-driven cars, was surely beyond his wildest dreams. Jerry Holtman, in an article in the May 4, 1961 edition of the *Corona Daily Independent*, noted that "the United States was speed mad" during the 1910s, when the emergence of the automobile and the airplane took this country by storm.

THE CORONA GRAND PRIZE RACE OF 1913

The official announcement of the first Corona Grand Prize Race was made in April of 1913. Corona residents were thrown into a whirlwind of activity preparing for the event to be held on September 9, 1913 — California Admission Day. Grand Boulevard was leveled and oiled in preparation for the big race. Because some residents were concerned about the safety problems that might have been caused by a pack of race cars rushing around the circle at the mad pace of 70 or 80 miles an hour, an official from the American Automobile Association (AAA) was called in to inspect the track. He declared it to be the safest in the world.

City officials hoping to draw attention to Corona, claimed that the Circle was a natural race track and that the races would be a positive event for the city to sponsor. The Corona Auto Club was founded to promote the event. Fortunately the members were able to get the backing of the AAA elevating the race to national status and guaranteeing a choice field of drivers and cars of national fame.

Besides the resurfacing of the boulevard, foot bridges were built across the track at about Sheridan Street on the west side and Third Street on the east side. The bridges allowed people to cross the street during the race. The grandstands were set up on the north side of the northwest quadrant of the Circle. The judge's stand was positioned across the street on the inside of the Circle about where West Third Street ends. This was the starting point as well as the finish line. Large scoreboards were erected behind the judge's stand. The pits were located at each end of the judge's stand. Residents volunteered their yards for parking and the churches all agreed to have their restroom facilities open for the use of the ladies in the crowd. Banners, refreshment, souvenir booths and the Corona Brass Band added color and spirit.

J. H. Flagler, a millionaire steel magnate who owned the El Cerrito Ranch, donated a perpetual trophy valued at $5,000 to be given to the first prize winner. The purse was $11,000 the largest ever offered up to that time. The favorites, including Earl Cooper, Teddy Tetzlaff, Ralph DePalma, Barney Oldfield and Spencer Wishart, received a lot of attention. The day before the race, the Riverside and San Bernardino Hotels were filled with excited race fans. The crowd was estimated at 100,000 with each patron required to pay 50 cents for an entry badge.

The first of three classifications, the Light Cars (engine displacements under 231 cubic inches), followed the pace car driven by A.M. Young, a prominent Southern California race promoter for the pace lap. The cars streaked along the oiled track at speeds as high as 75 miles per hour. When the race was over, an hour and a half later, Ed Waterman, driving a Buick, won the race, setting a world record averaging 63 miles per hour. Near the end of the race an anxious R. H. Rhodes, in a Studebaker, pushed his car to the limit trying to pass Al Caldwell's Maxwell. The steering gear on Rhode's car suddenly snapped creating Corona's first road race accident.

The excitement grew as the cars for the combined Medium Class (231-450 cubic inches) and the Free-For-All or unlimited class began the Medium Class race was to be 251.97 miles long with the Free-For-All race 50 miles longer. Among the 16 racers lined up were Barney Oldfield in his yellow Mercer, Felix Magone in a red Stutz and Earl Cooper in a white Stutz all waiting for the starting gun.

By the time the race neared the end, tire and mechanical failures had eliminated most of the cars. Oldfield and Cooper, in the heat of competition, were heading around the track at

speeds over 90 miles an hour. Suddenly, a boy appeared in the middle of the track. Oldfield, in an effort to swing around the startled boy, lost control of his car. Luckily, the injuries to Oldfield's mechanic and two spectators were not fatal but the accident put Oldfield out of the race. Earl Cooper won the $8,250 prize money and a $1,000 bonus for setting a new world's record. Corona was on its way to becoming the "Indianapolis of the West Coast."

THE SECOND CORONA GRAND PRIZE RACE- 1914

Held on November 26, 1914 with the hope that the Thanksgiving holiday would bring more spectators, the second annual race was eagerly anticipated by most Coronans. Special trains coming from several cities converged on Corona. A new highway connecting Corona directly with Los Angeles helped the expected crowd of over 100,000 to get to the city.

However, not all Coronans were enthusiastic about the race. There were those who were concerned about the safety of holding such an event on a city street with crowds lining every inch of the course. With this in mind, a five-foot-high

wire fence was built along the edge of the sidewalk. Again, the country's most famous race car drivers arrived in a flurry of excitement. Eddie Richenbacker, Ralph DePalma, Harry Grant, Earl Cooper, Barney Oldfield, Bob Burman, Eddie Pullen and Harry Babcock were among those who showed up to compete for the $12,000 purse.

Oldfield, Eddie O'Donnell, Richenbacker and Arthur Klein formed the first row. Again, blown tires and engine trouble plagued the favorites. The average speed was 86.5 miles per hour. Pullen, in his No. 4 Mercer, sped across the finish line with a new world record of 87.76 miles per hour. O'Donnell was second and Oldfield third. The following day, a thorough look at the record determined that Oldfield was actually second and O'Donnell third. Oldfield had, however, set a new kind of record. He was the first driver to complete a non-stop road race without any pit stops.

NO ROAD RACE IN 1915

There were no road races around the circle in 1915 because the city was unable to find someone to run the event. In view of the many new road races being established all over the country, the decision turned out to be a big mistake. The crowds moved on to new races, new cars and new places.

THE GRAND PRIZE ROAD RACE OF 1916

W. H. Peeler, a pioneer Corona auto dealer, stepped forward to take charge of the race to be held on April 8, 1916. To raise the necessary funding, the Citrus Belt Racing Association of Corona sold shares. In anticipation of an enormous crowd, a grandstand half a mile long was constructed around the circle. Brightly colored race posters were widely distributed and the event was advertised extensively in the newspapers. As a special feature, an air show was added to the festivities.

Since the 1913 race the average speed of the race cars had increased by ten to fifteen miles per hour. In the practice runs the cars were running the course at more than 100 miles per hour. It was obvious that all previous records would be shattered. The $12,000 prize money was the second largest offered outside of Indianapolis. Twelve cars were set to compete in the race. "Wild" Bob Burman (Peugeot), Eddie Pullen (Mercer), Hughie Hughes (Sunbeam), Ed Waterman (Grandy Special) and Barney Oldfield (Delage) were among the favorites.

Stunt pilot Tex LaGrone was hired to drop handbills over major cities in the Inland Empire. Sadly, while completing the task he crashed and the aeronautics show had to be canceled.

Corona shopkeepers, their shops festively decorated, and concessionaires were prepared for over 100,000 spectators even though the Inland Empire was in the midst of a heat wave. When all was said and done, race organizers admitted that there were only about 25,000 paying customers.

As soon as Frank Lowry waved the starter flag at 1:01 p.m., the race became an exciting struggle with the leaders frequently changing positions. Tire problems developed in almost all of the cars because of the hot surface of the race course and frequent pit stops were necessary. "Wild" Bob Burman determined to win the race, was clocking speeds over 100 miles per hour. With only 12 laps remaining, he was pushing his Peugeot as fast as he could. Then it happened — the left rear wheel collapsed sending the car out of control. Horrified race patrons ran as the car careened toward them. Burman's mechanic, Erick Schroeder was thrown into the street. The car, at a speed of 90 miles an hour, continued its rampage for three blocks before slamming into the crowd near the alley between Fourth and Fifth streets. William Speer, a security guard, was killed instantly and

Grand Boulevard (The Circle) as it appeared in 1915, the second year of the road races. Note the gasoline station sign in the lower left hand corner. *Courtesy Marsh Collection*

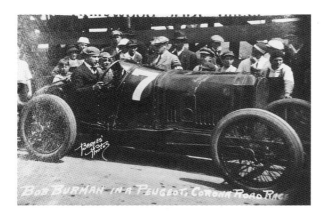

"Wild" Bob Burman, in one of the two Peugeots entered in the race, sits beside his mechanic, Erick Schroeder, just before the 1916 race began. They did not know that they had but three hours to live. *Courtesy Heritage Room, Corona Public Library*

The wreck of "Wild" Bob Burman's car, is shown on Grand Boulevard, between Fourth and Fifth Streets. Burman, his mechanic, Erick Schroeder, and a security guard were killed that fateful day. Five others were injured. The accident stirred public opinion and brought an end to the Grand Prize Races. *Courtesy Heritage Room, Corona Public Library*

five spectators were injured. Bob Burman, still clutching the Peugeot's steering wheel, was unconscious. Taken from the wreckage, he was sent to the Riverside County Hospital where he died a few hours later. Erick Schroeder died 20 minutes after the accident in the emergency hospital set up in City Hall.

The death bell of the Corona Grand Prize Race had been sounded. The accident was the final straw for many Coronans who had previously supported the races, causing them to switch their support to the opposition. Corona was not destined to continue as the Indianapolis of the West.

1911-1915: CORONA COMES OF AGE

The 1910s not only brought the excitement of the road races, but also continued prosperity on the agricultural scene. To the south of town, neat

rows of orange and lemon trees marched up the hillsides creating a verdant backdrop rising above the town stretching into the foothills. To the north and west were walnut groves, dairy lands and alfalfa, grain and vegetable farms.

During 1913, Corona orchards shipped more fruit than any other town in Southern California. In one week, 52 railroad cars containing citrus were sent east. There were approximately 7,500 acres of citrus surrounding Corona; 2,800 acres of Navel oranges; 1,700 acres of Valencia oranges; 2,400 acres of lemons and 600 acres of grapefruit. In 1915, the Lemon Exchange By-Products Company, the first of its kind in the country, was formed by Corona businessmen. The new plant produced citric acid, lemon juice, pectin and lemon oil.

Downtown Corona was prospering as well having over 50 retail businesses. There were livery stables and blacksmith shops for those who had horses as well as bicycle shops and the first automobile salesroom for those interested in the newer forms of transportation. A Wells-Fargo Express Company, two newspapers, a telephone system and no less than seven doctors and three dentists were important to the day-to-day functioning of the city. A glorious Neoclassical Revival City Hall was built on the east side of Main across from the equally elegant Carnegie Library.

The Majestic Theatre featured movie classics by such stars as the Keystone Cops and Charlie Chaplin. The excitement of serial dramas brought patrons to the theatre on a regular basis. The Congregational Church engaged Laurent the World's Greatest Magician for a performance in early 1915. For 25 cents per student and 50 cents per adult, the audience was treated to a two-hour program that included 30 flower tricks.

On February 13, 1915, the first Pacific Electric car arrived from Riverside and Colton. Between Arlington and downtown Corona the

cars stopped at Quarry, Porphyry (named for the local mineral), Grand Boulevard, Rilanco, Indian Farm and Buchanan, Pierce, Filmore, Tyler and Harrison streets.

Two new large elementary schools, Lincoln and Washington, opened. The Mission Revival-Style Washington School built in 1913 was located at Third and Grand. Lincoln School was built one year later in 1914. Several new churches were also built during this prosperous era.

In 1915, the Protestant churches banded together to engage two famous traveling evangelists from St. Louis for a series of Revival meetings. A 60- by-90 tabernacle able to seat 1,110 persons was to be erected by church members on the corner of Eighth and Main streets. When the army of volunteers arrived at the scene hammers and saws in hand, they were met by the local building inspector. He turned them away telling them that they had to have a permit. An emergency session of the Board of Trustees (City Council) was held and special permission was given for the erection of the tabernacle. Evangelist Guise and Price arrived amidst much fanfare and were welcomed by huge crowds at every service. A 100-voice choir of local singers performed each evening.

On January 26, 1915, headlines read, "Telephones Across the Continent: Human Voice is Heard From Ocean to Ocean." President Wilson had the honor of making that first call heard over the entire nation. It was noted that the tele-

phone system had gone from two miles in 1876 to 3,400 miles in 1915.

A Corona woman, Mary Grow, who came to Corona in 1891 and graduated from Corona High in 1908, was the first woman in Southern California to be elected to public office. Serving as deputy city treasurer under Captain John Merriam for two years, she was elected to serve as Corona's city treasurer and tax collector in 1915 and served until 1923. It was ironic that she was elected to office five years before women even had the right to vote. In 1921, she married E. A. Stobbs, the Mayor of Corona.

Unfortunately, Corona also had its share of disasters. The freeze of 1913 left many citrus trees in poor condition and caused a disastrous crop for that year. In February of 1915, more than three inches of fain fell over a two-day period causing several roads to be washed out. Downtown stores and many homes were flooded and the Santa Fe Railroad tracks incapacitated.

Additionally, Corona had a "hobo" problem. In early 1915, Reverend Reynolds and Reverend Roys felt that Corona churches should take responsibility for the hobos and volunteered to organize labor bureaus to help the men find jobs. The Methodist, Congregational, Baptist and Christina churches each agreed to conduct a labor bureau that would direct the hobos to places of prospective employment.

In 1913, the City of Corona purchased the land for its long-awaited city park. A lemon grove on the north side of East Sixth Street owned by

It took three years to gather the stones to build the second St. Edward's Catholic Church. It was dedicated on July 19, 1919. *Courtesy Heritage Room, Corona Public Library*

A car emerges from the Queen Colony Garage which specialized in both bicycles and automobiles. O. A. Huxsaw was the proprietor. *Courtesy Heritage Room, Corona Public Library*

the San Jacinto Land Company was selected as the best site because it would provide a clear view of the park by persons entering Corona from the east. A representative for the company remarked that the grove was "one of the worst looking groves in the entire colony," due to the freeze of 1913. He announced that the land could be purchased for $9,500 on the condition that it be used only for city park purposes.

The Woman's Improvement Club along with the Chamber of Commerce led the quest to establish the park. A committee consisting of some of Corona's most prominent citizens was formed to work on the project. Among the members was L. L. Nichols, the owner of Rhody Grove. As a surprise, he donated a strip of land 200 feet wide and 400 feet long that would connect the park to Grand Boulevard. Corona's city park was about to become a reality.

Unfortunately during 1914-1917, the threat of war was sending a black cloud over the whole country. Headlines and major stories of local newspapers focused on the events of the rapidly escalating war in Europe. Many Americans were

anxious about the possibility of sending U. S. troops overseas. At the same time most citizens believed strongly that it was important to save the world from the Germans.

AMERICA ENTERS WORLD WAR I

During World War I most Americans were intensely patriotic. Corona residents were no exception. War bond drives, parades, a community kitchen and the eagerness of residents to participate pervaded the air. President Woodrow Wilson put out the call to "make the world safe for democracy."

The outbreak of the Great War in Europe, in August of 1914, at first stunned Americans. A full-scale war seemed unthinkable in the modern age of progress. For almost three years President Wilson managed to keep America out of the war by issuing a proclamation of neutrality.

However, on April 2, 1917, with his usual crusading zeal, he asked Congress for a declaration of war. He explained the country's grievances: Germany's violation of the freedom of the seas, disruption of commerce, attempt to stir up trouble in Mexico and the killing of innocent Americans abroad. Congress quickly declared war against Germany by a vote of 373-to-50 in the House and 82-to-6 in the Senate. Congressional representative Jeannette Rankin, the first woman ever to sit in Congress, voted no. She declared that "peace is a woman's job."

Congress, in May of 1917, had already made plans to create an army. On June 5, 1917 men from all over the nation, including Corona, signed up for the "great national lottery."

There is no record of how many Coronans went into the service. We do know that 10 soldiers from the city died as a result of being in the war. Chester Husted, for whom Husted Park was named, grew up in Corona and entered the Army on January 9, 1918. He was sent into battle in France, won four medals for his great courage and

died on October 5, 1918. His Lieutenant buried him there near Mont Blanc. Also dying overseas during battle was Charles Nichols. Robert Curly, who enlisted in the Army in October of 1918, died a short time later on November 26 in a U. S. Camp. Elmer Tye, the first Corona soldier to die and be buried in France, there was cited as a hero because he and a friend went back onto the battlefield to rescue injured comrades. Crossing an open field, Tye was struck by a shell and died the next day, September 29, 1918. Lanning Ross McMillan was also killed overseas by a shell and was buried with military honors in "a pretty little French garden," nearby at Fisines on the Vesle River. Before he died he wrote to his mother:

"Do not worry mother, if anything happens. I hold most constantly this thought that I am doing and about my Father's business. It is a great cause and if I go out, it's a far better end than I have ever hoped to attain."

The worldwide influenza epidemic of 1918 took the lives of three Corona soldiers. Reports say that about half of the casualties died from influenza and pneumonia. Eaton Walter Blickhahn was one of those who died from Pneumonia as a result of being gassed during battle. A member of the Ambulance Service, he was sent to Chateau Thierry the first battle of Belleau Woods. Words of highest praise for his sense of duty and his fearless courage came from his captain, chaplin and fellow soldiers. John Henry Provensal died of influenza on December 7, 1918, at Camp Mead, Baltimore. Floyd Sandifer, a member of the Medical Officers Training Corps at Fort Riley, Kansas, died from influenza and pneumonia in October of 1918.

THE HOME FRONT

President Wilson declared, "It is not an army that we must shape and train for war, it is a nation." Even though the United States was only involved in World War I for 19 months, the war had a tremendous impact on Americans.

Corona received this World War I artillery gun because the city had done so well in fulfilling its war effort duties. The Woman's Improvement Club worked to obtain the gun from the federal government. The young man posing in front is Walt Goode. *Courtesy Heritage Room, Corona Public Library*

The state was forced to intervene in American life as it had never done before. Hundreds of new government agencies, staffed mostly by American businessmen, placed never-before-seen controls on the economy in order to shift the nation's resources to the war effort. For example, the Food Administration led by Herbert Hoover launched programs to increase production and conserve food, set prices and regulate distribution. The Fuel

a big thermometer in the center of town. As donations came in, the mark would rise from $10,000 to $20,000 and so on."

Bridges goes on to tell us about the time the Army set up headquarters in an empty field where the civic center is now located. They brought cook wagons, ammunition wagons and mounted guns, all pulled by horses and mules. Showing true Corona hospitality, several families invited

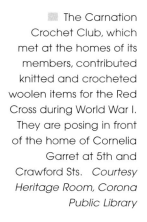

The Carnation Crochet Club, which met at the homes of its members, contributed knitted and crocheted woolen items for the Red Cross during World War I. They are posing in front of the home of Cornelia Garret at 5th and Crawford Sts. *Courtesy Heritage Room, Corona Public Library*

Administration rationed gasoline and controlled coal supplies. The Railroad Administration was founded to organize the country's railroad system.

According to Joe Bridges, who served as Corona's unofficial historian in the 1920s and 30s, "a patriotic fever for World War I was stirred up almost immediately among Corona's 3,800 residents."

He describes a war bond drive that began soon after the war started.

"During an early part of the war, a Liberty Train came to Corona with Sousa's band selling bonds. Even the school children contributed. The train carried a replica of the original Liberty Bell. Corona had a certain goal and it was recorded on

the soldiers to dinner. About 8 o'clock a soldier rode through town blowing a bugle. As Bridges reports, "they were running around like a bunch of quail getting horses and guns hooked up and left during the night."

In Corona, a food conservation unit was organized under the sponsorship of the Public Library. Called the Corona Food Shop or Community Kitchen, the program helped women how to preserve their own vegetables and fruits, provided help to community residents and assisted the Red Cross by providing food when needed. It was organized under the library system because that organization was considered the most community-oriented and well-organized. The Community Kitchen was a good example of the way people pitched in to help regardless of their previous knowledge. A real learning experience for those involved, the program was headed by a librarian and five people who had no experience in running a community kitchen. However, as Helen Lockwood Coffin in California Southland expressed it, "another intangible talent developed by the Kitchen was the ability to do things by faith."

The Corona chapter of the American Red Cross was very active during World War I. The Gray Ladies, more than 100 strong, rolled bandages, knitted warm woolen socks and caps, operated a motor corps and canteen, assisted the USO with emergencies related to servicemen and performed other services needed by the military. After the war, the Red Cross continued to aid causes and emergencies within the local community. Red Cross members had a strong empathy for the soldiers overseas and often served as the only method of communication between a soldier and his family.

Germany, with its ground war a shambles, its submarine warfare a dismal failure, its allies dropping out and its cities mutinous, accepted an armistice on November 11, 1918. America joyfully celebrated the end of the war with parades and parties.

AFTER THE WAR: CHANGES AND DISORGANIZATION

In *California Southland*, Helen Lockwood Coffin writes of the situation in 1919 after the Armistice was declared on November 11, 1918:

"Last year we were salvaging for war purposes the prodigality of Peace; this year our problem is to utilize the spirit and experience of war in behalf of peace. Last year we had the spur of imminent dangers which demanded self-defense, the inspiration of martial music and flying banners, the appeal of the military organization. This year

everything is in chaos, seething with possibilities but disorganized and changed. All nations, all communities, every individual is caught whirling in the process of reconstruction. All the bewildered world of us are trying to find a way out to something stable and enduring."

Although Coffin might be exaggerating a bit, her statement does point out a situation which must have been true.

CORONA ENTERS THE NEW ERA OF THE 1920s

By the end of 1920, the confusion and disorganization cited by Helen Coffin was becoming a thing of the past. The returning soldiers settled into civilian life with the hope and excitement of a new beginning. Many got married, got a job, bought a house and soon had a baby on the way. Corona went about the business of learning to live in peace.

Young architects returning home from overseas began designing in new styles of architecture inspired by the English Tudor cottages and castles, Spanish Colonial Revival houses, Norman cottages, Byzantine churches and other exotic styles they had observed as soldiers foreign countries. These romantic interpretations of the timeless

A young student who lived in the farm lands to the north of Corona gets ready to board the school bus. *Courtesy Heritage Room, Corona Public Library*

architectural styles of foreign lands became the latest architectural trend throughout our country. Corona had its share of impressive Spanish Colonial Revival buildings constructed during this period.

The Woman's Improvement Club in 1920 celebrated its 21st anniversary with one of the most memorable parties of the year. A piano duet, readings, a cornet piece and vocal renditions of "Somewhere a Voice Is Calling" and "Nymphs and Fauns" were included in the program. The Woman's Improvement Club, in conjunction with the Chamber of Commerce, applied for and received a large cannon in commemoration of the valor and bravery of Corona men and women who had served in World War I. Some sources place the cannon on a concrete pad in the city park, while others say it was placed on a concrete base in front of City Hall. It was returned to the federal government for scrap metal at the beginning of World War II.

In April 1921, Miss Corkhill opened the first Corona Hospital at 1002 South Main Street. The hospital was much needed by the colony. In those days, it was the custom of local doctors, of which there were several, to see the majority of their patients during house calls. We've all heard those stories about appendectomies being performed on a kitchen table. A safe, sanitary operating room was a great improvement that resulted in the saving of lives. In 1926, Miss Jessie Toogood took charge of the facility. Eight years later, in 1934, it became an emergency room for the Metropolitan Water District.

Arriving in Corona in 1927, Dr. and Mrs. Henry Herman opened a three-bed maternity home. Because of the great need for a hospital in the city, the facility grew to a 30-bed hospital, located at 812 South Main Street. Dr. and Mrs. Herman continued to serve Coronans for several years.

In the 1920s the hills between Corona and Chino drew a lot of attention because of the revival of oil development. Several companies started operations at distances varying from one to six miles from town. The Chino-Corona United Oil Company struck oil in the Puente Hills between Chino and Corona, In San Bernardino County. The first well was called the "best oil gamble in California today" and had a total cap-

RIDE THE BIG RED CARS

ital stock of 227,000 shares offered at a $1 a share. The well brought in oil at 3,646 feet but the oil was too heavy to pump successfully from such a great depth. Drilling was resumed after the heavier oil was sealed off with concrete. A light gravity oil was discovered between 3,878 and 4,228 feet. The prospect of finding an even better quality of light oil at an even lower level inspired the company to continue to drill. On April 15, 1923, good quality light oil was found at 4,547 feet. Although the well was in use, a major oil field has never was developed in that location.

In 1921, Mr. F. L. Kinney, realizing that Corona needed a second hotel, secured a five-year lease on the Corona Securities Building, remodeling it and refurnishing it as a hotel. The dining rooms of the establishment were a popular gathering place for those having special celebrations.

The same year, Corona experienced another flood. Roads were once more impassable and all of the bridges were out except for the Prado Bridge, the only crossing between Colton and Olive for several months. The dam at the end of the large reservoir at the W. J.

Hole Ranch collapsed, spreading a flood of fast-moving waters loaded and 20 tons of black bass over the landscape.

Coronans, always interested in quality education, missed a $150,000 bond issue for a new high school in 1922. The vote was 10-to-1 making the bond issue a remarkable success. The new school which stretched along an entire block on the north side of West Sixth Street, was designed in the latest Spanish Colonial Revival style. Progressive education was a topic that roused intellectual arguments among educators and parents. According to the *Riverside Press-Enterprise*, retired teacher Lucy Arnold saw it as an attempt to "individualize" instruction. She recalls that while some saw it as a complete farce, others swore buy it.

The 1920s were the heydays for civic and charitable organizations. Almost every resident belonged to at least one and many belonged to five or six. The Red Cross ,which had contributed so much to the efforts on the home front during World War I, continued to be active in the 1920s. Volunteers with over 800 hours of service were honored by local chairman T. C. Sias. The Corona Rotary Club, founded in January of 1923, had two slogans: "He profits most who serves best," and "Service Above Self." Charles Scoville was the first president. One of the principle activities of the organization was the raising of funds to help crippled children. Most of the funds were raised through fines levied during club meetings. The club established scholarships for worthy students.

The 26 charter members of the Lions Club, founded on September 20, 1923, first met at one of the downtown hotels. The organization con-tributed to many civic projects including land for a park, funds for the building of the band shell in the city park and the scout house. Youth activities sponsored by the group included speech contests and scholarships.

After several years of discussion, Corona was to have a municipal pool at last. On May 6, 1925, the contract for the pool was awarded to Mr. Burner for $15,000. The ornate exterior was designed to look like a castle with elaborate crenelated towers on each end and a dramatic arched entrance. The year 1926 brought to fruition the often-discussed Santa Fe railroad line between Corona and Elsinore. A celebration to mark the beginning of construction was held on August 30, 1926. The line snaked its way through Temescal Canyon.

Another fine example of the Spanish Colonial Revival style was the Parkridge Country Club located in the hills a short distance to the north-east of town. Built in 1925, it was a building with a prominent tower, an arcade across the front and slanted wings on each side. Behind the building, the club had a covered shooting range for those who wanted to do "blue rock shooting," as well as a flying field for private planes. Built by Dan Gilken, the club survived for only a few years. Gilken sold Golden Life Membership cards for $50 each in an endeavor to keep it open. However, the venture failed and by 1928 the building had become a sanitarium. By the 1960s, It had became known as the Cresta Verde Country Club.

Jefferson School, a beautiful example of Spanish Colonial Revival architec-ture, opened its doors in January 1928. W. Horace Austin, a prominent architect, was the designer of the

school located on Vicentia Street. On February 17, a formal dedication was held. Music, speeches and readings by the students were heard by the large crowd. The library wing, fronted with an elaborate slanted bay featuring large arched windows, was added in October 1931.

One of the few large new buildings constructed in the downtown area in the 1920s was the Corona Theater/ Landmark Building. Of Spanish Colonial architecture, the building was designed by architect Carl Boller of Ingelwood and dedicated on August 29, 1929. Several Hollywood celebrities attended the ceremony including Laurel and Hardy, Al Jolson and Irving Berlin. The building also held professional office space, store frontage, and a meeting room for the Masons.

In 1928, the Metropolitan Water District was formed by 13 Los Angeles and Orange County cities to bring Colorado River water to Southern California. A giant aqueduct was being designed for the purpose. Corona decided not to join the district because the city felt it did not need additional water. Coronans contended that Colorado River water would be of lower quality than that already being obtained through the Temescal Water Company.

The 1920s, was perhaps Corona's happiest era. There were fine schools, new homes, prosperous ranches, an active commercial center, an improved telephone system and a hospital. Plenty of black Model T Fords traveled the streets.

CORONA, STILL THE LEMON CAPITAL OF THE WORLD

The 1920s were the glory years of the citrus and agricultural industries. Even in the 1930s, in the midst of the Great Depression, Corona managed to survive by growing citrus and other crops, keeping most of the packing houses open.

The citrus industry, controlled by forces such as the weather, the economy and the size of the crop, had its ups and downs. During the 20s, citrus crop revenues were in the $2 million plus range with a dip in 1924-25 due to a Christmas freeze and another in dip in 1928 because of the appearance of the Mediterranean fruit fly.

During the Depression revenues were cut somewhat by the economy. As usual, the weather contributed the most to fluctuating revenue. In 1930-31, a cold spell in December, a small crop and poor sizes resulted in a total revenue of $1,812,994, down from $2,300,000 in 1929-30.

A "heavy freeze with considerable snow" caused the revenue for 1931-32 to hit a new low at $1,422,150. A large crop was produced in 1932-33 but heavy winds in January caused a lower grade and a loss of fruit. The revenue that year was $1,274,189, the lowest seen since the late 1910s.

Workers pick Washington navel oranges for the American Fruit Growers Association ranch in 1931. Note the Blue Goose label on the boxes. *Courtesy Heritage Room, Corona Public Library*

It was not until 1935-36 that the revenue was once again above the $2 million mark. In spite of low orange prices, the wind and low humidity during October and a lower grade of fruit, total revenue was at $2,363,997. Reports claim that the unusually hot summer in the East and Midwest provided a good market for lemons because people made more lemonade.

WATER: A CONTINUING CONCERN

In 1920, the water in the Ethanac Wells became saline (salty) and Corona, whose entire economy was based on the supply of irrigation and domestic water, had to search for new ways to provide both. In 1921, the Temescal Water Company drilled its first well inside the city limits at Joy and Third streets.

In a plan to harness the runoff from the San Jacinto River, Temescal Water Company built a dam in Railroad Canyon. With 4,500 acres of citrus groves to irrigate, the water company acquired 2,000 acres in the canyon, 500 of which were to be used as the surface area of a reservoir. The land was purchased and financed through an arrangement with the Santa Fe Railroad Company which had installed tracks in Temescal Canyon connecting Corona and Elsinore in 1926. Much of the Ethanac land was sold to help finance the rest of the project. Many Elsinore citizens were

unhappy about the damming of Railroad Canyon because they were afraid Lake Elsinore might dry up. Unfortunately, the lake did become dry for several years, and it was not until the 1960s that water from the San Jacinto River was routed down Railroad Canyon, to fill the lake again.

CORONA GREETS THE GREAT DEPRESSION OF THE 1930s

Almost every part of our nation was hit hard by the Great Depression that began with the stock market crash in October of 1929. Unfortunately, the worst was yet to come. In 1929, 659 banks closed their doors. In 1931, 2,293 banks closed, and, in 1932, another 1,453 ceased to do business. The Red Cross and Salvation Army opened soup kitchens to feed the hungry.

Between 1929 and 1933, farm prices over most of the nation dropped 60 percent. Tenant farmers and their families, having nowhere to go, wandered the roads of the South. Thousands hopped freight trains and headed west to California. The California Unemployment Commission reported in 1932 that an army of homeless had arrived in the state and were moving from town to town as residents often forced them to move on.

Corona, for the most part, didn't suffer as deeply as much of the rest of the nation because of the lemon, citrus, and agricultural industries. There were signs, however, that let us know the community was suffering from money problems.

Some high school students had to drop out of school and work to help support their families. The school district, in an effort to cut expenses, decided that it had more teachers than it needed. All of the women teachers who had husbands working for the school district were laid off. Additionally, the board demanded that all school personnel shop

only in Corona stores. Even when things got better, the school board refused to hire teachers who would have tenure if they were re-employed. Many teachers objected. The public sided with the teachers on the last two items, and the policies were soon eliminated.

Corona had its share of unemployed and itinerant workers, in desperate need. The Red Cross, always prepared to help in an emergency, handed out tickets for free meals. The organization also acted as a conduit for information, connecting those in need with agencies that could help the. Many Coronans helped out by spending many volunteer hours with the Red Cross.

As the need for food, clothing, and shelter increased in the early 1930s, the Settlement House, previously organized by the Woman's Improvement Club, did much to help those in need of those items. The W. I.C.'s Well-Baby Clinic provided much-needed medical care for families with young children. Corona's churches stepped forward to help those in need, providing emergency food and clothing banks.

When the Social Security system was inaugurated in 1935, Red Cross workers helped applicants fill out the paperwork. These same Red Cross workers, including Ida Field and Emily Hastings, worked tirelessly for hundreds of hours, finding food, clothing, and shelter for as many of the needy as they could.

Many itinerant workers found work at the farms, dairies, groves, and packing houses surrounding Corona. To house those who came to California to work in Corona's packing houses, a new community, Home Gardens, sprang up to the east of Corona. People managed, by raising their own food, to survive on the small farms in Norco and the land between Corona and Arlington.

The State and Federal government had programs to help put people back to work and provide emergency help for those in dire need. The State Emergency Relief Agency provided funds through local organizations. The W.P.A. (Works Progress Administration) provided many jobs in a variety of fields, including those requiring skilled workers, office personnel, artists, historians,

and those in the manufacturing field. Public works projects, such as improvements at the Corona City Park, storm drains, and landscaping financed by the W. P. A., giving jobs to Corona citizens.

CORONA'S WELL-ESTABLISHED SCHOOL SYSTEM

By 1936, Corona had a total of six schools with 2,237 students and 84 teachers. Younger students went to Jefferson, Lincoln, Washington, or Norco Elementary, while 956 junior high schoolers attended Letha Raney in Corona. The junior high was organized in 1923. Corona High School had an enrollment of 435 students with 60 graduating in 1936. Records show that in 1900 school costs totaled $8,476.57. Thirty-six years later, the costs had risen to $157,358.44.

CORONA CELEBRATES ITS GOLDEN JUBILEE

As Corona approached its Fiftieth Birthday, May 6, 1936, the nation as well as the community, was beginning to get back on its feet. Numerous

East Sixth Street, as it appeared about 1930. *Courtesy Marsh Postcard Collection*

president. The company turned out more than 1,200 garments weekly, and carried a stock of cloth valued from $30,000 to $ 50,000.

CORONA GETS A NEW SANTA FE DEPOT

On April 13, 1936, Santa Fe Railroad officials announced that Corona, in celebration of its jubilee year, would have a new depot. In the process, the old depot, built in 1877, would be demolished.

Plans were unveiled that showed a 191-foot-long Spanish Colonial Revival style building, topped with a red clay tile roof. Designed by M. C. Blanchard, chief engineer, and H. L. Gilman, architect, the features of the new depot "represented the most modern developments of railroad station facilities." The plans included attractive landscaping and paving of large platform with black pavement. The building, which featured a open waiting

activities, including plays, concerts, dances, a rodeo, and a plaque dedication celebrated the anniversary.

One of the key events of the celebration was the American Legion's Third Annual Sheriff's Rodeo. One of the races was a potato race with the posses from Riverside and San Bernardino counties competing for the top prize. To immortalize the success of the pioneers who founded the town, a bronze plaque donated by the 20-30 Club, was placed on a boulder in the city park, where it still exists today.

The *Corona Daily Independent* put out special issues of the newspaper featuring articles about the history of the Corona area, both before and after the city was founded.

In 1936, a few new businesses were relocating in Corona. The Sun-Cal Cloak and Suit Company, which moved into a large building on East Sixth Street, was one of these. Max Isonberg was the

area on the west end, was to be built of frame with a stucco exterior. A large freight room, a baggage room, offices, and a dispatcher's room occupied the east end, with the waiting room and ticket sales located next to the open passenger waiting section on the west end.

THE JOY AND JAMESON FAMILIES VITAL TO CORONA

Of the founding fathers of South Riverside (Corona), George L. Joy, along with his daughter and son-in-law, William and Hetty Jameson, was the only one who stayed to live out his years in the colony. The Joys and the Jameson families played a vital part in almost every aspect of the development of the area.

William, who arrived in 1887, became the superintendent of the South Riverside Land and Water Company that founded the colony. He and his wife, Hetty, had six children, all talented and hard-working. Hetty invested substantially in property within the town.

Joy Jameson, who is credited with many improvements and changes in the city, was a business and civic leader, and a devoted member of the Baptist Church. The Corona Daily Independent said of him upon his death in 1955, "A man who went beyond his own interests to give quietly and unselfishly of his talents, his time, and his heart to his church, his community, and his fellow man."

He was one of the ablest leaders of the citrus industry in California. His activities included the management of the Jameson Company, the development of alfalfa and vegetable lands in Imperial Valley, president of the Temescal Water Company, president of the Exchange Lemon Products Company, director of the Queen Colony Fruit Exchange, president of the Corona Investment Company, and service on the boards of the Sunkist Growers, California Fruit Growers Association, Fruit Growers Supply Company, and the Corona City Water Company. As a volunteer he served as president of the University of Redlands, president of the Riverside Council of the Boy Scouts of America, on the Board of

Pausing for lunch in 1939, the occupants of this car have set up a table and folding camp stools. *Courtesy Heritage Room, Corona Public Library*

Trustees of the Baptist Church and several other boards. The Jamesons had six children: Joy Gilbert Jr., Walter T., Charles Henry, Miriam Margaret, David, and Edith Ann.

William Henry Jameson Jr. was born in Corona on September 9, 1893. After graduating from Cornell University in 1916, he enlisted in the military service and served in the Machine Gun Battalion. After returning to Corona, he was president of the Jameson Company until he went into real estate with the Corona Investment Company. His wife, Mary Gard Jameson, who graduated from Stanford University, was known for her success in business, particularly after Williams died at the age of 39. She managed a 320-acre ranch, several apartment houses in Hollywood, and a large building and contracting company. She was an accomplished fencer, a member of the Professional Woman's Club, and the Woman's Club of Corona. Their children were Evelyn, Mary Joy, Frank Gard, and Adelaide.

Thorndike Jameson, the brother of William Henry, came to Corona about 1894. During his 40 years in the city, he served as president of the Citizens Bank and a director of the First National Bank. He was a successful citrus farmer and involved in several Corona business interests. He and his wife, Maud, were the parents of Emily, Carol, and Ruth. Carol, who graduated with a degree in medicine, became a medical missionary in India.

Jameson family members through the years have continued to pioneer in the citrus and agricultural fields. The land for the Crown Ranch was purchased in 1937, with further purchases of lands substantially adding to its size. Jim, Eloise, Adelaide, Frank, and Walter Jameson, and Crawford Teague participated with the Richfield Oil Company in the development of Rancho California and at Horsethief Canyon in the 1960s and 70s. The Jameson Packing House remained open until the 1960s, after the final division of the property among Joy's heirs, Eloise, and Adelaide. It is easy to see why the Jameson family has left an indelible and significant mark on the city of Corona.

Corona and Norco were just beginning to develop in the late 1950s. The region was beginning to shift its emphasis from agricultural to development, as large sections of orange trees were removed and a sea of new houses began to cover the land.

WORLD WAR II—
DRAMATIC CHANGES FOR CORONA

World War II was a turning point in Americans' lives and in the history of the United States. For the 45 months Americans fought abroad to subdue the Nazi and Japanese aggressors, Americans did all they could to aid the cause.

For Americans living on the West Coast, World War II was even more real because of the proximity to Japan and the long, exposed and vulnerable coastline. The danger of Japanese subs and planes bombarding the West Coast contributed to a constant climate of fear and urgency. Local groups and business leaders provided bandages and knitted wear. Most residents did their best to cooperate with a complicated rationing system, going without necessities to help the soldiers and the war effort. Stirring war bond drives and parades encouraged everyone from small children to senior citizens to invest in financing the war.

The *Riverside Press-Enterprise,* in an article printed on December 7, 1991, interviewed several veterans who were members of the Pearl Harbor Survivors Association. This select group of men described their participation during a significant time and

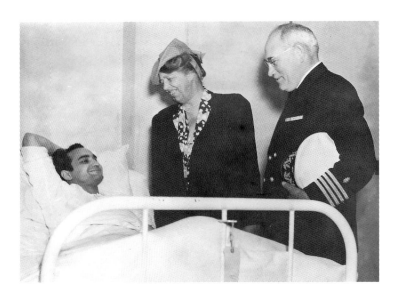

place in history. They expressed their feelings of shock, disbelief, sorrow and tragedy as the unprepared Americans saw Japanese planes swoop from the morning sky. There were approximately 80,000 soldiers and aviators stationed at Pearl Harbor in 1941, and the losses were great.

KNOW YOUR AIR RAID WARDEN!

A pamphlet titled "Know Your Air Raid Warden" was given to all Corona residents. It advised them to let the warden know the details concerning the number of people in the family, where one could be reached in an emergency, if there were any disabled, and where the gas and electric shut-off switches were located. The pamphlet gave these instructions in bold letters:

KEEP CALM AND COOL, STAY HOME. PUT OUT THE LIGHTS, LIE DOWN, STAY AWAY FROM WINDOWS, DON'T TELEPHONE. The directive also requested no screaming and no running.

THE AIRCRAFT WARNING SERVICE

The Aircraft Warning Service was serious business for towns on the West Coast. They mapped the flight of all aircraft, identified them,

and reported the details to an information center. All information was placed on a huge map called the filter board. The hundreds of volunteers who were active in this organization were called plotters and filters. Observers often worked as partners in order to make sure the lookout posts were manned on a 24-hour basis. Classes, lasting eight weeks, were held to teach citizens how to identify different kinds of aircraft.

An observation outpost was established at Prado. A weekly newsletter, called the Prado Post Patter, gave the latest information about what was going on at the post at Prado Dam. Among those who served there were biology teacher Miss Katherine Stewart, junior high principal Letha Raney, and J. Lorin Farmer, school music instructor.

WOMEN'S VICTORY SERVICE

One of Corona's most active organizations during World War II was the Women's Victory Service. The members were determined to keep in touch with every service person from Corona. They remembered birthdays, sent food and warm clothing, and kept tabs on the soldiers' whereabouts as much as possible

A large scrapbook in the Heritage Room, compiled by the Women's Victory Service, is full of clippings about the city's service personnel. Among those is the story of Lt. Vincent Shank, the son of Nancy Shank. She was chairwoman of the Corona Prisoners of War Committee. Vincent Shank was taken prisoner when his plane was shot down over Sicily, and he spent 22 months in a Nazi prison camp. While there, he organized a band, using instruments provided by the War Prisoner's Aid, a division of the International YMCA.

Mrs. William Loranger designed a huge flag covered with stars representing all who served from Corona during the World War II. It hung in City Hall for many years.

THE WAR AND PRICE RATIONING BOARD IMPACTS EVERYONE'S LIVES

Anything containing rubber or oils, including tires, automobiles, bicycles, boots, shoes, stoves, and gasoline, was rationed. Foods such as meat, sugar, cheese, lard, and butter were also on the list. The War and Price Rationing Board was headed by Ben Sampselle from January 1941 to October 1944, and by Daniel Hogan from October 1944 to September 1945. A hoarder (someone who stockpiled rationed goods) was despised and treated like an outcast.

Corona celebrated the closing of the War Rationing Board, ordered by O. P. A. chairman Chester Bowles, with a grand party on September 21, 1945. What an important day that was!

THE AMMUNITIONS DUMP

John Overbeck, now of Cincinnati, Ohio, remembers the days he spent in the 575 Ordinance Ammunitions Company in 1943. The job of the Company of 180 was to supply ammunition for the Western Defense Command, Southern Sector. The dump, which contained everything from artillery to small arms, was located off of Magnolia Avenue. There were several buildings on the site, including a headquarters building, approximately five barracks, a mess hall, a recreation hall, a shower, and a PX.

For recreation the men would either go to Riverside, Los Angeles, or Corona. Overbeck remembers the USO headquarters located two doors south of Sixth and Main streets, in an old store building. He often went to dances at the Woman's Improvement Club. The young women who volunteered to attend and dance with the soldiers were called Coronettes.

THE RULES CHANGE AT THE PLUNGE

A 1969 article in the Corona Daily Independent describes how the rules at the Corona City Park Pool changed during the war. Mrs. Nettie Whitcomb ran the plunge for years, as well as giving swimming lessons.

At that time, Hispanics were only allowed to use the pool one day a week. On December 7, 1943, Joe Dominquez, who became Corona's first war casualty, was killed during the battle of the Arawe in New Britain. When the news reached the city plunge, Nettie and her staff took down the segregation signs and burned them in the city park.

A NEW DOOR OPENS

As is often true, the closing of one chapter opens the door to another. During the war, thousands of soldiers had seen Southern California for the first time. They liked what they saw.

The Municipal Plunge, built in 1925. *Courtesy Heritage Room, Corona Public Library*

Municipal Plunge
Corona City Park

Chapter 6

Norco, El Cerrito, Glen Ivy and Fuller Ranch

NORCO: "ACRES OF NEIGHBORS"

Norco, one of Riverside County's most unique communities, has been home to a diversity of groups, from the Lusieño Indians to the owners of the many small ranches existing there today. In between were the Rancho La Sierra, prolific fruit orchards, chicken ranches, and a fabulous luxury hotel, the Lake Norconian Club.

THE INDIANS AND THE MISSIONS

Conclusive evidence found by archaeologist shows that the Luiseño and Gabrielino Indians occupied the land. Members of the Shoshonean linguistic group, which appeared in Southern California around 500 A.D., were attracted by and used the rich resources of the Santa Ana River. Paxauka, an Indian village, was located on the east side of the Temescal Wash and Pasinongna was a little north of where Prado Dam now stands.

The old site of an Indian camp, marked by a metate, near hills on the east side of Norco was discovered by Elsie Deand and Suzanne Gould. It was in a grove of cottonwoods along a winding road at the foot of the hills. The metate was a large boulder, polished smooth as a jewel, and containing five grinding holes.

As the missions were established, the Indian tribes received new names, depending on which mission claimed the territory in which they lived. The Gabrielino Indians, named for the Mission San Gabriel Arcangel, and the Luiseños, who occupied the territory given to the Mission San Luis Rey, both frequented the Norco and Corona areas. For more details about the Indians and the missions, please see Chapter 1.

RANCHO LA SIERRA

Most of what would become Norco was part of the Rancho La Sierra Sepulveda, a Mexican land grant given to Vincenta Sepulveda on June 15, 1946, by Governor Pio Pico. She was the widow of Tomas Yorba, and the rancho was part of her inheritance. The rancho line ran along the Santa Ana River on the west and north sides, and along a line where Parkridge

Road is now located. La Sierra is the Spanish name for "the saw-toothed mountain range", and was given to the ranch by the Yorba brothers, Bernardo and Tomás , as early as 1825. Bernardo and Tomás Yorba originally shared the entire Rancho La Sierra, grazing cattle there. In 1845, Bernardo Yorba asked that the land be divided because Tomás had died and the cattle grazing on the land had passed into the hands of others. Tomás' widow, Vincenta Sepulveda, who had resumed her maiden name, asked Governor Pico to grant her half (four square leagues) of the rancho. On June 15, 1846, Pico granted the eastern half to Vincenta Sepulveda and the western half to Bernardo Yorba.

BY 1916 — VISIBLE GROWTH

In 1912, according to records, there "was not a single house or shack of any description; not a tree or shrub and no water" on the flat plain owned by the Citrus Belt Land Company.

Three years later, in the spring of 1915, large ads appeared in the *Corona Courier*. They painted an inviting picture of the area then called Corona Farms and offered 5, 10, and 20-acre parcels for $275 an acre and up. Advertised as the ideal place to plant orange, lemon, peach, and apricot orchards, the ad also mentioned the opportunity to raise hogs, chickens, vegetables, and fruit. It further claimed that the finest steel and cement irrigation system was ready for immediate use. By

1916, at least 40 families had settled in the tract and had begun to set out fruit trees and raising animals such as chickens, turkeys, and rabbits.

THE CITRUS BELT LAND BECOMES ORCHARD HEIGHTS

After much experimentation, it had been discovered that most of the area was not suitable for citrus because the night time temperatures were too low and the winds were too strong. Clearly, the area needed a new name.

In February of 1920, the Corona Chamber of Commerce offered a prize of $10 for the best suggestion for a new name for the Citrus Belt Tract. Over 147 names were submitted to a special committee of land owners consisting of Ray Haddock, J. V. Bird, J. Grant, H. G. Phillips, and Mrs. L. M. Persons.

On April 3, 1920 the name "Orchard Heights" was suggested by H. C. Jones. It was chosen because it encompassed the wide variety of trees that could be grown. Rev. C. E. Maimann won the $3 second prize for his submittal, "Hillsdale". Anna Dwyer was third, with the name "Orchard Park", and received $1.

Orchard Heights lived up to its new name. Apricots, peaches, apples, grapes, pomegranates, and pears were among the best crops. From 250 acres of full-bearing apricot trees, nearly 200 tons of apricots were harvested in 1920. The Ontario Canning Company bought 80 tons for canning and drying. Altogether, 100 tons of "cots" were dried on wooden racks. In addition, over 500 tons of very fine peaches were harvested and sold to the canning company that year.

The farmers who lived in Orchard Heights held a meeting once a month at the Citrus Belt Land Company's boarding house. In the 1920s, they won many prizes for their fancy fruit at the Southern California Fair in Riverside. Norco was on its way to becoming a successful agricultural community, as well as a good place to raise a family.

HAMNER AVENUE, NORCO'S MAIN STREET

In the good old days, before the I-5 freeway was completed, those going to Norco headed north on Hamner Avenue, passing the intersection where River Road juts off to the northwest, and continuing north through the center of town. The pepper trees that lined both sides of the two-lane road created a peaceful country-like scene. Who was the "Hamner" for whom this main artery was named? He was John Thomas Hamner, who moved from Alabama to the Corona-Norco area in 1887. Hamner, who was on his own very early in life, headed west when he was 18, having sold a mule, his only possession, to his Uncle Jake for $50. After a few years in Texas, he got a job as a brakeman for the railroad and lived for a short time in the Los Angeles area. He settled in Corona at the age of 25, buying a team of mules and hauling clay to the railroad station. In the winter he farmed on leased land. Competent and responsible, he had taken the first step to becoming a prominent civic leader in Riverside County.

Hamner began buying parcels of land in that area. By 1912, he owned 540 acres of land. Hamner was elected to the Riverside County Board of Supervisors in November of 1902. He was reelected several times and remained on the Board for 18 years, retiring on January 3, 1921. He was one of the organizers of the Corona National Bank, promoter and director of the Corona Home Telephone Company, and a director of the Riverside Water Company. Hamner Avenue was named for him because of his many contributions to the county of Riverside. He died in 1949 at the age of 87.

CAPTAIN GULLY LAYS OUT NORCO'S STREETS

For those who live on one of Norco's older streets, it is interesting to know that Captain C. Gully, a civil engineer, was responsible for the layout of most of the original streets. Captain Gully learned civil engineering while working for the San Jacinto Land Company, which had control of the land that would become Norco in the 1890s. He laid out most of the streets on the east side of Hamner and built an irrigation system. Orange trees were planted, but the wind, winter frost and poor soil caused the attempt at orange ranching to fail.

Captain Gully, who got his title when he served in World War I, was Corona city engineer for a few years before he joined the Army. In 1919, he returned to Riverside County and became assistant civil engineer.

A pair of mules, on their way to work, pauses beside the road in Norco in 1924. Peach trees occupy the property to the left and eucalyptus trees, used as a windbreak, can be seen on the right. *Courtesy Norco Historical Society*

In May of 1915, ads appeared in the *Corona Courier* advertising the small farms available in "Corona Farms". In 1921, when Rex Clark bought 5,504 acres, he named the town Norco and built several buildings near the corner of Hamner Avenue and Sixth Street. *Courtesy Heritage Room, Corona Public Library*

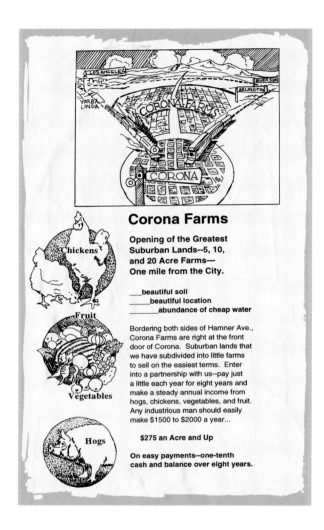

Corona Farms

Opening of the Greatest Suburban Lands--5, 10, and 20 Acre Farms--- One mile from the City.

_____beautiful soil
_____beautiful location
_____abundance of cheap water

Bordering both sides of Hamner Ave., Corona Farms are right at the front door of Corona. Suburban lands that we have subdivided into little farms to sell on the easiest terms. Enter into a partnership with us--pay just a little each year for eight years and make a steady annual income from hogs, chickens, vegetables, and fruit. Any industrious man should easily make $1500 to $2000 a year...

$275 an Acre and Up

On easy payments--one-tenth cash and balance over eight years.

Norco, as it looked in 1925, from the hill to the west of Hamner Avenue. The Grammar School is at the left edge, and the Norco Store is the two-story building in the center. The building to the left of the store is the machinery shop owned by the north Corona Land Company. Old Hamner runs in front of the store, and Sixth Street runs along the line of trees in the background. *Courtesy Norco Historical Society*

When Rex B. Clark bought the land for Norco, Captain Gully went to work for him, laying out more streets and creating the first practical water system. Retired in 1952, he can be credited with most of the community's early engineering improvements.

REX B. CLARK BUYS ORCHARD HEIGHTS

After becoming interested in the valley in December of 1920, Rex B. Clark began negotiations with the Orchard Heights Land Company. In 1921 he bought 5504 acres of Orchard Heights. After resurveying the town, subdividing the unsold land into 2½ acre plots, and reha-

bilitating the irrigation system, he held a grand opening for his new town of Norco. "Norco" is short for North Corona. He advertised it as "the ideal place for family chicken ranches." His plan, at that time, was to build a large chicken ranch for himself on the hills to the west of Hamner.

THE NORCO STORE

In March of 1923, the Norco Store, was built on the east side of Hamner Avenue, near sixth Street, by Clark's North Corona Land Company. The two-story rectangular building, made of poured-in-place concrete, featured a wide pergola built across the entire front.

The Norco store served as the company headquarters and supply center for residents of the valley. Almost everything, including groceries, feed, dry goods, hardware, and farm supplies could be purchased there. Housing the post office and the library, the store also served as a social center for the community. Some of the employees lived in the hotel rooms above the store. Businessmen who came to see Clark were frequent visitors to the hotel. Tradition says that the people came from as far as Los Angeles to partake of the delicious meals at the Norco Grill, a restaurant in the hotel. Sadly, the building was abandoned in the 1960s, and demolished shortly after.

Company. New modern pumping plants and reservoirs greatly increased the water supply.

In 1922, a machine shop to repair agricultural equipment was opened. A large crowd gathered to view the new development. Lots had been split from 5 to 10-acre parcels and made into 2-and-a half-acre mini-ranches. The first home resulting from this opening was built on Fifth Street, east of Hamner, in September of 1923.

On a hill to the south, Clark had installed a large beacon, used to mark the way for people seeking his new development. The children called this hill "The Chocolate Drop."

Norco's first business center, a building containing three units, was built along the west side of Hamner Avenue, near Sixth Street. It was constructed of brick and topped with a frieze of red clay tiles. The Orchard Heights Water Company occupied the north half of that building for several years. In 1930, the rooms on the south side were occupied by the Upham Drug Company and the Norco Poultry Supply. In 1964, the northern half became Norco's first city hall.

■ (Top Left Image) The Norco Grill above the Norco Store, often drew people from as far away as Los Angeles. The second floor also served as a hotel for employees of the North Corona Land Company. *Courtesy Norco Historical Society.*

■ (Left Image) Norco's first shopping center, built in the late1920s. The Norco Historical Society and the Norco Branch Library now have facilities in the rear half of the left section. *Courtesy Norco Historical Society.*

CLARK DEVELOPS NORCO

One of the Clark's first improvements was the drilling of two 26-inch wells. He employed E. W. Parsons as manager of the development. In March of 1921, a large cement plant for making concrete pipe was established at Sixth and Sierra streets. At the highest rate of production, it turned out 40,000 drainage tiles a day. When Parsons resigned, Rex S. Clark, a son of Rex B. Clark, was made manager of the North Corona Land

NORCO'S FIRST GRAMMAR SCHOOL

Norco's first school, built by Rex Clark in 1925, was a pleasant Spanish Colonial Revival-inspired building located on Acacia Street, overlooking Hamner Avenue. Covered arcades extend from each side of the centered entrance portico. the four classrooms opened off of the back of the arcade. The auditorium, located on the south end, was frequently used by the community for club meetings and events.

175 students, and taught a combined third and fourth grade class. Teachers were paid an average of $1,100 a year.

When the children moved to the new Sierra Vista Elementary School on Corona Avenue, she became its first principal.

She says that she enjoyed the 36 years in Norco, liked its rural atmosphere, and remarked that it was an ideal place to teach. The Norco Community Center was renamed in her honor in a ceremony in 1990.

WALTER AND CORDELIA KNOTT SETTLE IN NORCO

In 1924, Walter and Cordelia Knott bought 10 acres and planted blackberries on the south-west corner of Hillside Avenue and Third Street. Recognizing their crop's need for water, the Knotts bought 85 shares of stock in the Orange Heights Water Company. The only way the berries could survive in the sandy soil in that part if Norco was to have water every day in the summer.

The Knotts sold their berries at a stand on Hamner Avenue and third. For three years Walter argued with the Orange Heights Water Company

"Norco was pro-school. The people just gave me the support I needed to run the school," said pioneer educator Mildred Whiteside Fluetsch, who served the Norco district for almost 40 years.

"Everybody, including senior citizens, supported education. When we had a bond election, people would come on crutches to vote for (the issuance of bonds)." Mrs. Fluetsch said. Beginning her teaching career in 1933, she soon became the principal at Norco Grammar School. She was one of five teachers for 150-

Built in 1928 by Rex B. Clark, the Lake Norconian Club, located on 640 acres, brought the majority of its members from Los Angeles and Hollywood for the first couple years. The grand entrance is between the wings on the left. The ballroom is at the lower level on the right, with the lobby and dining room stacked on the two levels above it. *Courtesy Marsh Postcard Collection*

THE LAKE NORCONIAN CLUB, "THE RESORT SUPREME"

The first step toward the establishment of Clark's new chicken ranch was to dig wells at the location, in the hills west of Hamner. Surprisingly, his engineers discovered an underground lake of hot mineral sulfur water. Rex Clark, a creative man with big visions and dreams, began to make plans for a luxury resort which would be a playground for the wealthy from Los Angeles and movie stars from Hollywood.

Clark enthusiastically went ahead with his dream of the Lake Norconian Club, a luxury health spa and hotel to be built on the hilltop, surrounded by a golf course, a lake, manicured gardens, and an air strip. He envisioned that his private club would some day be surrounded by palatial estates. The first building to be built, in 1928, was the Tea House, built on the south side of the area that would become the parking lot. The semi-circular design was created to give each room the benefit of a maximum view of the manicured gardens. Ladies in short 1920s flapper dresses and gentlemen wearing suits had lunch and dinner in the new restaurant. Many patrons came from Los Angeles and Hollywood. For those having a private plane, a landing strip, with tents to shelter the planes, was prepared on the north side of the hill.

The Tea House was enough of a success that Clark set to work planning his 628-acre club, including a 62-acre lake. Dwight Gibbs, prominent architect from Los Angeles, was selected to design the Lake Norconian Club buildings. The second building to be built was the charming

for more water. In the end, the Knotts gave up their plans for settling in Norco and moved to 20 acres of leased land in Buena Park.

THE NORCO NEIGHBOR'S CLUB AND THE WOMEN'S PROGRESSIVE CLUB

One of the reasons that Norco was known for its neighborliness was the Norco Neighbor's Club. Founded in 1926, it was the first civic club in the valley. The name was soon changed to the Norco Women's Progressive Club. Contributing much to the culture and development of Norco, the organization was founded by Mrs. Amelia Gersback who served as its first president in 1926 and 1927. In 1928 the club became a member of the 23rd De Anza District of the California Federation of Women's Clubs. The group incorporated in 1964.

The organization, active in many civic affairs, was responsible for the founding of the public library. Some of these accomplishments were the establishment of playgrounds, the purchase and donation of the Senior Citizen's Center, scholarships, and other community activities.

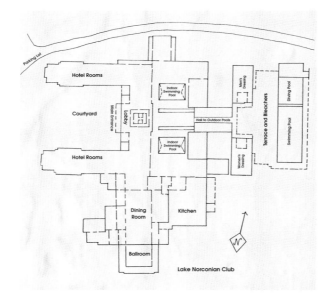

Lake Norconian Club

eight-sided Casino pavilion, cantilevered over the east side of the lake. The first formal event held there was a combined meeting of the Riverside Coroner's office and the Riverside Chamber of Commerce. The casino was open on Friday nights for dances and entertainment. Rex Clark often attended, participating in the skits and plays.

During an impressive ceremony on January 2, 1928, the water to the lake was turned on, rapidly filling the 62-acre area. The 18-hole golf course became a reality and the boat house, constructed on the north side of the lake, was christened during a big celebration on July 4, 1928. Clark's son, William, was put in charge of the boat house and water sports such as rowing, sailing, motorboat racing, fishing, and aquaplaning were held there regularly.

The main hotel, seven stories high, was built of poured-in-place concrete and topped with a red-tile-clad roof. Designed in the Spanish Colonial Revival style, the hotel had spacious rooms and large windows. Architect Gibbs planned the public rooms so that they had beautiful views of the gardens and hills. The hallways and rooms used by waiters and servers were hidden along the north side of the building. If a guest needed something, a member of the staff would appear quickly, emerging from the staff area on each floor, and disappear as soon as the guest was served.

The public rooms of the hotel were lavishly designed and decorated by Anthony Heinsbergen of Los Angeles. He and his employees decorated several of the ornate theatre buildings in the Los Angeles-Hollywood area. They decorated the ceilings, walls, and beams of the Norconian Club with classic Spanish and Italian themes. The richly-carved Spanish-style furniture was imported from Spain and Italy. The dining room, with its striking black-and-white diamond-patterned floor and high ceiling looked out over the lake and gardens.

The ballroom, lined with french doors on three sides, featured a special hardwood floor installed over springs for ease in dancing. Gold draperies and hardware complimented the lavish decorative ceiling, beams, and columns.

Twin indoor swimming pools were sheltered by ceilings made of glass set in wood frames. Small rooms, opening from the halls leading to the pools, were equipped with spas filled with hot mineral water. Ornamental tile in rich colors surrounded the spas.

The two olympic-sized out-door pools had seating for 800 spectators. Clark hoped that by building the pools to olympic specifications, the swimming and diving venues of the 1932 Olympic Games, held in Los Angeles, would take place at the Lake Norconian Club. Although that did not happen, many of the swimmers and divers who participated in the games used the pools during practice sessions. $50,000 was spent on a very expensive bar built near the pool. The three floors of hotel rooms, located in the wings on each side of the courtyard, were designed and furnished as if they were in the castles of Spain and Italy. In addition to the regular guests of the hotel, conventions and picnics were held regularly by various groups, including some of the prominent Hollywood studios. Some guests had rooms reserved for them year round. Room prices ran as much as $50 a day.

Clark offered an arrangement for local residents by which they could use the club's recreational facilities and dine there. Local organizations from Corona and Norco held parties at the pavilion.

Tunnels, stretching from underneath the hotel to the lake and pavilion, were built before the hotel was started. Rumors said that the tunnels were built so that Clark could entice Al Capone and the mob to stay at the resort, using the tunnels as escape routes, if needed. It does appear that Capone and his friends did stay at the club several times, but the tunnels were probably for the use of the staff, and allowed them to move from the hotel kitchen to the pavilion without being seen by the guests.

Rex B. Clark wrote, in a brochure advertising the club: "This chapter concerns America's 20th Century Aladdin, Mr. Rex B. Clark, and his dream

Rex. B. Clark, the founder of Norco, purchased 5,504 acres of land in 1921. He built the store, school, shopping center, and other main buildings of the town including the Lake Norconian Club. *Courtesy Norco Historical Society*

(Bottom Left) The public rooms of the Lake Norconian club were decorated with friezes, ornamental ceilings and beams, and murals designed and executed by the well-known Heinsbergen Company of Los Angeles. The ballroom, whose entrance is shown above, has a special dance floor built over spring trusses. *Courtesy Norco Historical Society*

of creating a legacy to the world of esthetic people a Golden Castle on the hilltop, wreathed in the perennial smiles of a California sun; to fashion from nothing, as it were, an Earthly Paradise whose beauty should not only excite the wonder and admiration of Mankind, but should echo

down the years like the sweet refrain of an old song. No man, but with the soul of a Byron, could have planned the Levantine Dream castle, dedicated to the Recreations."

NORCO'S FIRST CHURCH

The late 1920s Norco Community Church begun as a Sunday School of the American Sunday School Union and has served as a cornerstone of the community for more than 60 years. Officially incorporated on January 27, 1947, it is an independent non-denominational church that, since 1956, has been affiliated with the Independent Fundamental Churches of America. In the 1930s, the church had grown to over 60 members. As the congregation grew, the church was established on the corner of Sixth Street and Valley View Avenue.

NORCO GETS A LIBRARY

One of the signs of a stable community is the founding of the local library. The Norco Library, a community project sponsored by the Norco Women's Progressive Club, first opened its doors on July 9, 1930. The North Corona Land Company provided a roomy space on the second floor of the Norco Store. The club purchased used tables and chairs and assembled, stained and varnished the shelves for the 500 books loaned to the new facility by the Riverside County Library. The Library was supported by fundraisers featuring literary readings, musical entertainment and book socials. The N. W. P. C. acted as volunteer staff, performing every task needed to keep the library open. During World War II, the library was open every evening for the use of the men stationed at the Naval Hospital. Writing materials were provided and the men were assisted with writing letters to their families. The cookie jar, always kept full, and hot coffee helped the sailors feel at home.

When the Norco Park District was incorporated in 1950, the old Norco school building was purchased for use as a community center. The library was given a spacious rent-free room. It reopened on March 29, 1951, with Ethel Luttrell and Genevieve Sandiford serving as volunteer librarians. It was not until 1954 that the County of Riverside supplied a salary for the staff. On December 28, 1967, the Norco Branch Library celebrated the opening of a facility of its own, located on Hamner Avenue.

One of the proudest possessions of the Norco Fire Department is this lovingly-restored fire engine. It has been used in Norco parades and special occasions for many years. *Courtesy Norco Historical Society*

THE NORCO CHAMBER OF COMMERCE

In 1932, the Norco Chamber of Commerce was formed by citizens who wanted to bring new businesses to town. At the same time, they realized the importance of retaining the country atmosphere of the valley. Always working to promote Norco, the Chamber organized the first Norco Valley Fair in 1947, beginning an important tradition that continues to the present.

NORCO RESIDENTS SURVIVE THE DEPRESSION — THE LAKE NORCONIAN CLUB HOLDS ON

The Great Depression, which started with the stock market crash of 1929, deepened as the 1930s progressed. Those were lean times in Norco, as well as much of the nation. Luckily, many residents were able to survive by raising their own fruit, vegetables, eggs, chickens, and rabbits.

Mildred Fluetsch, then principal of Norco Grammar school, was aware that nutrition was the key to education. She initiated a soup kitchen at the school, ensuring that the students got a hot meal every day. "We charged two cents a bowl (for soup), but if they didn't have the two cents they could have the soup anyway. It really helped the kids during the Depression times."

Mrs. Fluetsch also helped students who needed eye care, clothes, shoes, medical care, and other necessities.

In the mid-1930s, the W. P. A., one of President Franklin Roosevelt's most successful New Deal programs, built the school playground, lunch area, and soccer field at the school. Mrs. Fluetsch remembers the Cod Liver Oil Project of the 1930s. Because of the concern that children were not getting enough vitamins during the Depression, Dr. Bernice (Jameson) Todd, the school doctor, set up a program which provided a spoonful of the cod liver oil per child each school day. The P. T. A. mothers came each morning to cut oranges into eight pieces. The children would line up on the veranda at recess, receive a mouthful of cod liver oil, and then be given the piece of orange to suck on. Many of the children would run eagerly out to the playground so they could find a place to spit out the oil and juice.

An act of neighborliness on the part of the North Corona Land Company is shown in a letter dated May 21, 1931. The company gave Clarence Swann permission to pasture his cow on the alfalfa owned by them, providing he maintained the alfalfa in good shape. It was signed by C. Gully, engineer.

Rex B. Clark barely held on to the glamorous Lake Norconian Club. During the Depression it was sometimes closed for periods of time. Many of the patrons tired of the drive out from Los Angeles and Hollywood. Others began going to Palm Springs — was the new "in" place to go. The name of the resort was changed to "Clark Hot Springs Hotel and Spa," and later, "The Rex Clark Hotel."

One of the most popular and useful features of the hotel was the swimming pools. Because they fit the parameters of an Olympic swimming pool, they were used as practice pools for as long as Clark owned the hotel.

THE LAKE NORCONIAN CLUB BECOMES A NAVAL HOSPITAL

In the months before the bombing of Pearl Harbor, the Navy was searching for a hospital site on the west coast. Clark offered to sell the club and property to the Navy for $3 million. After much bickering and negotiations, Clark sold the hotel for $1.6 million, and the Corona Naval Hospital was on its way to becoming established.

In October of 1942, the 268-bed hospital was officially opened. Hotel rooms were converted to hospital rooms, and larger spaces were converted to operating rooms and nurse's stations. The Navy sent servicemen to the facility to recover from rheumatic fever, polio, tuberculosis, malaria, and other chronic diseases. The hospital became the second largest Naval hospital in the nation.

Over the next six years, the Navy spent another $10 million on additions and improve-

ments. Expanding to 1,000 beds in the spring of 1943, the Navy built several new buildings to house hospital wards and to serve as headquarters for nurses and corpsmen. A 500,000 gallon water tank was built and a new sewer system installed. Wooden barracks were brought in to the lake house the 500-plus tuberculosis patients. They occupied the area where Clark's landing strip was previously located.

The hospital was teeming with patients and staff during World War II. By 1949, however, the need for the facility faded. It was closed in November of 1949 and the building stripped bare. The furnishings, draperies, and pictures belonging to the old Lake Norconian Club disappeared. Wiring, plumbing, and equipment was removed and used elsewhere. The magnificent hotel and grounds became a ghost town.

THE SCHOOL BECOMES A COMMUNITY CENTER

In 1947, state officials declared the Norco Grammar School an earthquake hazard. The students were moved immediately to the U. S. Naval Hospital, on the other side of the hill, and attended school in temporary classrooms. Mrs. Fleutsch remembers, "that was the most unique thing that happened to us. We marched the kids through the guard gates, and they played on the hill."

During Easter vacation in 1949, the teachers moved into the new Sierra Vista on Corona Avenue, near Fifth Street.

In 1947, a Community Center Committee was formed to work with the Corona Unified School District to turn the school into a community center. The residents of Norco had to agree to clean up and maintain the center while the final arrangements were made for the sale.

According to an article in *This is Riverside County-Corona-Norco*, local organizations and interested individuals formed work parties to restore the grounds and the interior of the building. The volunteers raised $4,000, the amount needed to complete the sale, and, in 1950, the building became a much-needed community center.

The first governing board elected to the newly-created Norco Park, Recreation, and Parkway District consisted of Kirk Parkmenter, Earl Copenhaven, and Jack Killen. In January of 1955, two trustee seats were added. Betty Sowell, William Kennedy, and Harry Brinton, in addition to Parmenter and Copenhaven, became members of the board. The grand opening/dedication was held on June 17, 1950. That year 136 meetings were held at the center. In 1954, the number had risen to 649. Not only had the residents of Norco preserved a significant historic building, they also provided an important center for the community, used by many clubs and organizations, as well as individuals.

In 1955 a second special district was formed to purchase the Orange Heights Water Company. The Company's water sys-tem had become badly deteriorated and needed drastic improvements. $1,750,00 worth of bonds were sold to buy the company and construct a new water system. Many Norco residents feel that these improvements marked the turning point in the growth of the valley.

Every community needs a fire department. The Norco Volunteer Fire Department was founded in 1957. As the community grew, the need for paid professional fire fighters became apparent.

THE CIRCUS WINTERS IN NORCO

For many years, during the 1940s, 50s, and 60s, Norco served as the winter grounds for a circus. The performers and animal handlers lived in the Norco Trailer Park on Hanmer Ave., and the animals were farmed out to various pastures in Norco farms. Particularly fascinating were the huge elephants that could be seen from Hillside Avenue.

NEW CHURCHES ARE FOUNDED IN NORCO

The Church of Jesus Christ of Latter-Day Saints began meeting in the Corona-Norco area in the mid-1940s, at the Woman's Improvement Club in Corona. In 1951, when it became apparent more room was needed, the congregation moved to the V. F. W. Hall at First and Hamner however,

The raising of nursery stock, as illustrated by this greenhouse and field, was important to the economy of Norco. *Courtesy Heritage Room, Corona Public Library*

The second grade class of the Norco Grammar School poses sedately in 1935. The teacher, shown in the back row, was Alice Clegg. Edna Johnson Velthoen, who donated the photo, is sixth from left, second row. *Courtesy Norco Historical Society*

they longed for a building of their own. They raised the needed funds by selling firewood, raising and selling pigs, hosting a Wild West Show, making and selling chocolate Easter eggs, and selling Christmas cards. In 1970, the Norco church became a separate ward, and, in the spring of 1984, it moved into a new church on Norconian Drive.

Until January of 1959, when St. Mel's Parish was established by the Most Reverend Charles Buddy, Bishop of San Diego, and Msgr. Thompson, the Catholic families from Norco attended St. Edwards Catholic Church in Corona. The latter, who was the pastor at St. Edwards, was instrumental in the naming of the new church. He had been born in the Diocese of Ardaugh in Ireland, which was once served by St. Mel, and went to college there. The first mass was celebrated in February of 1959 in the Grange Hall, with Father Samuel Engl, officiating. On February 1, 1960, St. Mel's conducted a ceremonial ground breaking for its first building.

In September of 1966, St. Mel's realized its dream of a school when the Benedictine Sisters from Ferdinand, Indiana, arrived to conduct the school. That first year, 195 students were enrolled in grades one through six.

The First Baptist Church of Norco was a mission church founded on September 16, 1955. With 32 charter members, the congregation met at the Community Center and the Grange Hall before purchasing land on Sixth Street. Brother Jim Adams, their first Pastor, came to them in May of

1957. The Norco Seventh Day Adventist Church, with 30 charter members, organized their church in July of 1960. Led by Pastor John Van Denburg, they met at the Community Center and the Baptist Church for the first 14 months. In April of 1961, the congregation purchased five acres of land on Corona Avenue. The Youth Chapel, the first building constructed, was finished in September of 1961.

Norco, a family-centered community, is proud of its churches.

THE NAVAL HOSPITAL BECOMES A REALITY ONCE AGAIN

In June of 1950, seven months after the Navy Hospital was closed, the Korean War began. Suddenly, the Navy needed the hospital again, and spent $3 million to renovate and get it ready to reopen. A year later, the hospital was recommissioned as a general hospital for Navy personnel and their families. Between 700 and 800 beds were in use. Navy wives sometimes had to be driven from as far away as Los Angeles and south Orange County to have their babies in the hospital's very busy maternity ward.

THE NAVAL ORDINANCE LAB WAS ESTABLISHED

In the early 1950s, the National Bureau of Standards Missle Development Division, learn-

The Norco Fire Department, which started as an all-volunteer organization, poses in front of the fire station with their Dalmatian dog. *Courtesy Norco Historical Society*

For more than 70 years, Norco has attracted those who love horses. The half-acre and larger parcels allow for the keeping of horses and other animals. *Courtesy Norco Historical Society*

ing that the hospital had been vacated, made plans to move from Washington D.C. to Norco. $1,540,000 was alloted by the federal government to rehabilitate and building as a weapons center. When the Korean War broke out in June of 1951, the Navy once again claimed the hospital. Forced to divide up the property, the Bureau of Standards was given Unit II in which to set up its development program. The Naval Ordinance Laboratory, with 7,700 employees,

was formed to give technical direction for the Navy's guided missile fuze research and development program.

THE NAVAL HOSPITAL CLOSES AGAIN

The Naval Hospital, situated on 607 acres, closed again in 1957. The property included 21 buildings that had once housed over 700 employees. The buildings, again stripped, sat empty except for the rats, foxes, bats and other animals that made it their home.

The Naval Ordinance Lab, which was continuing to grow, was given the clubhouse, lake, wells, reservoir, golf course, sewage system, and much of the original grounds. The Lab made a portion of the old Lake Norconian Club grounds available for community use, with permission from the Navy. Dinners and parties were held in the pavilion, and the tree-shaded grounds around the lake were used by the scouts for day camp and campouts. By 1970, there were over 1,000 employees at the Lab. The operating budget was over $40 million.

NORCO IN THE 1960s

In the early 1960s, Norco suddenly began to grow by leaps and bounds. As the two-and-a-half-acre plots were subdivided into half-acre mini-ranches, new streets were created, leading off of the established streets. Families who wanted to be able to have animals moved into the new ranch-style homes on half-acre lots. Special zoning allowed residents to have farms, animals and pets on lots one-half-acre or larger. Most of the grapevines and fruit trees were gone, but the chicken, turkey, egg and rabbit ranches were doing well. In the early 1960s, Norco farmers marketed more than 1 million dozen eggs, 100,000 fryers, and 3 million baby chicks.

The 4-H Cub Scouts, Indian Guides, and Indian Maidens had programs which attracted families. Active clubs for adults included the Norco Grange, American Legion, Fleet Reserve Association, Women's Progressive Club, P. T. A. and others. Riding groups were available for all ages, and the churches were gaining members. The Norco Hoof Beats, formed in 1961, with seven charter members, gave fascinating and lively demonstrations of square dancing on horse back. The Peruvian Paseo Club, started in 1970, specializes in the showing of Peruvian Paseo horses, and often appear in the Rose Parade in Pasadena.

The Norco Rotary Club, founded in March of 1968, is known for its community service. Certificates to reward children for improvement in class work during the year, encourage students to do well in school. The club has done much to help the handicapped and senior citizens. The Soroptimist Club, part of a worldwide organization of executive, business and professional women, was formed in Norco in 1981. Their goals are the betterment of the community, high standards in their professional lives, and forming friendships among other women executives.

NORCO HISTORICAL SOCIETY

For several years, the Norco Chamber of Commerce served as the official historical body of the City. It gathered and preserved important documents. After incorporation, Lois Richards was appointed official historian. For the next 21 years, she held the position, keeping records and gathering photographs.

After Mrs. Richards resigned in 1985, the Chamber of Commerce was officially appointed as the keeper of the historical materials. In early 1987, a special subcommittee of the Chamber was formed and began collecting and preserving items of historical significance.

The Norco Historical Society, an independent non-profit organization, received its non-profit status in March of 1987. The first task was to elect a nine-member board. The second was to look for a place to display and store the many historical materials gathered in past years. The Norco Museum, located next to the public library, on Old Hamner Avenue, has an especially fine photography collection, and display cases of Norco memorabilia.

THE CALIFORNIA REHABILITATION CENTER

In 1960, several government agencies were eyeing the empty and abandoned Lake Norconian Club/Naval Hospital, and several possibilities were considered for it future use.

On March 2, 1962 Governor Brown announced that the federal government would donate the hospital to the state of California. The State would proceed immediately to turn the facility into a narcotics addict rehabilitation center. Although not everyone was happy about the division, it did become a reality, and the rehabilitation center is still in operation.

If you visit the hotel today, you can still get a real sense of the dream castle that Rex Clark created. Most of the ornate painting exists on the ceilings and beams. The black-and-white marble floor in the dining room still provides an interesting pattern. The spring-based floor of the ballroom is in good condition. Several of the original light fixtures are in use. The indoor pools have been covered over and the spas and tiles removed, but the outdoor swimming and diving pools are still in place. The grounds are kept in immaculate condition and the view of the lake and pavilion, owned by the Navy, is still beautiful. However, the facility is obviously a prison, with multiple layers of razor wire and guard towers.

THE NORCO VALLEY FAIR

Perhaps the city's most popular is the Norco Valley Fair. The 1964 parade, which had 207 entries and 379 horses and ponies, managed to draw a large crowd. The Cub Scouts' Pack 174 captured the sweepstakes prize for the best float that same year. Country-western entertainer, Lucky Carson, served as grand marshal and the Camp Pendleton Marine Corps band led the parade.

Prizes were awarded in several categories of the decorative arts, including needlework, quilting, sewing, crafts, knitting, and crochet-

ing. The Norco Valley Agricultural Association gave prizes for the best vegetables, fruits, and animals. As examples, Luther Smith won the grand prize for his 50-lb pumpkin that year, and May Kay took six blue ribbons in the guinea pig division. There are special divisions for animals raised by children. The Norco Valley Fair is like the city itself. It is family-oriented and offers something of everyone to enjoy.

NORCO INCORPORATES

By 1962, talk of incorporation had begun. A supporter of the movement, Willard Love said in the *Corona Daily Independent:* "We must incorporate to save Norco and our way of life. Incorporation is the only way by which we can keep what we have and not be eaten away through annexation by the neighboring cities."

■ After Norco was incorporated in 1964, the City Hall was in the right-hand section of the old Orange Heights Water Company location. *Courtesy Norco Historical Society*

The cityhood and election of the first city council was finally set for December 15, 1964. The campaign had barely gotten started, however, when Riverside Properties, owner of considerable land within the proposed boundaries, brought a civil suit, claiming the incorporation proceedings did not comply with the law. The case was thrown out of court by Judge John Neblett. Another large property owner, the Marjan Company also campaigned against the incorporation.

Two days before the election, several hundred Norconians attended a combination dinner and incorporation rally, given by the Chamber of Commerce Committee for Incorporation.

Prospective council members campaigned vigorously. Gil Cox, Dr. John Konig, and Thomas Harris ran on the Western ticket, while William Range and Louis Hoefs ran on the All For Norco Ticket. All of these candidates promised that there would be no local property taxes. The City would be supported by sales tax and state subventions.

On December 15, the voters cast their ballots decidedly in favor of incorporation, with Gil Cox, Thomas Harris, Louis Hoefs, Dr. John Konig, and Bert Range elected to the first city council. Gil Cox served as the first mayor, followed by Louis Hoefs.

NORCO RETAINS ITS COUNTRY FLAVOR

Norco has truly lived up to its name "Acres of Neighbors". Four elementary schools, a junior high, a high school, and a junior college provide good educations for the community's students.

Ingalls Park, named in memory of George Alan Ingalls, a Norco hero who died in the Vietnam War, is geared toward horseback riders. Nellie Weaver Hall, located in the park, provides a center for various activities. Neal Snipes Park, named for a fallen Norco hero who was killed during World War II, was dedicated in April of 1973. The River Trails Park, a natural park located along the bluff above the Santa Ana River, is popular with horseback riders. Clark Field is a center of baseball activities.

With its large variety of clubs and organizations, Norco continues to be especially attractive to families with children. Horse trails border many of the streets, and the majority of the properties are in the form of mini-ranches, as was envisioned by Rex Clark in 1921.

THE FULLER RANCHO

The hills, valleys and flat lands around Corona continued to be developed in the 1920s. Visitors from the Los Angeles area were discovering the beauty of the rich countryside surrounding the 40-year-old community of Corona.

Olive Ransome Fuller and his wife Ione dreamed of a home in the country where they could spend their weekends entertaining their friends. They already owned a 3,000-acre ranch in Eastvale, seven miles northwest of Corona which they called the Fuller RanchO (this unusual spelling was on the letterheads and official documents). In the mid-1920s they built a fine Spanish Colonial Revival mansion on the bluff overlooking the river. The finest craftsmen were used to build the house. An Italian cabinetmaker, carved the beams and balconies. The ornate Spanish-style furniture and fine rugs were imported from Spain.

In 1925, O.R. and Ione Fuller built a Spanish Colonial Revival mansion on the Fuller Ranch. For several years it was their vacation home; however in 1932, because of the Depression, the family moved from Hollywood to the ranch, making it their permanent home. In 1937 the Fullers opened up a guest ranch, on which they entertained wealthy Angelenos and Hollywood stars. *Courtesy Marsh Postcard Collection*

They called their large Spanish Colonial house "Casa Orone", a combination of both of their names. Set in a verdant valley along the west side of the Santa Ana River, the house became the centerpiece of a recreational mecca, complete with a lake for the Fullers and their friends.

O. R. as he liked to be called, made his money as owner of several Auburn, Cord and Dueseberg dealerships in Southern California. During World War I, he established a White dealership. Soon after the war, he founded the Motor Transit Bus Company, establishing bus routes all over California. The Bus Company was eventually sold to the Greyhound Bus Company for $8 million. Fuller, who had arrived in California at the age of 18, liked to remind his friends that in spite of his many successes, he had only a third grade education.

O.R.'s father, Charlie Fuller, was an early pioneer in Southern California, coming here from Iowa in the late 1880s. A very successful businessman, he founded the Pioneer Transfer Company of Los Angeles. At the end of World War I, he purchased the ranchland in Eastvale. In 1925, because of failing health, Charlie sold the property to O. R. — his only child. O. R. purchased additional land bringing the total amount of acreage to about 3,000. He also leased property in the Santa Ana River bottom, bringing the total amount of land under his control to approximately 5,000 acres.

Sadly, the Fullers were greatly affected by the Great Depression. O. R. lost a fortune in the automobile business. By going into the agricultural business on a full-time basis, he was able to hold onto the ranch through sheer hard work and inventiveness. He raised a fine herd of dairy cattle and established home delivery routes in Ontario, Pomona and San Bernardino. He maintained the business until 1940 when he sold it to the Knudson Company. The *Corona Daily Independent*, in an article dated May 4, 1936, noted that there were several records established at the ranch:

"Adjoining Corona on the west is Fuller RanchO which produced 14,000 turkeys in 1935, the largest flock in Southern California. In addition the RanchO has a dairy head of 625 cows, the largest in the county. It also holds the record for the largest Barred Rock breeding flock —12,000 chickens and is believed to be the largest irrigated farm in the county."

Because of its reduced financial circumstances, in 1932 the family moved from Hollywood to Eastvale to live full time. O. R. opened his spacious home to the public in 1937 calling it the Fuller RanchO Guest Ranch and advertising the many outdoor activities available to guests, the fine meals and the charming character of the mansion.

Tradition says that gambling was one of the favorite pastimes for the ranch guests. Wealthy Hollywood stars flocked to the ranch finding it a great place to get away from it all. According to Mrs. Marcellie Thompson, O. R. and Ione's daughter, celebrities such as Groucho Marks, W. C. Fields, Red Skelton, Jack Oakie, Spencer Tracy, Mary Pickford, Buddy Rogers, Rachelle Hudson, Jeannette McDonald, Gene Raymond, Ken Murray, Garson Kanin and Clair Trevor were among the celebrities who enjoyed visiting the ranch. In 1938, O. R. subdivided the land along the bluff overlooking his large lake in the Santa Ana river bottom and created a row of very desirable view lots. Charles Grapewin, a well-known movie actor, built the first house in the new subdivision.

The ornate interior of the mansion, which featured a rich Spanish Colonial theme, was decorated by the finest craftsmen. The rugs and furniture were imported from Spain. *Courtesy Heritage Room, Corona Public Library*

Having 24 rooms, the impressive home was built for the considerable sum of $100,000. The street was named Grapewin Avenue. Other lots along the bluff were sold to a shipbuilder from Long Beach, a talent scout from Hollywood, a film director, an oilman and a mortician, also from Long Beach.

Several families living in nearby houses owned by the Fullers worked on the ranch and the resort. A store was established at the end of Chandler Street. The dance hall, called the Dog House, was a great place to go dancing on a Saturday night.

O. R. died of cancer in 1946 at the age of 66 and Ione married Harvey Weeks. She died in 1951 also of cancer. Three years later, their daughter Marcellie sold the ranch to a local dairyman named Walter Koenig in order to settle her mother's estate. In 1959 Koenig sold some of the property and Casa Orone to the Good Samaritan Retirement Center and the spacious house became the home of 66 elderly residents. On November 1, 1967 it became the Good Samaritan Home for Boys.

GLEN IVY HOT SPRINGS

Set against a backdrop of the Santa Ana Mountains on a narrow bench of land clad in lush greenery and live oaks, Glen Ivy overlooks the Temescal Valley. Through the years the springs and resort have attracted many generations of travelers and dwellers. It is located at the mouth of Coldwater Canyon, the largest canyon on the north side of the Santa Ana Mountains.

The Luiseño Indians frequently used the hot springs and named the valley "Temescal," which means "sweat house." For centuries the hot sulfur water bubbled out of the ground at a temperature between 85 and 110 degrees. Long after the Indians established the road, Spanish Dons and explorers traveled the road. In the late 1860s the Butterfield Stage had a stop near the springs. Accommodations could be found at the station occupied at that time by the Greenwades. As early as 1861 the *Los Angeles Star* advertised the springs, touting their medicinal value.

Captain Wheaton Sayward homesteaded the land in the late 1870s. He thought the waters would benefit his wife's circulatory illness. The couple built a 10-room adobe house for their seven adopted children. In 1887 the family moved to Canada after selling the property to Mrs. Newman and Mrs. Thorndyke. It was Mrs. Thorndyke, an ardent spiritualist, who built the small bath house and a three-story frame home. Sadly, the buildings both burned in 1884.

The Steers family opened the hotel and bathhouse in 1890 in the Sayward's adobe and are credited with being the originators of the name

"Glen Ivy". As the resort gained popularity, small wooden guest cottages were added and covers were built over the pools at the hot springs. In the 1902 booklet, *Corona, the Queen Colony*, the resort is advertised under the proprietorship of J. F. Mitchell. He called it "the finest pleasure resort in Riverside County especially for businessmen from Los Angeles who like to get away for a rest and a few days of shooting rabbits, quail and doves."

For Coronans, the canyons and swimming holes of the Temescal Valley were great places for picnics, summer holiday celebrations and get-togethers. The tally-ho, a large wagon which held a dozen or so people, often traveled down the canyon bringing people to what were called "talley-ho parties".

For a few years around 1910, the hotel and grounds were owned by a group of Los Angeles sportsmen headed by Jack Doyle of the Vernon Country Club. In 1913 Mr. and Mrs. Frank Johnson became the next owners. Under their ownership Glen Ivy Hot Springs continued to grow in popularity. As more families purchased cars, the trip out to the Temescal Valley became somewhat easier. In 1920 the Johnsons built the

three-story main hotel building, designed with historic character and charm, around the adobe. The huge fireplace was constructed of stones found on the property and inset with Indian metates. Murals of pioneer scenes decorated the walls of the dining room. The lobby was built around an existing palm tree.

By the 1920s and 30s Glen Ivy Hot Springs and Hotel was considered to be the best-known facility of its kind in Southern California. Prominent politicians and movie stars frequented the home, soaking in the pools and eating sumptuous meals.

In 1937 the Johnsons leased the entire facility to Florence and Axel Springborg. Five years later the couple purchased the property. In the capable hands of the Springborgs, who were experienced hoteliers and restaurateurs, the resort became even more successful. The hotel became known for its excellent meals and in particular, the Smorgasbord served every Saturday night. The banquet facilities hosted many Corona celebrations.

The Springborgs were often photographed with their huge St. Bernard dogs. They kept saddle horses available for hotel guests and often rode along the forested trails with them. The Springborgs owned a pair of matched Palominos and silver-mounted saddles which they rode in parades and shows. Alex, who was president of the Al Malaikah Shrine Patrol, named his horse "King of Glen Ivy". Corona residents were saddened when the Springborgs announced their retirement after almost 30 years as owners of the charming hotel.

Temescal Properties Inc. purchased the property in 1965, planning to continue the operation of the hotel, pools and extensive grounds. Unfortunately, the flood of 1969 which did extensive damage to the Temescal Wash, also damaged the hotel to the extent that it had to be closed. After two years of repair work, the resort was reopened in April of 1971. However in 1972, Temescal Properties announced that the hotel was no longer profitable and closed it permanently. A special era was gone forever.

Full of charm and an "Old World" character, the Glen Ivy Hot Springs Hotel, located 10 miles southeast of Corona, was constructed in 1920 and went on to become very popular and successful. It was built around an old adobe which was built in 1879 or 1880 by Captain Sayward, and featured a palm tree growing up through the lobby. *Courtesy Heritage Room, Corona Public Library*

The hotel, located high on the hill at the end of a lane flanked by two rows of stately palm trees, is now a private residence. The pools and bath house located on the middle level, are open to the public. An 18-acre recreational vehicle park is located on the lowest level next to Temescal Canyon Road.

EL CERRITO RANCH-TEMESCAL GARDENS

In Spanish El Cerrito means "The Little Hill." Before the freeway was built, the hill named El Cerrito could be seen from all directions. It was a landmark for travelers coming along the Old Temescal Road and starting to cross the bare alluvial plain along what is now Ontario Avenue.

The virgin land was part of the property purchased by the South Riverside Land and Water Company in 1886. In 1893 Robert Taylor, the founder of South Riverside, bought the property for himself and set out 14,000 lemon trees. It was he who christened the ranch "El Cerrito." and-built an impressive house for his family.

J. H. Flagler, who bought the property for $76,078 in 1896, was a wealthy standard oil and steel magnate. He built a packing house for his lemons, oranges and grapefruit. The packing house eventually was purchased by Sunkist Growers.

Mr. Flagler's daughter Anna, was married to Baron Hickey, the person who suggested the name "Corona" as the new name for South Riverside in 1896. Shortly thereafter at the age of 43, Baron Hickey committed suicide by ingesting poison while staying at a hotel in El Paso. He left behind a note which said, "I prefer being a dead gentleman to a living blackguard like your father."

In the early 1930s, Allen Davis planted the neighborhood's first avocado grove and built a house on what came to be known as Avocado Hill. At the same time he subdivided some of the land below the hill and called it Temescal Gardens. A few years later, the Transit Mix Company of Corona built a small tract in the area.

J. Midgley, in his paper "How El Cerrito Was Named," reports that renowned novelist Sinclair Lewis lived in El Cerrito in the late

Duke and Duchess, were two of the St. Bernard's owned by Florence and Axel Springborg, the owners and proprietors of the hotel from 1937 to 1965. Famous for their excellent meals and Smorgasbords, the pair everyone welcome at the hotel. *Courtesy Heritage Room, Corona Public Library*

1930s. In 1926 Lewis was offered the Pulitzer Prize for the *Arrowsmith* but refused it. In 1930 he became the first American to receive the Nobel Prize for literature. Lewis was one of the most influential satirists in America literature.

In 1945 Francis Stearns bought El Cerrito Ranch and some additional property. He subdivided it into lots, drilled water wells, built roads and named the new community El Cerrito Village.

As more families moved into the neighborhood, the need for the community's own school house arose. In 1959 the El Cerrito School was built, creating a focus for the community.

THE GHOSTS OF RINCON-PRADO

Look out over Prado Dam, to the north and you can envision the site of the crossroads town of Prado, known until 1907 as Rincon. By the time the dam was completed in 1941, the settlement had disappeared from the face of the earth.

Rincon, like South Riverside (Corona), was created during the "Boom of the Eighties". Planted in 1887, the town was touted by its promoters as a natural trade center because it was situated on the banks of the Santa Ana River at the junction of the Old Temescal Road, the Pomona-Rincon Road and the Santa Ana Canyon. Rincon became a station on the projected Riverside, Santa Ana and Los Angeles Railroad. Of the 600 acres subdivided by the Rincon Land and Town Company, 70 were divided into town lots. Nearly $80,000 worth of land was sold in the first few days. A wooden Victorian-style schoolhouse was moved to Rincon from Auburndale, a failed townsite less than a mile away.

By 1888 there were 50 people living in town. By 1890 the community had two stores and several houses all situated at three intersections near the center. There were several farms and ranches in the area, including the Campio and Fear ranches. In 1900 a new bridge was built across the Santa Ana River and the railroad finally was extended to Rincon.

It was in 1907 that the community's name was changed to Prado which means "plain" or "yard" in Spanish. In 1908, with the new railroad opportunities, Prado became a center for the shipping of hay, cream and carloads of clay. The railroad built a bunkhouse for railroad workers in Prado.

Does anyone remember Prado Beach? In 1915 a Labor Day Picnic on Prado Beach was advertised in the Corona newspaper. The ad, placed by H. F. Scott the manager, highlighted the new hardwood dance floor and band music. Also mentioned were free attractions, hot lunches and all kinds of concessions. If the visitor preferred, he or she could bring a picnic lunch as well as camp for a few days. Tents and bathing suits could be rented.

In 1921 Prado was first viewed as a potential site for a major dam by Orange County interests.

In the early 1930s Allen Davis planted the neighborhood's first avocado grove at El Cerrito Ranch. *Courtesy Heritage Room, Corona Public Library*

This was followed in 1925 by the first official study of the townsite as a flood control basin. However, the town continued to be a prosperous farming center with dairies and field crops as a focus. That same year J. J. Newberry sold his ranch to Excelsior Creamery and Orange County voters defeated a flood control measure.

Even though Orange County voters defeated a flood control measure in 1929, time was growing short for the community of Prado. The town post office was discontinued and the railroad agent was removed from the Prado Station.

The death bell of Rincon/Prado was sounded in 1938 when a series of storms from February 27th to March 3rd created a disastrous flood which did millions of dollars worth of damage in Orange and Riverside Counties. Leo Friis reported in *Orange County Through Four Centuries* that at the peak of the flood, shortly after midnight on March 3rd, water roared out of the Santa Ana Canyon at a rate of 100,000 feet per second. At

1 a.m. a wall of water inundated the small communities of Atwood and La Jolla near Placentia. In all, 19 people were killed. All of the county's automobile bridges were wiped out except the Chapman Avenue bridge. Over 40,000 acres of Orange County farm land were covered with the flood waters. When the waters receded, a thick coat of mud mixed with oil from the Richfield oil fields was left behind. The flood greatly speeded up the reality of the Prado Dam.

The Army Corps of Engineers was designated to head the dam project which was financed by the federal government. A few of the buildings, such as the post office now sitting on the same property as the Yorba Slaughter Adobe, were moved to other locations but most were demolished. Many of the surrounding ranches such as the Merideth, Hartshorn and Lillibridge properties were destroyed. The site of Rincon-Prado became the Atlantis of Riverside County, buried forever under tons of water.

Chapter 7

The Brink of Great Changes

IT WAS A MOST UNUSUAL DAY!

Anyone who lived in Corona in 1949 will remember the freeze and snow of 1949. It seems like everyone who owned a camera was out taking photographs of their favorite places covered with snow. On January 18, 1949, the city was covered with approximately three inches of snow, while the foothills to the south received as much as nine inches. The Robert L.Willits family, who owned a large citrus orchard south of the city, described it thusly, in a New Year's card complete with photographs:

"The 1949 freeze was our big story this year. It arrived with snow, ice, hail, and wind. The temperatures were in the low twenties. Hundreds of citrus trees were broken by the weight of the snow. In the Corona District we had 61 dangerous nights with orchard heating on 29 of these. At first it was very exciting — the cars, the oil tanks, the men with torches, the heaters looking like ten thousand candelabra, the droning of the wind machines, the hurry and bustle of it all. But soon it gets to be a grim struggle against the elements, a nightmare with weary men firing by night and filling by day.

"Ned is in the midst of it all, but R. L. W. for the first time in his long citrus career was not on the firing line. He found a nice warm bed and a telephone a marvelous combination and wished he had thought of it forty years ago.

"When it was over Corona had lost less than 5 percent of our fruit, compared with California's 30 percent loss. However, the fruit was of poor quality and small size because of the long cold spell. The cost of the frost protection was very high.

"In the national media Corona had one page in *Life* on February 14,1949...double page in the *National Geographic*...July 1949 was mentioned two or three times in Joe Jenks comics, and "The Miner From Corona" in *Mule Train*. Also *Storm Center* with Ginger Rogers was filmed here last month."

Orchard heaters, along with a lot of hard work on the part of those in the citrus industry, saved most of Corona's $4 million citrus crop.

1949 was not only the year it snowed in Corona. In 1928, there was almost four inches of snow piled in some parts of Corona. The next time it snowed was in 1932. After the 1949

snow and a long freeze, which lasted for almost two months, it was not until 1968 that snow appeared again, almost giving Corona a white Christmas. On December 22nd of that year, it snowed on the last day of school before Christmas vacation and caused a lot of excitement among the children. Most of them frolicked in the snow, throwing snowballs and laughing.

THE 1950s: THE BEGINNING OF GREAT CHANGES

By 1957, there were over 12, 750 people living within the city limits. Agriculture still dominated the economic base of the community. Corona was still surrounded by neatly-maintained groves of oranges, lemons, and grapefruit, and avocados were being raised in El Cerrito. Norco's egg and poultry ranches were doing well. Many will remember the Gobbler's Knob on Hamner Avenue, which sold high-quality turkeys.

The Santa Fe Railroad passed through Corona, providing access to the transcontinental line, and the Pacific Electric Cars still offered service from the Riverside, San Bernardino and Colton areas. The Greyhound and Metropolitan buses stopped at a station on Third Street to pick up passengers. The Municipal Airport was a popular place for local flyers. There were 12 motels and hotels for those who were passing through town.

The Corona-Norco School District listed 3,775 students enrolled in local schools in 1957. There were three elementary schools, one junior high, one senior high and two

parochial schools in Corona and a grade school and new junior high school in Norco. The Corona Public Library was home to over 30,000 books and pamphlets.

The swimming pool, located in the 20-acre city park on Sixth Street, was a popular place on hot days. In addition, there were three neighborhood playgrounds.

A new and improved business climate was just beginning to emerge. In the late 1950s, there were 478 businesses operating in Corona. Fifty of these were manufacturing plants which produced such items as lemon by-products, brick and tile, silica, sand and gravel and a variety of foods.

In the early 1950s, the Borden Plant was relocated to Corona's industrial park. Manager A.J. "Dutch" Velthoen was in charge of the manufacturing of crystallized lemon juice. It was packed into small cans which went into the rations of U.S. servicemen. The area's largest employer was the Exchange Lemon Products Company (Sunkist), which operated a large and active plant northeast of Grand Boulevard. With more than 600 employees, the plant processed about one-third of the total output of lemons and 80 percent of the lemon by-products in the United States.

The U. S. Naval Lab, located on the west side of Hamner in Norco, employed the second largest group of people, most of whom were engaged in electronic research.

Die Casting and machinery manufacturing companies were

becoming established in the industrial area between Corona and Norco. In 1958, parcels of land could still be purchased for as low as $3,000 an acre. Industrial land in Orange County cost about twice as much. Using this comparison, Corona began to promote the lands to the north of the city that had been zoned for industry.

The Greyhound Bus Lines sent their buses through Corona on a daily basis. This photo was taken in front of the station on Ramona Street in the early 1940s. *Courtesy Heritage Room, Corona Public Library*

FLYING HIGH IN CORONA

Occasionally a barnstorming pilot in a OX5 Curtis Jenny landed in the hayfields north of the city and offered rides to the residents for a few dollars. You can imagine the excitement of seeing a rare plane in the sky above.

By 1930, there were several local residents who had been bitten by the flying bug. Among them were Dr. Denver Roos, Glen James, and Harry M. Johnson Sr. They called their planes "Crates." According to Jim Greer, in an article in the *Corona Daily Independent*, the group was "just crazy about airplanes" and made a landing strip in a dirt field northeast of the circle. It developed into the city's first airport. Unfortunately for them, the advent of World War II brought an end to recreational flying on the west coast. After the war, George Dober established an airport near Magnolia Avenue, behind the Hickory Restaurant. When the property was sold, the airport was relocated to the old Kuster ranch. When Scott Thursby bought the ranch, the airport was named Thursby Field.

It was in 1958 that the city took over the airport, mandating that the facility had to support itself. When the Riverside Freeway took nearly 1,000 feet of the runway, it was once again time to move. A site, owned by the U. S. Army Corps of Engineers, was selected near Prado Dam. Being located in the flood basin brought a

few problems, namely the threat of frequent flooding. On the other hand, there were few houses near the airport. In 1969, $196,000 was spent to completely rebuild the facility. The airport has continued to be a popular place for local residents who have their own planes.

Jesse Hill, called "the greatest all-round athlete in the history of Corona High School," graduated from the school in 1925. He went on to become a coach at Corona High School, Riverside Jr. College, Long Beach College and USC. *Courtesy Heritage Room, Corona Public Library*

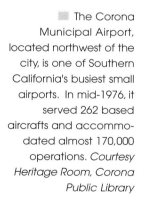

The Corona Raceway, which operated in the hills east of Corona from 1970 until 1975, was run by Felice, Laura and Tom Lipari. It was a popular place for family outings. *Courtesy Heritage Room, Corona Public Library*

In 1948 and 1949, residents flocked to the Old Corona Raceway, located at River Road and Corydon Street. Dan Nicholson, Mel Steiner and Walt Bowen, from Los Angeles were the builders of the half-mile dirt track. They had been looking for a racetrack location outside the metropolitan area and thought the Corona countryside would be ideal. According to Mel Beets, who used to announce the races, Parnelli Jones, who went on to become famous in the racing industry, got his start at Corona. Other drivers who went on to become well-known were Troy Pittman and Jack Austin, a three-time San Bernardino champion.

In 1971, the Lipari family opened the Corona Raceway, fondly remembered by many local people, in the hills east of Corona. Onlookers witnessed many nights of thrills, spills and speed. In 1970 the first race at the family-oriented track was held in 1970 and featured stock cars and motorcycles. Felice Lipari, along with his wife, Laura, ran the track for the first several years, until their son, Tom, took over the operation. Felice had been a Formula I racing driver in Italy 50 years prior, in the early 1930s. For awhile J. C. Agajanian, a big name in racing circles, was a partner in the running of the raceway. A movie about the life of race driver Richard Petty was filmed at the track.

The Corona Municipal Airport, located northwest of the city, is one of Southern California's busiest small airports. In mid-1976, it served 262 based aircrafts and accommodated almost 170,000 operations. *Courtesy Heritage Room, Corona Public Library*

In 1985, after 15 years of racing, it was announced that the track would cease operations. For the final event over 500 motorcycle riders turned out. A crowd of more than 1,500 saw the 300 qualifying riders compete in a tough race. All semblance of the track is now gone, and houses occupy the site that gave so many Corona families thrills and enjoyment.

CORONA-NORCO YMCA: AN ORGANIZATION FOR THE ENTIRE FAMILY

In the mid-1960s Corona had over 80 community organizations. Particularly active were the members of the YMCA. In 1962, Lloyd Jensen, after moving to Corona with his wife, Laura, and sons Larry, Ron and Randy, came up with a plan to revive the YMCA in the city. His incentive had been his previous experiences in the Reseda Y. Along with a committee consisting of Bill

Landry, Jim Cleveland, Lloyd Lay, Gordon Adams, Frank Rebello, and himself, Jensen worked with the Riverside YMCA to create a Corona branch of the organization. The first membership drive, in 1963, produced 113 sponsoring members.

The first official Y program was the 1963 summer camp, headed by a local teacher, Bill Michaelis. Jack Nichols was hired by the board to work as a YMCA secretary on a part-time basis. Lloyd and his son, Randy, through the cooperation of the elementary schools, organized the first Y-Indian Guide tribe, the Mighty Mohaves. Soon there were six additional tribes totaling 64 "Indians." One of the main reasons the Y became such an active organization was the cooperation and assistance of John Stallings, Superintendent of the Corona-Norco Unified School District.

In 1964, 191 youths became involved in the new Gray-Y and Jr. High programs. The following year, the Y began to gather great momentum. Van Carter, deciding that it was important to have a program for the girls, started the Y Indian Maidens. That year, approximately 1,000 young people were involved in Y clubs, summer camps, judo classes and other activities sponsored by the Y. Al Velasco was hired as part-time Secretary-

▪ Shown below is the first diesel-powered train to come through Corona. The sleek modernistic Engine No. 6 is shown in the late 1950s on the Santa Fe tracks north of town. *Courtesy Heritage Room, Corona Public Library*

■ Downtown
Corona, as it looked in
the early 1960s. The Lord
Building, built in 1911, is
shown on the right side
of the photo. The First
Baptist church tower
can be seen all the way
to the left of the photo.
*Courtesy Heritage
Room, Corona
Public Library*

fine yearlings that commanded top prices. Over $3 million in purses were won by the offspring of Four-and-Twenty, Nashville and Our Rulla. Azure Te, Chiclero and Nasharco were among the horses who won many winning stakes.

The ranch became a showplace when the Arnazes built a new five-bedroom 4,000-square-foot Spanish Colonial house.

Arnaz considered selling the ranch as early as 1970, but he wanted to be certain that the property would remain a horse ranch. In 1976, he sold the property to Dr. E. Jan Davidian, a prominent Orange County orthodontist and Arnaz moved to Baja California. From 1964 until 1967, Arnaz was the focus of a lawsuit brought by two employees of the Thunderbird Country Club near Indio. He was accused of slander, assault, battery, and false imprisonment, but in December of 1967 he was acquitted of all charges. The ranch was a great place for Arnaz and one that he had enjoyed and would always be fond of.

The Davidians moved to the ranch and renamed it Bar-D-Zok Quarter Horse Ranch. In 1980, they sold 17 acres to an auto parts manufacturer, and, in 1984, sold the remaining acres to the Golden State Cheese Company. The firm has since developed the world's largest cheese factory on the site.

Manager. As activities increased, Velasco was became full-time secretary. Alice Capdeville and Carole Halzle were hired to keep the office running efficiently. With their tireless devotion, they helped the kids and ran many activities.

In 1972-73, the Corona-Norco Y separated from the Riverside Y and began a building program. The groundbreaking for the new building took place on their plot of land on April 1, 1973. Two years later, the new building was dedicated to the youth of the area and the Christian ethics of the organization. The Y has continued to be very active, expanding its programs to serve the whole family.

DESI ARNAZ AND HIS RANCH

During the 17 years that Desi Arnaz owned the 50-acre Corona Breeding Farm on Rincon Road, he and his horses received frequent attention. Anaz who purchased the ranch in 1960 with partner Earl Mitchell, Arnaz was quoted as saying that the ranch could turn out some of the finest thoroughbred stock in the nation.

Brilliant racers, Nashville and Our Rulla, stood at stud. It cost the owner of a mare $3,500 to mate with either champion. The farms produced some

THE 1960s AND 1970s
BRING FURTHER DEVELOPMENT

Corona began to change rapidly in the early 1960s, and by the 70s, was developing at a fast pace.

Golf courses and parks were part of the new pattern. The 1,000-acre Butterfield Trail Park, then

strong economic force. Housing tracts were being developed rapidly, as more people moved from Orange County. They were attracted to the lower home prices, the view, the clean air, family atmosphere and the good schools of Corona. In 1972, the new type of development at Village Grove created a lot of interest. Built around a lake, many of the houses were constructed with the new concept of zero lotlines.

Corona had two newspapers by the 1960s. *The Corona Daily Independent* and the *Riverside Press-Enterprise* both had their share of subscribers. In 1964, the Corona Community Hospital was joined by a new facility, the Circle City Hospital. The next year the Community Hospital expanded, as was needed with the burgeoning population growth.

The number of restaurants was increasing as more families ate out more often. One of the most popular was the Live Oak Inn in Temescal Canyon. Featuring good food and a pleasant atmosphere, the tree-shaded restaurant also contained a large gift shop. Still further out toward Lake Elsinore was the De Palma Italian Village restaurant. Guiseppe De Palma had purchased several acres

the largest natural recreation park in Southern California, was established northwest of town. Baseball diamonds, camping facilities, hiking trails and horseback riding paths brought families to the park.

Three professional-quality 18-hole golf courses provided an illustration of the increasing popularity of the sport. The Corona National, Creste Verde, and Serfas Golf Courses, with their manicured green lawns, serene ponds and trees added a new beauty to the city.

For those who wanted to join a nudist resort, the Glen Eden Sun Club in Temescal Canyon offered privacy, wooded land, sports and activities. It was affiliated with the Western Sunbathing Association.

The City of Corona moved its offices into the picturesque Spanish Colonial Revival buildings that had been built in 1923 as Corona High School. The students moved to the new high school at Lincoln and Tenth streets.

Corona continued to be surrounded by orange and lemon groves. About 4,000 carloads of fruit were shipped out of Corona each year. The 400-acre plant of the Lemon Products division of Sunkist was very active.

By the late 1960s, the number of manufacturing plants had increased to 56, indicating that manufacturing was becoming a

so that he could build a small hideaway cabin and plant a garden. In 1961, he opened the small off-beat Italian restaurant that held 30 diners. Eventually he expanded the building until it included nine rooms and could hold 200 persons. In 1969 the building burned. The site where the restaurant was located is now covered by a large lake.

The Corona Music Theater Association, a talented musical group, produced many fine programs. Each fall the public waited in anticipation to see the show produced by talented singers and dancers. Well-loved musicals, such as *Brigadoon, Carousel, New Moon,* and others featured professional-quality artists.

Who could imagine the degree of growth that would take place in Corona and Norco during the 1970s and 80s. Large houses are now sprouting on the tops of the hills and in the valleys. Experts expect the phenomenal growth to continue well into the next century.

WHERE TO FIND HISTORY IN CORONA AND NORCO

Pictured to the left and on the next page are some of the places that tell us about Corona and Norco's rich history. Take the time to visit them. They will help you understand the unique past of the Corona Valley.

The Heritage Room, located on the second floor of the public library, contains a treasure trove of maps, books, photographs, and memorabilia depicting Corona's unique history. It is open six days a week, during specific hours. *Photo by Diann Marsh*

A Luiseño clay pot is displayed in one of the cases of the museum. Because most of the local Indian artifacts have disappeared long ago, this pot is a particularly valuable treasure. *Photo by Diann Marsh*

Partners In Corona

DynCorp

The U.S. Navy has been a vital presence in the Corona/Norco area for more than 50 years. On December 8, 1941, the day after Pearl Harbor, the Navy became the owner of the then financially troubled Lake Norconian Club (a.k.a. Rex Clark Hotel) and surrounding 700 acres.

Dedicated in April 1994, the Warfare Assessment Laboratory is a single site integration facility for weapons analysis and combat system performance.

Within months, the existing structures were converted to hospital use, more buildings were erected and a huge Naval hospital took shape. Through World War II and into the healing years beyond, tens of thousands of wounded Navy men were sent to Corona for treatment to regain their health and put their lives back together.

In 1951, the Missile Development Division of the National Bureau of Standards moved into the Navy's facilities to pursue research development and test and evaluation work on Navy tactical guided missiles — at that time, a field in its infancy.

In 1953, this work was transferred directly to Navy cognizance and a portion of the former Corona Naval Hospital facilities emerged as the Naval Ordinance Laboratory, Corona.

The Naval Warfare Assessment Station (NWAS) currently consists of approximately 1,000 federal employees, primarily scientists and engineers, with an annual budget of $150 million, making it one of the area's largest employers.

Serving as the Navy's Independent Assessment Agent, the NWAS's mission is to "gauge the war — fighting capacity of ships and aircraft, from unit to battle group level and to assess the suitability of

design, the performance of equipment and weapons and the adequacy of training."

From a scientific and technical standpoint, NWAS occupies the middle ground between agencies that design and manufacture weapons and the operating forces that utilize those weapons in combat.

During WWII, the Navy learned the hard way that weapons designed and produced by people who don't have to use them in combat may not perform as expected when needed. A paramount example of this is the poor performance of US torpedoes developed in secrecy before the war. At a time when submarines could have helped America most early in the war, the torpedoes suffered from major design defects unknown to Fleet operators with disastrous results.

The wisdom of retrospect turned the problem into a "never again" lesson for the Navy. Since 1954, the Naval Warfare Assessment Station has conducted independent analysis and evaluations

PHALANX (Close In Weapon System) gun firing system performance.

of weapons, particularly guided missiles and associated combat systems. This critical mission formalized a decade later when the former Missile Evaluation Department was established independent of the NOLC and renamed the Fleet Missile Systems Analysis and Evaluation Group.

Throughout the long years of the Cold War, the Navy squared off time and again against the Naval forces of World Communism, and thanks to the NWAS, always with the confidence of knowing the strengths and weaknesses of their weapons. During the Vietnam War, Desert Storm and other instances where weapons have been used in combat, NWAS support has had significant impacts on the outcome. The benefits of independent assessment makes the difference on the firing line.

In pursuit of its mission, the NWAS staff includes hundreds of scientists and engineers who rank among the best and most highly respected in the Navy as system analysts. Much of the work NWAS conducts must occur wherever the Fleet is deployed. NWAS maintains detachments to support telemetry sites, tactical aircrew combat training system (TACTS) sites, AEGIS analysis and data processing sites and technical offices worldwide.

NWAS is also responsible for other equally significant tasks, such as metrology systems and interface gauge engineering and serves as the Navy's worldwide scientific and technical authority to perform these important functions.

Since the hospital was established early in WWII, the Navy has been a strong economic and cultural force in the communities of Corona and nearby Norco. In the early years, the hospital brought hundreds of medical professionals to the immediate area. In the 50s, scores of scientists and engineers relocated to the region and more than 75 percent of the nearly 1,000 federal employees currently at NWAS hold college degrees.

The NWAS accounts for a tremendous amount of area business, from huge utility charges and purchases from local suppliers to contracts with local vendors for technical and scientific support. As many of the state's aerospace and defense contractors downsize, the NWAS retains a staff that numbers nearly as high as it did in the 80s when pressure from the Cold War was at its peak. Additionally, DynCorp, NWAS's primary engineering support contractor, employs 350 professionals and technicians in their Norco offices with an annual budget of $19 million.

The presence of the NWAS has had a major impact on the cultural ambiance of the area. Several generations of scientists, engineers, technicians, managers and support professionals have passed through the gates of the Navy facilities in Corona. While under the direct command of the uniformed military, NWAS is defined by a large civilian population, who put down roots, purchase homes, raise their children and retire here. Together, the young and old alike exert a well-educated and caring influence on this sparkling American community.

NWAS's future shines bright. Since the removal of the great threat of Communism and the collapse of the Soviet Union, defense spending has been dramatically reduced. While there is no single foe on the immediate horizon, history shows us that such a threat can appear quickly. The void left by the fall of the Soviet Union and associated Cold War is being rapidly filled by a more diverse and equally insidious foe in the form of terrorism by weaker nations.

As America faces off against this new foe, the Navy must reevaluate its tactics and learn to gain more from its ever-decreasing budget. This means getting the most of limited funds, a concept to which the Department of Defense is still getting accustomed. This places a premium on objective, scientific and independent assessment efforts — and NWAS has the corner on the scientific market for the Navy — and the Corona/Norco area is its home.

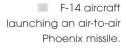 F-14 aircraft launching an air-to-air Phoenix missile.

A Standard missile being fired from a guided missile cruiser.

Watson Pharmaceuticals

atson Pharmaceuticals is not your average generic-pharmaceuticals firm.

Unlike many of its larger counterparts, this growing Corona-based company has consistently been cited by Forbes Magazine as one of the nation's top 200 best small companies in the country.

Since its inception in 1983, Watson bears the distinction of meeting or exceeding industry analysts' projections with steady revenue and earnings growth as a diversified specialty pharmaceutical company that develops, manufactures and markets both proprietary and generic products.

Much of the firm's remarkable rise can be directly attributed to the entrepreneurial spirit and vision of its founders, Dr. Allen Chao and Dr. David Hsia. Their success lies in having found and filled a niche in the highly competitive drug manufacturing industry.

Since 1993, Watson's payroll in Corona has more than doubled to approximately 550 employees. Companywide, the firm employs 1,100 individuals.

The consistent, steady performance is fueled by acquisitions that immediately contribute to the bottom line. Whether it's a new drug, technology or company with a well-established sales force, Watson's acquisition strategy has long turned heads.

To sustain growth, the acquisition-minded firm has shifted its focus from hard-to-produce generic drugs to branded or patented products. The company also has assembled a formidable sales force to sell and market its burgeoning lineup of branded products, which offer better profit potential.

Their mission is simple: "to develop, manufacture and market" conventional off-patent drugs such as tablets, capsules and liquids and the branded and off-patent products that employ Watson's advanced drug delivery systems. These systems are primarily designed to enhance the therapeutic benefits of pharmaceutical compounds.

Watson has met industry demands and responded to new competition by focusing on product niches that are technically more difficult to duplicate or require specialized manufacturing technology.

The Early Years

After working as a research scientist and pharmaceutical technology director for a major Chicago-based pharmaceutical company in the 70s, Chao took his mother's advice to follow his own "entrepreneurial instincts" and strike out on his own.

The company name is a tribute to his Chinese-born mother, whose

maiden name was Hwa, with a small concession to the English language: "Hwa's son" became Watson.

While still in Chicago, Chao put his Purdue University Ph.D. to the test, conducting research and development for his fledgling firm in 1984.

The next year, he moved the firm to Corona – making it one of a handful of drug makers in Southern California – to be closer to his family, who helped him raise the nearly $4 million he needed in start-up capital. Part of that initial investment immediately went toward renting a 25,000-square-foot space to begin developing generic drugs. The initial facility has since grown to incorporate a 165,000-square-foot manufacturing campus.

In December 1985, the company gained FDA approval and shortly after the New Year, the company founders and their 30-some-odd employees began growing the firm in earnest.

In 1990, Chao had purchased the company back from his family and moved into a 120,000-square-foot build-to-suit site in Corona, which has subsequently been expanded to nearly double the size. These structures serve as the company headquarters from which 600 employees work in the various divisions of administrative and product development operations.

Over the years, Watson has expanded into many major metropolitan markets, with more than 600 employees in offices from Miami and New Jersey to New York, Chicago, Texas and Georgia.

"I believe our success to date can be traced back to our corporate vision, strategies, employees and management," says Chao, who oversees the company's future growth and strategic direction. "The other key to continually growing in this industry is the ability of our firm to develop technically challenging products."

The company's management team believes that success and leadership evolve from a corporate culture that rewards achievement, respects and values individual employees and customers, and has a long-term focus on quality, technology, integrity and service.

Watson's success comes amid a continuing explosion in the use of generic drugs as substi-

tutes for brand-name medications. Growth is being propelled by patent expirations on brand-name drugs and by the growing use of generics by HMOs and other cost-conscious managed-care firms.

Part of Chao's two-pronged innovative business strategy includes studiously targeting drugs that are about to lose patent protection and focusing on those drugs that are difficult to manufacture or have relatively small market potential – and thus, few potential competitors.

From its earliest days, Watson generally avoided competing with traditional price-driven and commodity-oriented off-patent products. Instead, it leveraged its technical expertise and focused on products that offered less competition for three reasons: the drug targeted relatively small markets that were unlikely to attract multiple competitors; the drug required specialized

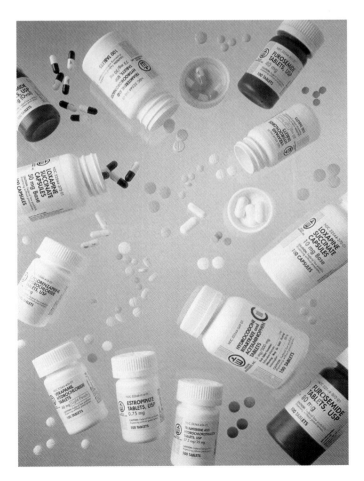

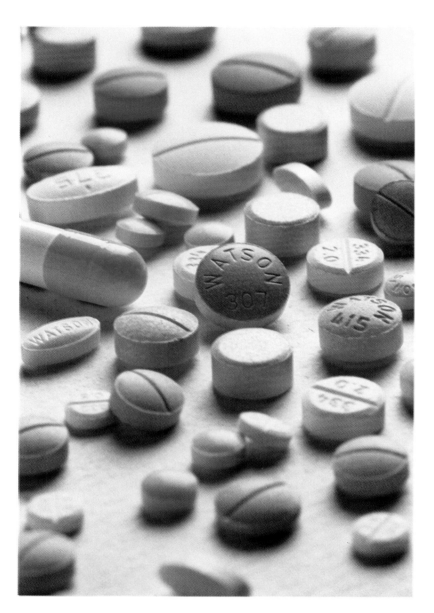

Watson entered the specialty area of dermatology in 1997 through the acquisition of Oclassen Pharmaceuticals. The overall dermatology market is growing consistently at a rate of approximately 10 percent each year.

Building on its expertise in developing and manufacturing hormonal oral contraceptives, the company created its Women's Health division when it branded three internationally developed products while its neuro/psychiatric division represents the largest market with important opportunities.

Watson also currently has over 90 generic products on the market, targeting five areas: analgesic, anti-hypertension, anti-ulcer drugs, hormonal regulator and tranquilizers. Generic drugs typically sell for a fraction of the cost of branded counterparts and pricing pressures and razor-thin margins make business tough.

But Watson rises to the economic challenge by concentrating on its niche products. For example, the firm not only makes narcotic painkillers but is one of the few generic drug companies that is also in the female contraceptive market.

The firm currently has one of the largest off-patent pharmaceutical portfolios in the country. This expanded offering allows its customers more choices and helps secure placement of its products among managed care, retail chain and independent pharmacy groups.

Chao has utilized cash generated from the company's profitable generics business to fund the development of proprietary drugs. An important area of research is the development of alternative drug delivery systems, in particular drugs that can be taken through the oral mucus membranes or other orifices instead of injection with needles.

manufacturing expertise; and the drug required significant technical skill to develop.

Watson's branded pharmaceutical line covers four distinct divisions: primary care, dermatological, women's health and neuro/psychiatric. Its products range from oral contraceptives to antidepressants and narcotic painkillers.

Launched in 1996 with the FDA approval of Microzide for hypertension, Watson's primary care groups account for the company's largest sales category and promotes products to 20,000 primary care physicians.

If patients can take the medications themselves through the skin or mucus membranes, it is less time-consuming and often less costly. Additionally, doctors are more likely to prescribe a drug that is more convenient for patients – boosting the drug's sales potential.

Watson's success can be traced to Chao's philosophy of understanding the marketplace, keeping an eye on the pulse of the industry and staying a step ahead of the latest trends. In 1997, the company experienced a sales increase of 45 percent to $324 million. Before one-time costs associated with its acquisitions, Watson achieved its 20th consecutive quarter of increased earnings and grew earnings by over 31 percent for the full year.

Watson continues to grow and broaden its off-patent product offerings through internal development and through the acquisition of Royce Laboratories. Additionally, the acquisition of The Rugby Group in early 98 substantially increased the firm's off-patent portfolio and provided a well-established telemarketing organization to support off-patent and branded sales.

Recent acquisitions have helped Watson reach a certain strategic mass that should enable it to compete more efficiently in the current healthcare environment. Acquisitions have allowed the firm to expand the breadth and scope of the company's products thereby reducing its vulnerability to changes in the competitive, regulatory and technological environments for any single product.

In 1997, Watson achieved record results while taking important steps to strengthen the firm for the future. Revenues increased 35 percent to $338 million and earnings per share rose 29 percent to $1.15, excluding non-recurring merger costs. That year marked the fifth consecutive year of record earnings since the firm's initial public offering in 1993.

Watson continues its transformation from a purely off-patent pharmaceutical manufacturer into a full integrated off-patent and branded pharmaceutical company, well positioned for growth into the next century.

Best Best & Krieger LLP

On April 11, 1891, the following appeared in the *Riverside Daily Press*: "Raymond Best, a young law student from Warsaw, Indiana, who has been living in Riverside a couple of months, has just passed a very creditable examination at Los Angeles and been admitted to the bar." One hundred years later, Best Best & Krieger has met the challenges of growth with both exceptional performance and promise, sharing a common future with the region as it shares a common history.

Raymond Best purchased the law library of John G. North, the son of the founder of Riverside, and opened his office for the practice of law on the second floor of the Evans Building at the corner of Eighth and Main streets. At the time, Riverside County had not yet come into existence, and Best had to take the Santa Fe steam train to the San Bernardino County Courthouse.

Best was an acclaimed public speaker. In the May 31, 1918 issue of the Riverside Enterprise, he announced his candidacy for Riverside County District Attorney. The reporter who wrote the story also commented that, "He has a powerful voice and is most emphatic in his delivery." He was also vulnerable to a good book sales man and loved to spend hours discussing the law and reading law books. By 1938, the firm had the best law library around. As late as 1950, the collection of law books had long outgrown the firms library, and law reports for every state in the nation lined the hallways.

■ Founding father, Raymond Best (right) with son Eugene Best.

Best's son, Eugene, took the bar examination in 1918 and passed with flying colors, although he never attended law school. He recalled that the examination that year consisted of oral questioning by three appellate justices in Los Angeles as well as a written examination of three questions. Later the same day, the candidates called the clerk of the court who gave them their results, accepted their $2 library fee, and obtained their signatures on the oath to practice law. Gene became a partner in the new firm of Best & Best in 1925. There were at that time 31 practicing lawyers in the Riverside area.

Before becoming a partner, Gene Best opened an office in Elsinore in 1923 which he operated on a one-day-a-week basis for over 30 years. He was appointed City Attorney of Elsinore in 1932, a position he occupied until 1954. From 1929 through 1940, he also served as City Attorney for the City of Riverside.

In 1938, John G. Gabbert joined the Bests and in 1941 the firm became Best, Best & Gabbert. From 1941 to 1943, Gabbert was Police Judge for the City of Riverside, a position previously held by Gene Best from 1926 to 1929. By that time, James H. Krieger had joined the firm which became known as Best, Best, Gabbert & Krieger. An office was opened in Hemet, and Krieger held office hours there one day a week. In 1949, Gabbert was appointed to the Riverside County Superior Court and left the firm, which then became known as Best Best & Krieger, its name to date.

In the 1950s distinguished attorneys such as John Gabbert, John D. Babbage, Arthur L. Littleworth, James B. Corison, Enos Reid and Edward Amschel joined the firm. Babbage had taken over the Elsinore office from Gene Best, and when he left the firm to take up his duties as State Assemblyman from Riverside County, Littleworth took it over. It was still a one-day-a-week office, housed in a private corner of an Elsinore bank. No secretary, no appointments. "People simply lined up and waited to see the lawyer — with every conceivable kind of problem," said Littleworth. A few years later, Littleworth took over as Elsinore

City Attorney from Gene Best and served until 1959.

The firm's current senior partner, Arthur L. Littleworth, was one of the two practicing lawyers appointed to the governor's commission to review California water rights law in 1977. He has tried a number of important water rights cases, including representing the State Water Contractors and their 20 million users who receive water from the State Water Project in the Bay-Delta hearing process beginning in 1987. He was lead counsel for Riverside County defendants in an action involving more than 10,000 parties brought by the downstream Orange County Water District to adjudicate all water rights within the Santa Ana River watershed.

The list of prestigious attorneys and their honors and public offices is a lengthy one for Best Best & Krieger. From Eugene Best's service as Riverside City Attorney, more than half a century ago, the firm has grown to serve as general or special counsel for more than 60 cities and public agencies from the Bay Area to the Mexican border. Municipalities, school districts, special districts and utilities have been well served by Best Best & Krieger's extensive governmental law experience and derive particular benefit from the firm's expertise in matters of redevelopment, land use, eminent domain, public works construction, governmental reorganization, employee relations and civil rights litigation.

Best Best & Krieger was appointed as Corona's City Attorney in March, 1976, replacing the former city attorney who was elevated to the local court and has served in that capacity since that time. They consider their longstanding relationship with the City of Corona is one of the crown jewels in the firm's history of providing high quality and cost effective legal services to municipalities.

For over 100 years, from Raymond Best's 1890s real estate and business practice to the present, the firm has also helped business clients identify goals and implement strategic plans to achieve them. Best Best & Krieger counsels and serves the full spectrum of business organizations from corporations whose shares are publicly traded to individual entrepreneurs. The firm has an outstanding reputation as a nationally recognized bond counsel firm, assisting public agencies with the financing required to meet the rapid demands of population growth and development. Also, trial lawyers at the firm have for generations successfully represented clients in state and federal courts, in virtually every area of civil practice, exhibiting their extensive experience before local, state, and federal administration boards and agencies. From James Krieger's key role in implementing the State Water Project, the firm has become a nationally recognized force in water, resources and environmental law. This practice has evolved to include environmental protection laws, including specific experience with federal and state environmental regulations, and hazardous waste management issues.

Over the past 100 years, lawyers at Best Best & Krieger have also served as leaders in their communities and even today, the firm's leadership continues to be recognized in both the legal community and the community at large.

The firm's focus on the future goes beyond the next generation of lawyers and the study of the law itself. It builds on the commitment of Best Best & Krieger to continue to grow professionally and to enhance the position and reputation of the firm in its service to clients in its second century, shaping its future through an ability to recognize the value not only of what is, but of what might be.

Best Western Kings Inn

et back from the freeway, the Best Western Kings Inn of Corona shares a parking lot with two restaurants and boasts a reputation for being "close to everything, yet away from it all."

Located just off the 91 Freeway at the Lincoln exit, this hotel is the perfect place for business travelers and tourists alike. Conveniently situated amidst many popular Southland attractions, the Kings Inn is a favorite stopover destination for tours from Los Angeles to Palm Springs, San Diego and Las Vegas.

Its central location near major freeways allows easy access to a number of area destinations including Disneyland, Knott's Berry Farm, the beautiful wine country of Temecula, Glen Ivy Hot Springs Spa and Ontario Mills, California's largest entertainment and outlet mall with over 200 specialty stores, restaurants and theaters.

Best Western Kings Inn offers visitors a high standard of excellence with 87 beautifully-appointed, newly decorated guest rooms and a friendly, professional staff.

The Best Western national hotel chain implements a "surprise" annual inspection designed to make certain each of its locations meet exacting service standards. Owned by Robert and Janet Lind, the Best Western Kings Inn of Corona has consistently scored in the top two percent of all the Best Western hotels nationwide. This fact is due in large part to the hotel's Executive Housekeeper, Elvira Rodriguez, who has been with the Best Western Kings Inn for over 17 years!

Personal in-room amenities include local phone calls and *USA Today* newspaper, remote control television with premium satellite stations, including Showtime, ESPN, CNN, USA, TBS, TNT and more. Telephones with dataports are also available.

The deluxe rooms feature a refrigerator, microwave, safe, hair dryer and in-room VCR with a wide selection of complimentary movies.

 Best Western Kings Inn of Corona is a favorite destination for business travelers and tourists alike.

Guests also enjoy a complimentary full continental buffet available every morning from 5 a.m. to 10 a.m. Other amenities include next day laundry service, an outdoor heated pool and spa, three adjacent restaurants featuring casual and fine dining options for breakfast, lunch and dinner as well as entertainment and banquet facilities.

Nestled in a hidden canyon just eight miles away, Glen Ivy Hot Springs Spa offers 15 relaxing mineral pools, professional body services, salon treatments and Southern California's only red clay mud bath.

The Best Western Kings Inn offers special packages with Glen Ivy Hot Springs Spa. This popular "Club Mud" mini-vacation includes overnight accommodations at the Kings Inn of Corona, spa admission and continental breakfast for one low price.

The popularity of this package led to the inception of "Club King," a VIP card program for frequent Club Mud–Mini Vacation guests which offers an array of added upgrades and amenities, including points earned for a free night's stay!

Business travelers will appreciate the convenience of an on-site conference room with seating for up to 35. Projection screen, flip charts and catering services are available.

A combination of outstanding service, a friendly, caring staff and welcome environment bring guests back time and again.

Convenience, comfort and personal service: three qualities that make the Best Western Kings Inn of Corona a perfect destination for all your travel needs.

Complas, Inc.

Complas, Inc. was founded in 1989, following extensive market research and plan development and is owned and actively managed by Monica Garcia who has extensive experience in the field of telecommunications and international marketing. Complas' objective was to become a quality provider of products and services in the rapidly growing and changing telecommunications industry.

The company's initial offering in early 1990 to be the Cable Systems International (then AT&T) cut center in California for Pacific Bell was a success, and the fledgling company was awarded a 10 year contract for copper cable. Later in 1990, Complas was awarded a contract for Alcatel Transmission Products and Pirelli Fiber Optic Cable sold to Pacific Bell, and in 1992, AT&T (now Lucent Technologies) Transmission Products were added to the Complas catalog.

Since its inception, Complas has grown from a startup cable services facility for Northern California to become the largest Value Added Reseller (VAR) of telecommunications products and services on the West Coast. The company is known for its ability to deliver on its commitment to quality service, and this has led to great customer confidence and respect.

Although Complas is a small company, it offers the advantage of low overhead and the inherent savings this produces. The size of the company, coupled with its experienced management and technical team, enables Complas to be flexible and to have the ability to customize a product or service to meet a customer's specific needs. Complas has assembled a team comprised of experienced, professional managers and a work force which is dedicated to providing the highest quality, most economic solutions to its customers.

Currently, Complas offers telecommunications products and services from two locations in California, one in Northern California and the corporate headquarters in Corona. The company expanded recently and added a new location outside Dallas, Texas to serve customers in the Southwest and to further diversify its offerings. Their facilities in California provide over 180,000 square feet of covered warehouse and high-tech custom assembly space while the Texas location is conveniently situated to address the customers in that region.

Complas' extensive inventory of cable and transmission products allows them to meet their customers immediate needs as well as providing the ability to custom assemble complete telecommunications solutions to meet specific requirements.

The core business of Complas is represented by a full range of outside plant products and services, including transmission equipment, copper cable and fiber optic cable. Complas is uniquely situated to address this particular market and offers products from a broad range of manufacturers, provides assembly and installation services and gives its customers complete turnkey, engineering, furnishing and installing total systems solutions. The company takes pride in following all projects from inception to completion.

Complas also has a pro-active development program aimed at providing new products and services to support the emerging technologies of the telecommunications world.

Some of the stock of state-of-the-art telecommunications products maintained by Complas.

All products and services from Complas have the added plus of carrying Minority and Women Owned Business Enterprise credit. Complas is a Cordoba certified M/WBE so that products and services purchased from Complas carry M/WBE credit which Complas' customers may apply towards their own M/WBE objectives. Many of Complas' customers have established goals for minority and female participation in the work they perform so Complas' status as an M/WBE is an added plus for those particular customers.

A unique feature of Complas is their New Product Updates and Outside Plant Training sessions, the first of which was held at the Tracy location. The session was designed to meet the needs of outside plant, engineering, construction, purchasing and others wanting to know what's new in OSP products and services. Complas enlisted the vendor community to assist in presenting their newest offerings and to discuss the latest in cost saving applications. The session included in-depth reviews of fiber optic and copper cable, duct and engineering, design and placement in the outside plant. The all day session included a tour of the Tracy facility and offered a perfect opportunity to ask the "experts."

In a demonstration of the trust and confidence its customers place in Complas, the company was contracted to design and assemble portable communication units to provide 6,300 voice circuits and broadcast media communications facilities for the 1996 Republican National Convention in San Diego, California. These communications "trailers" were constructed at the Corona facility and rolled into place at the convention. Following the convention, the trailers went into regular service with Pacific Bell as part of their emergency restoration program.

Complas' Corona base houses its distribution and assembly operations. Here, the company performs custom assembly and light manufacturing. It is also the center of Complas' operations and serves as the company's corporate headquarters.

Founder Garcia has defined Complas' commitment as: "The Complas Team is clearly focused on serving our customers and exceeding their expectations for quality and service."

Corona Regional Medical Center

The Corona Regional Medical Center is a superior provider of medical care, dedicated to the health, healing and wellness of community residents. As a not-for-profit facility, Corona Regional Medical Center is committed to delivering exceptional health care. It is guided by its philosophy of "people helping people."

Corona Regional Medical Center, as it is known today, came into existence in 1992 when Circle City Medical Center and Corona Community Hospital merged. Their mission was to become "Partners in Health and Healing" with the community.

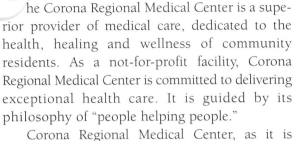

Although the center's modern history is relatively short, its roots go deep into Corona's past. The medical center began as El Nido Maternity Home which opened in 1933, offering only obstetric services. By 1940, it had become a general hospital, known as the Corona Community Hospital. In the mid-1960s the buildings on the center's Main Street site were remodeled and expanded. Another hospital in the area, Circle City Medical Center, was for-profit, physician-owned and located on Magnolia Avenue. When the two merged in 1992, they became a not-for-profit organization under Vista Hospital Systems, Inc.

At that time, the two facilities became Corona Regional Medical Center. Each campus was designated for different purposes, and services to the community were greatly expanded. The two campuses, Corona Regional Medical Center on Main Street for acute care and the Rehabilitation Hospital on Magnolia for rehabilitation, combine to make Corona Regional Medical Center one of the most comprehensive hospitals in the Inland Empire.

Corona Regional Medical Center offers the community everything from pre-natal care and wellness visits to hospice care and almost every service in between. In this way, a continuum of care has been established that allows Corona Regional Medical Center to meet the needs of all community members.

The Corona Regional Medical Center Main Street campus has a dedicated staff whose comprehensive expertise ensures that residents of the Corona-Norco area receive unparalleled care to meet their health needs. Armed with the latest advances in technology and training, medical and surgical specialists provide a full range of services, for example:

- 24-hour Emergency Room
- The Outpatient Pavilion — a centralized area for all out-patient services.
- Bloodless Medicine Program
- Full range of Diagnostic Services including a state-of-the-art Angiographic Laboratory
- Maternal Child Health Unit
- Medical/Surgical Unit
- Pediatric Unit
- Intensive Care Unit
- State-of-the-art Surgical Suites

The Corona Regional Rehabilitation Campus mission is to help patients rediscover ways of living, moving, working, coping and enjoying life. Whether the problem is due to injury, accident or disease, specialists at the Rehabilitation Hospital offer programs designed to meet individual requirements. The Acute Rehabilitation Unit is equipped to treat patients with stroke and head injury, in addition to patients in need of physical, occupational and speech therapies. The Long Term Care and Transitional Care Units provide skilled nursing for ventilator dependent patients or those with post surgical needs. As part of the Corona Regional Rehabilitation Hospital, the medical center offers a variety of Senior Mental Health Services, including inpatient and partial hospitalization programs. The goal of the inpatient unit is to restore optimum function for each individual. The partial hospitalization program provides high quality day treatment for seniors experiencing emotional anxieties and other problems associated with daily living.

Corona Regional Medical Center is proud of the continuum of care offered at its facilities. Patients can progress from hospital to rehabilitation to home care. A unique service of the medical center is its Home Health and Hospice Agency. Based on studies that healing is more successful in a patient's home, that's where Corona Regional Medical Center's team of Registered Nurses, Licensed Vocational Nurses, occupational therapists and physical therapists go to provide needed services.

Not only is Corona Regional Medical Center dedicated to superior performance, it is also in the forefront of patient health education. The medical center's programs, designed to educate residents about their overall health, include a Chaplain program, health fairs, wellness education, physician referral, and social services.

Corona Regional Medical Center's medical staff members represent virtually every major medical specialty and are highly trained and committed to their patients. All staff members, from physicians and nurses to therapists and technology specialists, are focused on ensuring that patients

receive the highest quality personal care in a compassionate, dignified environment. Carrying the sense of community at the medical center a step further are the enthusiastic volunteers. Volunteers play a vital role in medical center activities, and Corona Regional Medical Center is proud of its extensive volunteer program. The health care team at Corona Regional Medical Center would not be complete without the support of the Foundation, the Foundation Board, and the Medical Center Board of Directors, many of whom are leaders in the Corona-Norco community. Their dedication and generosity help many possibilities for the medical center become realities.

Striving to ensure that the complete medical, health education and prevention needs of the community are met in a comfortable, compassionate and efficient manner, Corona Regional Medical Center continues to serve Corona-Norco residents and to work with the entire community as "Partners in Health and Healing." Corona Regional Medical Center is an integral part of community life and just as its roots go deep into the past, its "people helping people" relationship with Corona-Norco will reach far into the future.

■ (Left Photo) 1998 Advanced Physical Therapy Equipment.

■ (Top Photo) Physical Therapy Equipment used in the 1970s was considered the latest advancement.

■ (Bottom Left) Radiology X-Ray machine was a diagnostic tool of the hospital in years past.

■ (Bottom) In 1998 a High-Tech Angio Lab allows greater visualization for more accurate diagnosis and treatment.

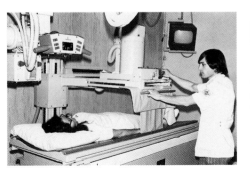
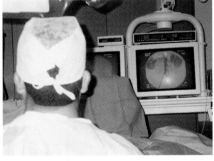

Corona Regional Medical Group

n addition to offering excellent medical care, CRMG has a feature that places it in the top ranks: physicians and staff who relate to patients as people, not simply medical cases. When seeking new physicians Corona Regional Medical Group looks for physicians who are not only American trained and Board certified, but are also good to their patients, good to their peers and good to each other. Outstanding customer service is its focus.

The name Corona Regional Medical Group was introduced to the public in April, 1998. Prior to that, the medical group was known as Corona Medical Group, Circle City Medical Group, Cambrils Medical Group, Norco Medical Group and Westlake Medical Group. The roots of the medical group trace back to 1978 when a local physician founded the first managed care physician practice in the Corona area. Through this single practice, physicians recognized the opportunity to improve the health care in the community through managed care.

Over the years, the network grew and expanded to include the following: Circle City Medical Group, located in Corona since 1981;

Norco Medical Group located in Norco since 1985; Cambrils Medical Group located in Corona since 1986; Westlake Medical Group located in Elsinore since 1989; and Inland Region Medical Group located in Chino Hills since 1995. In March, 1996, Vista Medical Foundation, Inc., a not-for-profit organization, acquired all of the medical groups. Subsequently, Sierra Sunrise Medical Group was also acquired and merged into the medical group. All medical groups now operate under the name Corona Regional Medical Group.

CRMG's main campus is in Corona, in close proximity to Corona Regional Medical Center. The hospital and medical group are both affiliated with the same not-for-profit health care company. As sister organizations, the hospital and medical group share various services and resources which allows them to contribute more to the community through their not-for-profit mission.

In addition to the Corona location, CRMG has its "four corners": Sierra del Oro, Norco, Corona Hills and Lake Elsinore. Another service provided by CRMG at the main campus is an Urgent Care Center which operates seven days a week with

 The main campus of Corona Regional Medical Group.

extended hours and on weekends to meet the urgent health care needs of the community.

In addition to the "four corners," CRMG features Magnolia Industrial Care Center (MICC) which caters to the 4,000 plus companies in the Corona/Norco area. Not only does MICC provide excellent care for industrial related medical problems, pre-employment drug screen and physicals, they also provide a wide variety of educational services. Doctors from MICC, visit businesses, conduct on-site safety checks and develop programs that prevent injuries and accidents from occurring. The physicians also conduct safety seminars for employees on topics such as how to lift, how to deal with repetitive motion jobs and how to prevent carpal tunnel syndrome. These seminars are popular and many Corona companies take advantage of them.

CRMG's Health Educator programs offer a wide variety of health education lectures and classes such as how to deal with Alzheimer's Disease, smoking cessation, congestive heart failure, instruction for stroke patients, education for diabetics, weight management and hypertension.

Nurse Educators conduct parenting seminars along the theme of "now that the baby has arrived, what do we do?" Registered nurses also present classes on dealing with the unique problems of adolescence and how parents can approach the problems of the teen years. These seminars are free and are offered both during the day and at night.

One thing that has stayed consistent throughout the years is that Corona Regional Medical Group has always been managed by a physician. The current Chief Executive Officer and Chief Medical Officer Albert B. Briccetti, M.D. has numerous years of managed care administration experience and medical director leadership.

CRMG has a core of 30 Primary Care Physicians with a full complement of over 200 specialty physicians to provide virtually any type of medical care needed. When a patient needs medical care not available through these physicians, the medical group makes arrangements to provide the medical care elsewhere. Loma Linda University Medical Center and UCI Medical Center are just two examples of the vast resources Corona Regional Medical Group has to draw upon to maintain the health of the community.

Committed to provide quality health care and superior customer service.

Responsible to our community, patients, physicians and employees.

Maintaining health through prevention, intervention and wellness.

Growing with the community we serve.

CRMG has grown from a single family practice office to a not-for-profit medical group currently responsible for maintaining the health of almost 40,000 people, approximately one-third of the Greater Corona area.

The medical group is entering the new century on a progressive course with new technology, including a website on the Internet. CRMG looks forward to fulfilling its mission to keep the community healthy well into the future.

Corona Rose Flowers & Gifts

*I*f you were to call Corona Rose Flowers & Gifts and ask to speak to Rose, you would be in for a big surprise when owner Ken Staudinger picked up the telephone. Ken was working for a can company in La Mirada as a maintenance mechanic when he and his wife Sandi purchased Robson's Flowers & Gifts in the Mervyn's shopping center, their first flower shop. Ken had been called "Spanky" prior to the acquisition of the flower shop but was later dubbed "Corona Rose" by his co-workers. Although Ken wanted to change the name of their new store to Sandi's Flowers & Gifts, Sandi felt that didn't really describe the store and suggested they use Ken's nickname. Thus was born Corona Rose Flowers & Gifts.

Sandi's aunt opened the family's first flower shop in the San Fernando Valley in 1969 just before Ken and Sandi met. Sandi had grown up working in her aunt's flower shop. When she and Ken married, their dream was to own a business in which they could work together, and the flower business was just what they were looking for. At the end of 1985, they felt ready to buy that first shop. Although they searched for some time for an existing place which had the kind of ambience they were seeking, nothing could be found. Just as they were considering leaving the Corona/Norco area, they heard of a flower shop available in the Mervyn's shopping center. They knew it would be perfect for them. By March 1, 1986, it was theirs, and they started making changes to create the business as they envisioned it. Within four years, the business had quadrupled its gross sales.

Trying to do that in 900 square feet became a problem, so they began looking for a second location and found "Hatton's Market," a 9,000-square-foot building on the corner of Main Street and Grand Boulevard. They, and the experts called in to examine it, felt it was perfect. Their grand opening had over 300 people on September 15, 1991. Unfortunately, a few months later, the Gulf War began and soon after, the major part of the 1990s recession hit Corona. Their flower business more than doubled in that time. With the burden of two locations and a very large debt, they were advised to downsize. After one and a half years, they closed the big shop, but what to do now with double the flower business.

Never one to accept defeat, Sandi found an available building on 6th Street just off Buena Vista and despite heavy losses, persuaded the owner to lease the space to them. Thus bloomed a third Corona Rose. Moving out of Main and Grand on New Year's Eve, they were open for business by Valentine's Day, 1992. Six months later, the original store in the Mervyn's center sold, which allowed them to concentrate everything on their present location. It is here they have continued their policy of giving good quality and top service to their customers.

Ken and Sandi divide the work load with Ken in charge of the delivery department, accounts receivable and most of the ordering, while Sandi does accounts payable, designing and marketing. They have two full-time and several part-time designers. In addition, they have two delivery vans and several sales clerks, including their oldest daughter, Heidi.

Heidi has been working in the flower business since 1986. She even went to work for a flower shop when she and husband Adrian lived in Barstow just after their marriage. She has the same keen sense her parents have about quality and service and now manages Corona Rose with Ken and Sandi. Theirs truly is a family business, including their grandson, Jacob, born to Heidi

■ Ken and Sandi Staudinger take ownership of the original Corona Rose Flowers & Gifts.

and Adrian June 11, 1996. He was at work three to four days a week until his sister, Katelin, was born April 10, 1988.

Wendy, Ken and Sandi's other daughter, worked for them until she moved to Irvine in 1995. She says the skills she learned from her parents about work ethics, sales and marketing earned her the respect she has now from her employers.

Sandi proudly explains, "Our staff can do just about anything with flowers, including European, Tropical, French, English garden, and various other arrangements." Corona Rose Flowers is well known for its large assortment of roses, generally carrying over 1,000 roses in five to eight different colors.

Ken purchases the flowers primarily from the San Diego area, directly from the growers, many of them located in Carlsbad. This assures him of the quality necessary for their shop.

Corona Rose Flowers has had its share of unusual requests. They have made arrangements in bedpans for hospital patients, funeral arrangements with golf clubs and band equipment, and even built an entire motocross motorbike for a memorial piece. An amazing accomplishment was when Sandi got a basketball inside of a 40" balloon for a customer, after everyone else said it was impossible.

Sandi and Ken consider Corona Rose Flowers a full service, everyday flower shop where people come to get flowers for family events. However, they specialize in corporate accounts having a large number of major businesses in and out of town doing not only birthday and anniversary arrangements for employees, but business thank you's and apologies. They handle special events for many businesses. Major holidays and wedding and funeral flower arrangements also keep them very busy.

During the 20 years they have lived in the Corona-Norco area, both Ken and Sandi have participated in many local activities. Ken has been a Deacon and Treasurer of their Church, is active in Corona Rotary Club, VFW, American Legion and Elks, and is currently on the Corona Chamber Board. Sandi is a member and past president of Soroptimist International of Corona, past board member of the Corona Chamber of Commerce, past member of the Ladies Elks and professional volunteer for Girl Scouts and a Norco Swim Team member. They belong to the Corona Norco Navy League, a group which supports Jr. & Sr. High Sea Cadets, and they are both certified FTD Master Florist Managers.

On July 7, 1998, Sandi was inducted into the American Institute of Floral Designers (AIFD), which acknowledges official validation of florists' abilities as a floral art designers. She is the current Chairman of the local FTD district, which includes over 1,200 flower shops in California and Nevada. In 1995, as Treasurer of the district, she organized the Wedding Show, called "Weddings of the Nations" which was attended by over 400 florists. In 1998, the "FTD in Concert" Design Show and Trade Fair will be Sandi's second year, and she hopes to top both of her past shows. In 1997, she was a program presenter for the National FTD Convention held in Hawaii, as well as a volunteer in the flower room and hospitality room. She gives talks to civic organizations, clubs and churches in the local area on such topics as marketing, goal setting, employee relationships and floral designing. Last, but not least, she has also been a feature designer at the Los Angeles County Fair for FTD and has commentated for other designers over the last eight years.

Corona Rose Flowers and Gifts is proud to be in the top five percent of FTD's 26,000 flower shops worldwide. Not only are they achieving their dream of working together but they have established a successful and respected business, known for its service, reasonable prices and quality. Ken, Sandi and their staff believe they don't just sell flowers, they sell emotions and deliver them next door and around the world and that's what makes the difference.

Youngest employee, grandson Jacob Whitehurst, is learning the family business.

Crossroads Christian Church

One of the state's oldest independent congregations, Crossroads Christian Church, enters the millennium as one of Corona's newest churches as well. With its many building projects gradually filling in the gently sloping campus-with-a-view, the church overlooks the broad Santa Ana River Valley.

Crossroads Christian Church continues the pattern of growth and expansion to ever-larger sites and bigger buildings. This growth has been part of the congregation's history since it was organized on October 29, 1892, as the First Christian Church of South Riverside by South Riverside Land and Water Company. A small frame building was moved from the old Lincoln school onto the property and a baptistery was added to it.

According to a history of the congregation complied by Dessie Harris and based, in part, on the recollections of Mrs. Ocie Taylor Songer, the new church at Eighth and Howard (dedicated March 3, 1895) was succeeded by a new building at Ninth and Main streets (dedicated June 21, 1908). This building, after being remodeled, carried the church into the 1960s.

The Church's current sanctuary named His Place, has a seating capacity of 1,500.

James Taylor Sr., I.A. McCarty, Miss M. Hand and Andrew Wheaton.

During the community's first century — since the area was separated from Riverside and incorporated as the city of Corona — the church has met at five different locations, each a little grander than the last.

In 1892, the church first met in a frame building on the east side of Main Street near Fifth. Boxes with planks across them served as pews, and a table was used as a pulpit. The first baptisms — 32 of them — were performed at Cold Water Canyon Swimming Pool, now known as Glen Ivy Hot Springs. H. Elliott Ward was called as the congregation's first full-time pastor.

In 1894, the church was installed at Eighth and Howard streets on three lots donated by the

Having voted on a name change to "Church of Christ, Corona" in 1932, the congregation purchased land at Rancho and Main streets in 1962 and dedicated the new facilities on December 6, 1964.

Timothy Coop was called to be the pastor in 1970 and the church took the name Crossroads Christian Church. In 1992, a century after its founding, the congregation gathered in an orange grove to break ground for the first buildings on its current site at Ontario and Kellogg avenues.

One of the church's elders, Brad Dupray, wrote for the August 6, 1996 edition of *Christian Standard*, "The church has grown up with the city (and)...after experiencing steady growth in the 1970s and early 1980s, the church stepped out in faith in 1983 to purchase 38 acres of land

than 200 children each week day. Off-campus facilities accommodate 480 students in Crossroads School, and future plans call for building a facility to serve the growing need for additional classrooms to house grades K-8.

A 60,000-square-foot auditorium to seat 3,000 people at a single worship service is being planned. It is expected to be constructed in the near future as Crossroads continues to develop its 38-acre campus as a focal point in South Corona's growth pattern. Additional building projects are also planned to meet the growing needs of the church and its outreach into the community.

The indomitable spirit that moved Crossroaders to a progressive building program over 100 years ago remains today. Any visitor to the Crossroads campus will find a warm welcome, dreams being realized, and an ongoing commitment to having a positive impact on the city and the surrounding community of Corona.

in a part of town that was projected to be a virtual new community of housing in the 1990s."

In 1994, the congregation called a new pastor from Australia, Barry McMurtrie, to lead the congregation into the 21st century. An internationally known leader who had built the largest Protestant church in Australia, Barry, along with his wife, Gay, moved his global base of operations to Corona.

In need of larger facilities, the congregation erected a huge tent on its new property where it met for nearly a year and a half. Despite the inconveniences of dusty and sometimes muddy parking, and rainy-season streams running under their folding chairs, Crossroaders persevered through the "tent meeting" days and their numbers grew in two years — from an average of 1,325 per Sunday for the first six months of 1995 to 4,000 plus. On March 17, 1996, the congregation held its first Sunday morning worship service in its new sanctuary, named His Place, a building with the capacity to seat 1,500 people.

Over 40 different ministries use the many buildings that have been constructed on the church's Kellogg Avenue property. Its preschool cares for more

Glen Ivy Hot Springs Spa

Glen Ivy Hot Springs is: "One of those rare places in the world where the Earth itself gives her gift of warm water to people, water warmed deep in her heart. That has made this a special place for many generations of people," exclaims CEO John Gray.

The hot springs have existed for several centuries and were very popular among the indigenous people whom the Spanish missionaries named Luiseños. Even to this day, many artifacts have been found on the grounds. Combined with the cool waters of Coldwater Creek, the local inhabitants were provided with hot and cold running water by Mother Nature herself.

In the September 8, 1860, edition of the *Los Angeles Star* (the Los Angeles newspaper of the day) was an advertisement: "Temescal Hot Springs Spa — Accommodations for those wishing to visit the springs can be found at the residence of Messrs. Greenwade and Co., proprietors of the Overland Stage Station." The earliest mention of Glen Ivy Hot Springs locally as a commercial establishment was in 1890 in *The Riverside Bee*, the newspaper of the era. At that time, Corona wasn't even Corona yet. It was called South Riverside.

A two-room bathhouse with zinc-lined tubs by the springs and a two-story frame "hotel" was built and run by a Mrs. Thorndyke in the early 1870s. The hotel burned down in 1884.

Following Mrs. Thorndyke, William T. Sayward and his brother Captain Wheaton Sayward bought the land. There they built a large ten-room adobe house which stood on the property until 1979. They dubbed the property Coldwater but later sold it to Mr. and Mrs. W.G. Steers. The Steers were from England where a canyon was often called a "glen." Thus, it was Mrs. Steers who renamed the Coldwater Hotel the Glen Ivy Hot Springs as she had also noticed the vines of ivy growing profusely at the mouth of the canyon where the hot springs originated. During the ten years the Steers managed Glen Ivy, it became a resort.

In 1898 the Mitchell Family bought Glen Ivy Hot Springs. As one of their features, they organized what were called Tallyho parties, large hunting expeditions in the area. They also built a large stone stable which was later transformed into a dance hall. Although the dance hall eventually burned down, the stone walls remained for decades.

At the turn of the century, Frank and Mabel Johnson bought Glen Ivy with the dream of turning it into a country inn. The only source of light in those days was kerosene lamps and cooking was done on wood stoves. Electricity and gas weren't introduced into the area until 1916. The resort grew and flourished under the Johnsons' ownership. They built guest cottages, added more mineral baths, built a massage building, cleared land and planted 30 acres of citrus trees, some of which remain standing today.

The Spa expanded again between 1913 and 1920 with the construction of a large bathhouse that contained eight colorfully lined tiled, sunken tubs, steam and massage rooms and a reception area. By the 1930s a renovation of the facilities was undertaken including the clearing of an airstrip along Glen Ivy Road. Then owner, Axel Springborg offered a Danish smorgasbord buffet on Sunday mornings which became so popular that flying enthusiasts would fly their private planes down from Los Angeles just to enjoy the feast.

By the 1960s the hotel and spa were beginning to show their age and were badly in need of costly upgrades required by new building codes. A sudden rainstorm brought a flash flood down from the Santa Ana mountains above the Spa in 1969 and washed away part of a tennis court, a number of cottages and the picnic grounds. Although the hotel closed for repairs, the pools were kept open briefly.

Glen Ivy Hot Springs began its return to paradise when it was purchased in 1977 by a group of private shareholders and incorporated as Glen Ivy Hot Springs, a day-resort open to the general public on a daily basis.

Since 1977 there has been a continual progression of upgrades to the facilities including the addition of new pools and deck areas, the addition of two massage buildings, the Spa Salon and Spa Shop, new locker and changing facilities, the lounge pool and Spa Pavilion. Later innovations were the Champagne Pools at the south end of the resort featuring bubbling spas surrounded by a grassy esplanade for lounging.

The facilities themselves offer about a dozen pools of different temperatures, water qualities and sizes. Guests who generally come to spend the day to relax, to be pampered, to get away from it all, can have a variety of water experiences. Along with "taking the waters," a selection of skin and body care treatments are offered. The combination of the waters and the various skin and body treatments, a simple, healthy cuisine and relaxed setting are inviting to all who visit the facility.

The Spa is open year round, closing only for major holidays such as Christmas. The size of the staff varies a bit by season but generally averages 100 employees year round.

Expansion since January 1977 has been considerable. Developed areas have quadrupled. The newest addition is a just completed multi-function building which provides an upgraded entrance to the Spa, a retail shop, cafe facilities and administrative offices. Men's and women's locker rooms will open in autumn of 1998.

The unique atmosphere of Glen Ivy Hot Springs, "Nature's Day Spa," continues to draw guests from all over Southern California and beyond. Attention is paid to preserving the traditions of rest, health and serenity first appreciated by the Native Americans who felt this was a sacred place where the warm natural waters offered healing for the body, mind and spirit.

As Gray emphasized, "We're in the 'feel good' business. Our objective is that all our guests leave after their day at the spa feeling good and feeling good about themselves."

A lovely fountain overlooks the Lounge Pool at Glen Ivy Hot Springs Spa.

Golden Cheese Company of California

Cheesemaking is one of the oldest methods practiced by man for the preservation of a highly perishable and nutritional foodstuff into a product not likely to deteriorate. Although the exact origin of cheesemaking is difficult to establish, archaeological evidence suggests cheese was produced as early as 6,000-7,000 B.C.

Nestled in the heart of Southern California's dairyland, the Golden Cheese Company of California operates one of the largest and most sophisticated, fully integrated cheese and whey processing facilities in the world, while still adhering to established cheesemaking principles.

Built and commissioned in 1985, Golden Cheese Company uses a modern state-of-the-art integrated control system to support some of the same ancient cheesemaking principles used thousands of years ago. The site is operated by over 200 employees and runs continuously seven days per week, 24 hours a day.

The company's 52-acre manufacturing complex in Corona is home to all facets of the company's business, ranging from cheese manu-

facturing, whey processing and ethyl alcohol production to quality control, cheese cutting, packaging and warehousing.

Milk is purchased from Southern California farmers and delivered to the factory daily. Before being converted into cheese, the milk is tested for purity and content. This is the first step in a rigid quality control program that is practiced on site.

In the course of a year a billion pounds of milk are processed into 100 million pounds of premium quality cheddar, Monterey Jack, mozzarella and reduced-fat cheeses.

Although each variety of cheese requires a particular series of steps to make them unique, there are certain procedures that remain constant in the art of cheesemaking.

All the milk is pasteurized before being used. When the pasteurization process is completed, enzymes are added to help the milk curdle and aid in establishing its ultimate taste and texture. This process forms a custard-like substance which is cut into smaller pieces to begin the separation of the curds and whey. They curd/whey mixture is

■ "Golden's Family of Cheese"

Golden Cheese Company uses a modern state-of-the-art integrated control system to support some of the same cheesemaking principles used thousands of years ago.

Nestled in the heart of Southern California's dairyland, the Golden Cheese Company of California operates one of the largest and most sophisticated, fully integrated cheese and whey processing facilities in the world.

Milk is purchased from Southern California farmers and delivered to the factory daily.

In the course of a year, Golden Cheese processes a billion pounds of milk into 100 million pounds of premium quality cheddar, Monterey Jack, mozzarella and reduced-fat cheeses.

cooked to further develop the desirable characteristics of the cheese and then the liquid whey is removed. The cheese curds are then salted and pressed into 40-pound blocks before being set in the warehouse for aging.

Every stage of the production process is monitored and checked by state-of-the-art analytical laboratory to ensure that the quality of the finished product meets the highest standards.

Golden Cheese utilizes all components of the milk. The whey that is removed from the cheese curds is processed into Whey Protein Concentrates. The residual milk sugar (lactose) is fermented and distilled into ethyl alcohol, which is used as a fuel additive. The remaining milk solids are concentrated into an animal feed. In the end, all that is left is water. This is then used to clean the equipment.

Golden Cheese currently serves multiple markets, including retail and food service for some of the nation's largest grocery chains and fast food restaurants. It is able to offer customers a selection of cheese varieties in a range of sizes and styles, including natural cheese in both block and slices, shredded cheeses, blended shreds and processed American cheese in loaf and individually wrapped slices.

Lucas Oil Products, Inc.

Centrally located and close to transportation corridors, Lucas Oil moved its corporate operations and offices to Corona in 1994.

Sputtering or leaking engines around the world are the target of Lucas Oil Products, Inc. Whether correcting a power steering problem in a school bus or stabilizing oil in a dragster, the quality products from Lucas Oil can be found in vehicles from Corona to Kentucky and around the globe.

Family owned and operated, Lucas Oil was started by Forrest and Charlotte Lucas after they saw a need for better lubricant and fuel treatments. For years the couple owned their own fleet of long distance trucks which hauled materials all over the continental United States. Based in Indiana, the company realized firsthand the lack of quality engine additives as their drivers would call from on the road with tales of breakdowns and complaints about engine mishaps. Every day a truck was stalled cost the company money so Forrest began to experiment in the 1980s with different oil products to solve the company's costly problems.

Working with the anthem, "Keep That Engine Alive," the Lucas' developed and perfected a line of oil and fuel treatments designed to save fuel and extend the component life in Americas heavy duty trucks. After the products were tested and proven they were then introduced to the American truck stop industry. With nearly every truck stop in America now selling Lucas products, the line is an overwhelming success. That success encouraged the Lucas' to sell their trucking business and design a separate line of products for automobiles in the late 1980s. This quickly became the fastest growing chemical line in the auto parts market. In the 1990s, Lucas again ventured into a new automotive field, making a line of racing oils for the high performance industry.

"Our forté is to make better products for industries and for situations that are not having their total needs filled by other oil products.

Believe me, the major oil companies left a lot of weak spots! We have an excellent staff and a world of technology that we have gained through years of research. We've done a lot, but we've got a lot more to do," President Forrest Lucas says.

Far from its humble beginnings in Indiana, Lucas Oil incorporated in 1989 and moved out West to Anaheim then Chino before settling its corporate operations in Corona in 1994. The company liked Corona because of the city's central Southern California location, nice community and business friendly environment. All Lucas products are manufactured and bottled on-site and shipped from their large, state-of-the-art facilities.

Not only is the company, its products and reputation for quality and service well known throughout the country, it is recognized around the world. The foreign demand for Lucas products is great because of the high price of gas and oil overseas. To meet that demand, in 1989 Lucas expanded into the international market, selling its fix-it products in countless countries including Russia, Germany, Asia and England. In addition, the company has an office down under in Australia — and continues to grow.

Along with the development of their various oil products, Lucas Oil has worked to produce more environmentally friendly products that help conserve the earth's resources. One of their goals has been to develop additive packages that allow engines to go much longer between oil changes. Through their research, the company developed a fuel treatment that allows engines to save up to 20 percent of their fuel when they operate. The stop leak products also help the environment, as they are 95 percent effective at stopping leaks in power steering units, automatic transmissions and hydraulic systems.

As a leader in the oil industry, Lucas is a major player in the American racing industry, participating in events and serving as a sponsor for many racing teams. Lucas products are used in thousands of high performance racing cars, from NASCAR, NHRA, USHRA, IHRA and SODA Truck Racing circuit.

Although Lucas is closely associated with racing, a wide range of customers use Lucas' products. They include Pomona Unified School District, which uses the engine additives in its fleet of school buses, farmers, factories, construction and towing companies, car repair shops and interstate trucking businesses, to name a few.

Southwest Airlines Co. also uses Lucas' products in their ground fleet to help solve oil consumption, engine wear and hydraulic related problems. "It's a good feeling to have products that help people," says Forrest Lucas.

From its Heavy Duty Oil Stabilizer, Fuel Treatment, Transmission Fix, Power Steering Stop Leak and Tool Box Buddy, Lucas products are developed to maintain and prevent engine damage. From a professional race car to a mother in charge of the school carpool, Lucas Oil is a family owned and customer friendly company that makes quality products that help ensure safety, longevity and engine performance.

Owners and founders of Lucas Oil Products, Inc., Forrest and Charlotte Lucas.

The Lucas name and products are known throughout the United States and around the world.

MediaOne

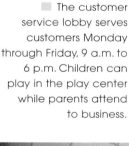
■ Customer service center located at 425 S. Corona Mall since 1993.

■ The customer service lobby serves customers Monday through Friday, 9 a.m. to 6 p.m. Children can play in the play center while parents attend to business.

*I*n the year 1964, America steps up the race to the moon. Satellites orbit the earth and beam color television programs to Europe and Asia.

Television served as the window to the American experience, emerging as the single most important source of current events and entertainment.

But for the residents of rural communities who lived beyond the range of broadcast television, the national and world news could only be found in black-and-white newsprint. For them, there was no Ed Sullivan show to introduce them to the Beatles and Elvis. No Dick Clark and the American Bandstand.

Two young Harvard Business School graduates recognized the niche that needed to be filled and formed a company designed to bridge the gap in the broadcast technology of the time. Amos B. Hostetter, Jr. and H. Irving Grousbeck erected a 520-foot antenna in an Ohio cornfield to offer ten channels of television over a coaxial cable.

Although the entire service area only encompassed five square miles, this pair of entrepreneurial visionaries named their burgeoning business "Continental Cablevision."

By 1996, Continental Cablevision evolved to become the nation's third-largest multiple system operator, serving over 4 million customers in more than 750 communities.

Purchased in 1997 by U.S. West Media Group, and renamed Media-One, the premier cable company is emerging as an important international provider of cable television and other communications services.

Technology may have changed since the company's humble beginnings over three decades ago, but its core philosophy has stayed the same. MediaOne remains committed to providing local communities with the highest quality cable television services.

But as its new name suggests, MediaOne strives to be a telecommunications leader capable of delivering the most sophisticated interactive, multimedia products and services on earth. From remote towns to major cities, from country to country, across the street and around the world, tomorrow's technology is ready today.

For many people the Information Superhighway is more of a fantasy than a reality... a yellow brick road of technological wizardry. But what MediaOne knows is that the Information Superhighway has been under construction since before the days when the founders of the firm were putting up their first antenna.

Long before TV's grand entrance into the American living room, the telephone company built a national telecommunications system that used "twisted pair" lines to transmit switched, narrow-band telephone calls. These lines had enough capacity to handle a telephone signal, but not much more.

Then along came coaxial cable. Since a single video signal is approximately 2,000 times bigger than a telephone call, high capacity coaxial cables provided the perfect conduit.

Today MediaOne offers most customers 54 or more channels of television programming, and each "average" cable system easily carries more than 100,000 times as much information as a conventional telephone line.

Because of this size difference, two different "wired" telecommunications infrastructures were set up across America, a narrow-band, two-way switched audio service (the telephone system) and a wide-band, one-way, unswitched video service (the cable TV system). Their designers may not have realized it at the time, but these infrastructures would have wide-ranging, long-term effects.

Contemporary cable systems are constructed of more than just coaxial cable. MediaOne's current system relies on a high capacity fiber optic "backbone" that interconnects individual cable system "head ends" for improved signal quality and increased reliability. Together, they form the cable network of the future.

MediaOne's commitment to technology has paid off. The company was selected by GTE to distribute its interactive television service to more than 550,000 homes — making it the largest such service in the country.

Traditionally, cable TV has been a one-way, subscription-based service. But today cable is quickly becoming more of a two-way street to include residential and commercial voice, video and data communications, as well as high-speed access to the Internet, a global network of computer databases.

One of the true marvels of modern technology is the way it changes the way we work and live. MediaOne has emerged not only as a leading provider of communications services across the country, but spans the globe from Singapore to South America.

Although MediaOne is increasing its global presence, the cable company continues a strong tradition of local services. Its corporate structure is highly decentralized, with regional offices across the country and around the world. Supported by more than 10,000 employees worldwide, local management in each of MediaOne's operations is entrusted to make their own decisions about the specific entertainment, cultural, educational, business and public service needs of each individual community it serves.

In fact, for all its technological prowess, MediaOne's real expertise lies in its people skills. MediaOne is known throughout the industry as being "close to the customer" and customer service delivery is considered second to none. This is evidenced in the number of industry awards the company received over the years for customer service, overall management excellence, marketing, technological innovation and financial acumen.

MediaOne's systems across America bring students the world through "Cable in the Classroom," quality, commercial-free educational programs teachers use to enhance and enliven the learning process.

The company also launched a national media literacy effort to improve children's TV viewing habits and help parents take charge of their family's TV viewing options. MediaOne believes that teaching children how to use televisions must be a national priority which leads to a society that is literate not only in the printed word, but also in the use of electronic media.

In a world accustomed to moving at the speed of sound, MediaOne responds at the speed of light.

The Technical Operations center opened in 1995 and is located at 2320 Pomona Rincon Road.

Nature's Recipe Pet Foods

ature's Recipe Pet Foods was founded in 1981 by Jeffrey P. Bennett when his prized Samoyed, Tasha, developed life-threatening skin and coat problems from an allergic reaction to commercial pet food. To save the dog, Bennett began a daily routine of vegetarian cooking to personally nurse Tasha back to health — and simultaneously created one of the most innovative developments on the pet retail scene.

Virtually overnight, Bennett became a pioneer in the premium pet food industry, formulating home-cooked, vegetarian meals for his pet. With one product, Non-Meat Dog Kibble, and an initial $100,000 investment from a second mortgage on his mother's home, Bennett turned his small, one-man operation into a thriving multi-million dollar business with more than 70 employees.

Today, Nature's Recipe is one of the most successful pet food manufacturing businesses in the world with revenues in excess of $60 million. Headquartered since 1990 in Corona, California, Nature's Recipe is located in a 148,000-square-foot distribution center that was chosen due to the opportunities it provided for expansion.

Between 1986 and 1991, Nature's Recipe grew by a phenomenal 1,640 percent and *Inc.* magazine featured Nature's Recipe Pet Foods four times as one of America's 500 fastest growing privately-held companies. Mr. Bennett was honored twice by Ernst & Young, receiving the "Entrepreneur of the Year" award once for manufacturing and once for the category of "socially responsible."

Nature's Recipe Pet Foods has always put the health and well-being of pets first, formulating products for purity — offering quality natural nutrition to dogs and cats. In the years since its inception, Nature's Recipe has continued to lead the premium pet food category in industry "firsts." In 1985, Nature's Recipe introduced the first lamb and rice kibble dog food — with other manufacturers subsequently responding with their own versions. Other product innovations include Rabbit and Rice for Dogs and Cats, and Venison and Rice for Dogs — ingredients that eliminate many health problems in pets. All Nature's Recipe pet food products are produced without the use of artificial preservative, artificial colors and flavors, sugars and dairy products.

In March of 1996, Bennett sold his company to H.J. Heinz Company, one of the world's largest leading food processors and purveyors of nutritional services. Nature's Recipes' acquisition by the $10 billion Heinz company resulted in giving the city of Corona its first Fortune 500-related company. Bennett currently serves as president of Heinz's newly-established Nature's Recipe Division.

Nature's Recipe Pet Foods are available throughout the United States, Canada, Mexico, Scandinavia, Europe, Japan and Taiwan. The Nature's Recipe Pet Food list now includes more than 30 premium pet food products.

In November of 1992, Bennett was elected to the Corona City Council where he has brought a no-nonsense, action-oriented approach to his responsibilities. As a member of the city council, he has drafted tough anti-crime ordinances and was an effective proponent of a statewide funding measure that provided support to local public safety and law enforcement services. In 1996, he was overwhelmingly re-elected with more than 69 percent of the votes from Corona voters.

Quality of life is the foundation of Nature's Recipe — whether it's pet foods that provide a better quality of life for pets and their owners, or involvement in social issues that affect the quality of life for an entire community. Jeff Bennett's commitment to quality of life includes extensive involvement in Say No Together; The Starlight Foundation, an organization that grants last wishes to terminally ill children; and God's Kitchen, a provider of hot meals to the homeless.

He also supports his community by serving on organizations including the American Cancer Society, Alternatives to Domestic Violence and the March of Dimes. He has been recognized with the Distinguished Citizen of the Year Award by the Boy Scouts of America. In 1995, he was given the Richard Baseheart Award by Actors and Others for his significant contributions to the welfare of animals. Bennett also serves on the National Advisory Board of Mothers Against Sexual Abuse (MASA). In 1996, he received the Albert Schweitzer Humanitarian of the Year Award from the Riverside Humane Society and Governor Pete Wilson appointed him to the State of California Advisory Committee on Juvenile Justice and Delinquency.

Mr. Bennett lives in the city of Corona with his wife, Nan Eisley-Bennett and two daughters, Jillian and Jocelyn.

NuTrend Homes

When you first drive onto the lot of NuTrend Homes, you can see evidence of the owner, Peggy Whittenton Domasin. It's as though each home has her personal signature on it. You find yourself surrounded by beautiful, spacious and exquisitely decorated homes. Each home has an exclusive NuTrend touch to it. Why? Because the homes sold at NuTrend are manufactured by Silvercrest, in Corona, and can be custom designed. Each sales executive representing NuTrend Homes has been qualified as a Design Specialist and will assist in any changes the buyer elects to make to any of the designs offered or can start with the buyer's desired square footage and design the home with the buyer's own personal signature.

The world of manufactured homes has evolved from the days of paneling and metal to drywall and stucco, from 12 feet wide to 54 feet wide. Cathedral ceilings, gourmet kitchens, pantries the size of bedrooms and "retreats" off the main bedroom where a mother of a two-year-old can find some peace and quiet are all possible. Even two stories are available for those long skinny lots by the beach or tree filled lots in the mountains.

The history of manufactured homes began with the commonly known phrase "trailers" which were constructed and brought to locations for G.I.'s returning from World War II who faced a severe housing shortage. The "trailers" were hauled to a spot, unhitched from the truck, hooked up to electricity and water and became "Home Sweet Home." Today things are much different. The homes purchased from NuTrend can be set up in much the same way in a planned community (a Mobile Home Park). However, today the wheels and axles can be removed and set up as low profile, looking exactly like the homes seen every day when traveling through housing developments. The normal park setting usually has two or three steps up to the home and the under area is concealed with matching exterior. Although NuTrend is regarded as master of all settings, its specialty is Land and Home projects. In this setting, the home is placed on a foundation and becomes real estate. If desired, two, three or even four car garages can be constructed and financed all in the same package. Two of the major differences between purchasing a home through NuTrend and locating a trustworthy contractor to build your home are time and cost, and NuTrend will take the lead every time.

Peggy Whittenton Domasin will not compromise her standards. She prides herself on her product, Silvercrest, and her team of executives. The buyer can start their day at the Silvercrest factory tour, given every Saturday, drive two miles to NuTrend, custom design their home including land improvements (if needed) and drive off knowing the cost of the project from beginning to end. The contractor puts the final touches on the project by visiting the site with the buyers and determining where their new home will go and what will be needed to provide the buyer with a "turnkey" project. During that time, the finance department is locating the best form of financing available, sometimes using the buyer's equity as a down payment. Then, in about six weeks, the buyer will be watching TV in his new home. And all it took was one Saturday in Corona.

When Peggy started her career as an interior designer in El Paso, Texas, she wouldn't compromise her standards. Her designs were her signature and her reputation, and she held both precious.

She relocated to California in the early 1980s and entered the real estate market in Riverside. She still held onto those high standards, and they proved successful. Associates in the manufactured home industry encouraged her to research a manufacturer that held the same high standards. She discovered Silvercrest and felt confident they would up hold the reputation she had established for herself. For a period of time she represented both industries, real estate and Silvercrest. Eventually, she focused solely on her new endeavor, NuTrend Homes, proudly offering Silvercrest. How far did she take this new endeavor? In 1993 she had her own dealership. In 1997, her sales exceeded $4.5 million.

Her accomplishments go beyond the norm and the old cliche "You can't fight City Hall". Peggy doesn't know the world "can't" and loves a good fight with City Hall. She was involved with the first FHA Loan in California to finance manufactured homes. Today, an FHA loan is very common practice in the industry. As she attempted to spread her wings, she found some cities and counties still had that World War II outlook on her homes. Today, manufactured homes can be located anywhere in the State of California. There are no financial or locational differences whatsoever between an "on-site" constructed home and a factory manufactured home. Manufactured homes accommodate 30 percent of the housing market in the United States, and those within the industry predict that by 2003, that figure will increase to 50 percent of the market.

Peggy Whittenton Domasin sees no limits to her future. She still holds tight to her standards and keeps growing. She recently established two other products that are in great demand. "Park Models" which are under 400 square feet and qualify as a recreational vehicle (less the

motor and steering wheel) because these homes serve as weekend getaways in R. V. parks. Her other product "Welcome Home Flats" or "Granny Flats" are designed to be a second home on a property. They were originally called "Mother-in-Law Flats" but husbands seemed to be very reluctant to discuss a purchase with that name. So the name was changed but not the concept. She also has a company that constructs sheds with various designs such as a red barn or a play house with planter boxes and tulips. Because her homes are so beautiful, she wanted to provide storage units that would compliment, not embarrass.

Customers are Peggy's priority. By process of elimination she has established a working relationship with a small group of contractors who meet her high standards. Once the home leaves the factory, she has to trust others to perform their duties with her business in mind. She is proud of her accomplishments, and she is proud of the individuals who work as a team to provide the public with the best service and product available. Her motto: "To compromise one's standards is to reevaluate and lose."

The team at NuTrend Homes sees no limit to their future expansion.

ProChef, Inc.

roChef barbecues are to the barbecue industry what Mercedes is to the automotive industry — the top of the line. If you are lucky enough to be the owner of a ProChef barbecue, you not only can barbecue a meal, you can roast, bake, deep fry or grill as well. A ProChef grill is like an outdoor kitchen.

Although ProChef came into being in 1990, its parent company, Grand Hall Enterprise Company, Ltd. was established in 1976. Grand Hall began exporting cast iron burners and gas cocks from their home base in Taiwan to Australia and first produced barbecue grills for Rinnai Corporation of Australia. In 1983 they produced their first diecast aluminum barbecue grill for Jacuzzi. However, when in 1986 Jacuzzi terminated its grill line, Grand Hall decided to market its own line of grills under the ProChef label and founded Grand Hall USA in Dallas, Texas.

ProChef was established in 1990 in Corona, a desirable location for a business which needs easy access to both major highways and rail lines. At that time, Charlotte Lin, President of ProChef, Inc. purchased property and a building on Railroad Street. The Corona plant is a facility of about 46,000 square feet, and it is here that ProChef manufactures, assembles and distributes its products nationwide. Recently, a customer service center has been added to the local facility so that distributors, retailers, or even consumers can visit if they need to implement their warranty policy.

From its beginning, ProChef has had a strong commitment to research and development in order to produce state-of-the-art products for the serious outdoor chef. ProChef was the first to use a patented cast brass burner in an outdoor gas grill. In 1991, ProChef introduced and patented the first "No Assembly Required" grill. By 1995, ProChef was producing one of the most popular outdoor gas grills in America.

ProChef buys component parts made of stainless steel and heavy brass and aluminum castings from several parts of the world. Stainless steel and brass castings come from Taiwan. Cast iron components come from Mainland China. From Australia they purchase wheels and Jarrah Wood (a type of teak) for shelves and carts. Packaging, printed materials and cardboard cartons are obtained locally. All these component parts arrive at the Corona plant where they are then assembled, tested, packaged and shipped. For ProChef the advantage of purchasing castings from overseas is that it keeps their prices lower. The castings and other component parts are brought into the US as component parts rather than finished products, thereby lowering the duty. Also, many more items can be put into a container for the same freight costs. These cost savings are then passed onto the consumer. The consumer gets a higher quality product at a lower cost.

From Corona, ProChef ships its products nationwide to companies who are traditional distributors of hearth products such as fireplaces, patio furniture, casual furniture, barbecues, and air conditioners. These distributors generally have a network of retail dealers who purchase from them and that is how the ProChef products reach the consumer. ProChef does not just sell its barbecues and other products to retail customers. It sells in truckloads — 300 to 400 products at a time.

However, ProChef does not just produce barbecues. They also manufacture and market portable patio heaters and gas fireplace logs. Patio heaters are used extensively in the party rental trade by caterers and restaurants who produce

A ProChef grill is like a fantastic outdoor kitchen.

outdoor parties, weddings and other social events. The gas fireplace logs are found in fireplace and hearth products stores. The gas fireplace log is used by home owners who want the beauty and warmth of a fireplace but do not want the mess of a traditional wood burning fireplace. All of ProChef's products have been approved by the American Gas Association and the Canadian Gas Association for design, safety and function.

ProChef is a business which operates in a traditional two-step distribution marketing concept. An example of their operation can be found in the operation of AES, a company based in the state of Washington. AES sells traditional hearth products, fireplace parts and accessories, gas logs, barbecue grills, patio heaters, air conditioning equipment and casual furniture (such as patio furniture). Every year, AES purchases three or four truckloads of gas grills from ProChef, some 1,000 grills. In turn, they then distribute those through their network of dealers which are located as far away as Montana. AES distributes hearth products into Northern Oregon, all of Washington, and parts of Canada and Idaho, to approximately 1,000 retail stores.

In the Southwestern region of the United States, ProChef acts as the distributor. A network of approximately 125 retail establishments in Southern California, Arizona and Southern Nevada display and sell the ProChef product line. ProChef does maintain a showroom at its Railroad Street location but does not sell to retail customers. Locally, you can find ProChef products on display at fine specialty retailers from Ventura to San Diego. In the Corona area you can find ProChef grills displayed at Hearth & Home in Riverside and Patio World, also in Riverside.

ProChef's sales force consists of an in-house management team and a network of independent manufacturers' representatives. This sales team works in cooperation to insure that ProChef products are available nationwide. They have pushed the expansion of the business from ground zero when they opened in 1990 to $7.6 million in sales today. In addition to the sales teams, there are approximately 15 permanent employees responsible for advertising, accounting, shipping and production. During the busy production period, temporary help is added to bring the staff to approximately 30 people.

ProChef begins marketing its products in September, begins building in October, and delivers to distributors in December, January and February. Local retailers will begin to take delivery of product in March and continue through August.

When asked about future plans, a ProChef spokesperson said, "Our future plans are to make our products the best on the market."

Smittybilt®, Inc.

Producing superior quality products since day one, Smittybilt®, Inc. manufactures products that serve the four-wheel drive industry from California to the East Coast and around the world. The rugged design and craftsmanship that defines Smittybilt® truck bars, tube bumpers, sidebars and other accessories can be seen on four-wheel drive vehicles on and off the road from the Grand Canyon to Moscow's Red Square.

From its small beginnings in Smitty's South El Monte garage, Smittybilt has grown to be a leading manufacturer of four-wheel drive products and accessories around the world.

Family owned and operated, Smittybilt started out Rock-ett Products in 1956, in the El Monte garage of Basil "Smitty" Smith. The four-wheel drive enthusiast mainly operated machine work and helped to develop special four-wheel drive equipment. He perfected overdrive adaptations for four-wheel drives, automatic locking front hubs for Jeeps, full floating axle conversions, a variety of engine adaptations and hangers, oversize brakes, improved soft tops for Jeeps and tow bars.

With his added inventions, Smitty soon found the need for more space, moving his operations from his garage to a larger lot on Lee Avenue in South El Monte. There, the business continued to flourish and within three years, Smitty had hired several employees to work with him. As Americans discovered the thrill of four-wheel drive vehicles, the demand for Smitty's parts grew. In 1973, he tore down his house and built a new building to accommodate even more employees and his rapidly expanding business. That same year, the company incorporated and changed its name to Smittybilt®, Inc., the moniker that is known around the world today.

As a leading force in the off-road movement, Smittybilt® continued to grow with the aide of Smitty's son Tom, who joined his dad in 1967 and took over operations in 1973 when Smitty officially retired. Tom Smith, with the help of his wife and co-owner Debbie, introduced new and innovative ideas and products to the four-wheel drive industry. By the 1990s, not only had the company's product line increased, but the market for four-wheel drive parts and accessories had risen 400 percent since the days of the old Smith garage.

Still owned and operated by Tom and Debbie, in January 1992, Smittybilt moved its offices and operations permanently to Corona. With the city's Southern California location and easy access to transportation corridors, Corona was a perfect match to meet the company's growing logistical needs. In addition, all of Smittybilt's® employees followed the four-wheel drive accessory producer to its new home, electing to move to the family-friendly area.

All Smittybilt® products are made by the company employees on-site, from manufacturing the various parts, to wrapping and shipping orders to customers. The large production center also includes state-of-the-art technology, including automated machines and robotics that weld parts, which help to produce the company's signature Ultra-bars, Outland products, Sure-Steps, front and rear bumpers, front guards and other four-wheel drive products.

The Smittybilt name stands for quality four-wheel drive products and superior customer service.

Servicing the whole four-wheel drive market, the Smittybilt® name is known throughout the United States and to distributors and dealers worldwide. Smittybilt® tubular parts and the accessories that go with them are sold in countries around the globe. From Japan, France, Saudi Arabia and Russia and Australia down under. Parts like Sure-Step™ sidebars, nerf bars, tube bumpers, cage kits, grille guards, brush guards and tow bars as well as Outland™ front guards and tail light guards can be seen on Jeeps climbing distant mountain tops or on four-wheel drive vehicles navigating foreign roads.

Smittybilt® also participates in off-road racing, sport truck shows and jamborees. The company sponsors the "Hummer" and "Big Foot" specialty trucks which tour the country and put on demonstrations. A conscientious corporate citizen, Smittybilt® is also involved in the community. The company participates in local car events and is a member of the Corona Chamber of Commerce, the

Specialty Equipment Manufacturers Association, CORVA and the Four Wheel Drive Association, to name a few.

Although products have changed and developed over the years, Smittybilt® remains on top of the four-wheel drive industry because of its honesty, quality products and dedication to serving its customers. Even though Smittybilt® has grown to be "the name brand in tubular parts," Tom Smith says that it is not the focus of the company. "Anybody can build a tubular part," he says. "It's serving the customer that's important."

Keeping in touch with the latest engineering, technology and design, the company continues to be on the forefront of the four-wheel drive industry. With a new 207,000-square-foot building in November 1997, a name and reputation that stand for quality and a commitment to customer service, Smittybilt® maintains the tradition of excellence that started back in 1956 in a South El Monte garage, and continues on into the 21st century.

USA Waste of California

An example of the American dream come true, USA Waste of California is a corporate leader and friend of Corona, offering thousands superior waste disposal services. A decades-long resident of the community, USA Waste has grown from a one-truck operation to an army of thousands operating in states all over the country.

With its fleet of trucks, which includes the familiar orange haulers, USA Waste transports tons of refuge, recyclables and green waste for residential, commercial and industrial entities. The company services include waste collection, recycling programs, transfer facilities, construction services, landfill design and operation. From its commercial scout service and automated waste collector to its cost-efficient transfer vehicles, USA Waste's mission is to create loyal customers by providing the highest quality of service possible.

USA Waste was first established in 1955 as Western Waste Industries, Inc. by Kosti Shirvanian. In the beginning, Kosti cleaned bins and hauled refuge with the help of one flat bed, wooden-paneled truck. With his sister doing the company's books, Kosti's business soon developed into a trusted small hauler in the community. By 1963, the company had grown and incorporated thanks to the determination of Kosti and his siblings who built the company from the ground up to become the largest Southern California integrated waste service company.

In 1996, Western was bought by USA Waste of California, one of the largest companies in North America. Ever expanding, USA Waste operates more than 100 landfills in around 36 states. With the help, experience and insight from an industry leader like USA Waste, officials said the merger would allow Western to provide enhanced services to residents and businesses in Corona and other areas.

Following Kosti's example, USA Waste works to continually upgrade its operations, while maintaining the hardworking values from yesterday. The disposal company operates automated collection and recycling systems that minimize waste. At USA Waste's Material Recovery Facilities, waste that would typically go to the landfill is presorted, separated and sold as recyclable material. The company also employs trucks that allow for cost-effective programs which are customized to meet the needs of the communities it serves. In addition, through unique public, private and municiple partnerships, USA Waste has developed and now operates public landfills across the nation. Responsible and safety conscious, all landfills developed and operated by USA Waste exceed federal, state and local regulations.

With an eye toward the future and technology, the company is constantly developing new equipment and state-of-the-art waste disposal and recycling programs. USA Waste took the industry lead in recycling management strategies and operation in the early 1980s, piloting a curbside collection program. The company also recognized the importance of residential recycling, reaching out to the community with informational materials to educate the public on the subject. USA Waste explained the who, what, when, where and why of recycling to encourage participation, comply with state recycling regulations, and most of all, help the environment. For example, in Norco, where there are many horses and large plots of land, USA Waste assists residents in recycling horse manure and green materials from their lots. Residents with hazardous waste are also helped in disposing of their materials. In addition, the company works in the community to encourage people to look for and buy recyclable products.

The company also recycles material at the California Institute for Men in Chino and the California Institute for Women in Frontera. At the men's center, green waste and wood material are turned into viable alternative fuels and compost material. Ten prisoners assist in the process, sorting through the material, grinding the wood down to turn into boiler fuel. Nearby at the women's facility, 47 acres of compost steer manure is processed, bagged and then sold to department stores.

As illustrated through its community outreach, USA Waste has a long-standing tradition of strongly supporting Corona and its residents. Since its first days of operation in the city, the company has made it an unofficial policy to give back to the community. With half of its work force living in Corona, Western has made civic participation a focus and priority, as a good neighbor and responsible member of the community that has provided so much to the company.

USA Waste participates in many nonprofit organizations, including the Corona Boys and Girls Club, Corona Neighborhood Center and the Corona-Norco YMCA. The company is also very involved with the local library, medical center, schools, law enforcement and fire department, and senior programs. As a positive influence in the corporate community, USA Waste and its employees volunteer their time, services and money to local service clubs, the Corona Chamber of Commerce, American Cancer Society, Corona Christmas Parade, Corona 4th of July events and Wings & Wheels show, just to name a few.

As an industry leader, USA Waste also led the push into the classroom to educate students about

recycling. The company has aggressively pursued its educational program in local schools since the early 1990s, finding that if students are motivated to change their habits and recycle, they will make their parents follow suit.

A friend of the community, USA Waste has provided a myriad of integrated waste disposal services from its Corona headquarters since 1955. Through its innovations and hard work, the small refuse hauler started by Kosti has developed into an industry leader, representing superior quality and service committed to helping serve its customers and improving the quality of life in the communities where it operates.

USA Waste vehicles are customized to provide communities with special programs like curbside recycling and commercial waste removal.

The waste disposal company provides a myriad of services for the city of Corona and communities across the United States.

With its environmental focus, USA Waste takes pride in reducing the amount of waste that goes into landfills by turning green waste, wood and other materials into viable conditioned soil for public consumption.

In an ongoing effort to educate the public about waste and its effect on the environment, USA Waste of California works with the community and in local schools to promote recycling and waste reduction.

Alfredo Rodriguez

Alfredo Rodriguez is known internationally for his outstanding paintings of the American West. His vivid images of mountains, deserts, Indian villages are always show-stoppers. Winner of top awards from the most prestigious organizations in the art world, Rodriguez's work is included in the books *Western Painting Today* and *Contemporary Western Artists*. He has been featured in such magazines as *Art of the West, Western Horseman, Informat, International Fine Art Collector* and *Wild West*.

The Pathfinders
Oil 30"x40"

Recently, Rodriguez was a featured artist at the Autry Museum of Western Heritage, in Los Angeles, in association with the American Indian and Cowboy Artists.

Rodriguez was born and raised in Tepic, Mexico. His career as an artist began at the age of five when he was given a small set of watercolors. His mother saw that he had a God-given talent for painting and scrapped together enough money for him to have a few lessons from Santiago Rosas, a well-known Mexican artist.

Navajo Stress
Oil 30"x40"

Rodriguez has found in Corona an environment conducive to his lifestyle and his painting goals. He established his home and his wife and three daughters here and continues his work in a self-designed studio on his premises. Being close to his family is one of his greatest pleasures.

The City of Corona honored Rodriguez in 1993 by commissioning him to paint a massive mural for the Children's Area of the Corona City Library. The mural was unveiled in 1993 and was received with tremendous admiration.

Although Rodriguez enjoys international response and critical aclaim to his work, career and family come first. He recently said, "If I had the chance to say anything to people in the world, I would say I want to be remembered as an artist who loved beauty, children, nature and the world in general — an artist who strived for perfection knowing he would never attain it, because only God is perfect."

Campbell Plastics Engineering and Manufacturing, Inc.

State-of-the art molding machines whir and hum around the clock in a sprawling 37,500-square-foot facility known as Campbell Plastics Engineering and Manufacturing, Inc. (CPEM) of Corona. Some are fully automated, others require a human operator. And every 30 to 60 seconds, each high-tech machine pumps out a plastic component for cellular phones, digital pagers, even revolutionary gas masks used by the US Army to protect against chemical warfare.

As one of Southern California's leading plastics manufacturers, CPEM capitalizes on a unique collection of in-house capabilities including research and development, engineering services, injection, insert and silicone molding, mold design, fabrication and repair.

CPEM employs a highly skilled staff of professionals who design and engineer products for some of the nation's largest telecommunications, automotive, computer, aerospace and medical companies. Their client base includes AT&T, McDonnell Douglas, Hughes Radar, Baxter Healthcare and the US Army.

Established in 1981 as Venture Plastics Inc., CPEM initially operated from a 10,000-square-foot site in Santa Ana. Fifteen years later, the multi-million dollar firm changed its name to better define the broad range of services offered. To meet growing demand, CPEM moved into its current Corona location in July of 1996.

Today, CPEM's capabilities include close tolerance injection and insert molding utilizing a myriad of resins. Silicone molding is also available as well as a wide range of integrated value-added services such as engineering, computer aided design (CAD), real time monitoring, sonic welding, optical inspection, printing and product assembly.

CPEM also meets and exceeds the highly stringent ISO 9000 standards, an international quality standard which outlines the minimum requirements a company must have in place. Over the years, CPEM's quality system has been refined to include detailed document control with step-by-step manufacturing instructions and computer-generated real time analysis.

Being on the cutting edge of technology helped CPEM seal a multi-million dollar deal with the Department of Defense for the design, development and testing of plastic and silicone components to replace existing metal features and attachments for a gas mask to be used by the US Army as protection against biological and chemical warfare.

Campbell Plastics Engineering and Manufacturing Inc. was selected as the prime contractor to produce the new M-45 Gas Mask in 1997. As such, CPEM is responsible for in-house production, selecting sub-contractors, product assembly and final testing.

From concept to production, CPEM of Corona has emerged as an industry leader in quality innovation, customer service and responsiveness.

■ Since 1981, Campbell Plastics Engineering and Manufacturing, Inc. has emerged as one of Southern California's leading plastics manufacturers.

Citizens Business Bank

itizens Business Bank is the "Bank Business Banks On" in Corona and throughout the Inland Empire. Citizens Business Bank is the principal subsidiary of CVB Financial Corp. CVB Financial Corp. is listed on the American Stock Exchange under the symbol CVB.

Citizens Business Bank and CVB Financial Corp. are headquartered in Ontario. The Bank has more than $1.3 billion in assets and 23 branch offices. Branches are located throughout the Inland Empire, San Gabriel Valley and North Orange County. Citizens Business Bank is the largest independent bank in its markets.

The Corona office of Citizens Business Bank

Citizens Business Bank began as Chino Valley Bank on August 9, 1974. It was organized by seven local businessmen and community leaders. Five of the seven organizers remain on the Board of Directors today.

The Bank has earned both local and national recognition as one of the safest, strongest and best managed banks in the United States. It has received the designation of "Premier Performing Bank" for 23 consecutive years and "Super Premier Performing Bank" for six years from the Findley Reports. The Bank was rated the highest performing bank in California for the 10-year period from 1985 to 1995 in a study by the highly regarded consulting firm of McKinsey and Company.

Citizens Business Bank was named Entrepreneur of the Year in 1995. It also has received wide recognition for its commitment to the communities it serves. This includes the Economic and Social Development Award from Soroptimist International and the Lincoln Award. In addition, many of the officers and staff have received awards for their individual contributions to the communitites served by the Bank.

The Bank has grown with its markets. It has opened seven offices and acquired 16 offices during its 24-year history. Since 1991, the Bank has added 11 offices and more than $800 million in assets.

Citizens Business Bank offers a complete package of financial services to business, professional and individual clientele. It specializes in services to businesses and professionals. Services include all types of deposits, loans and investments. In addition, the Bank offers comprehensive asset management and traditional trust services, as well as international banking accommodations. Citizens Business Bank is also the bank for many agribusinesses and dairy clientele.

The future of Citizens Business Bank is to be the premier relationship financial institution for business and professionals by delivering the finest in financial products and services to its customers in the Inland Empire, San Gabriel Valley and North Orange County. This will be achieved through an unqualified commitment to its four core values of financial strength, superior people, customer focus and cost effective operation.

Citizen Business Bank is "The Bank Business Banks On!"

City of Norco

The City of Norco was founded on a vision, a vision of people who wanted to maintain a rural lifestyle among the growing urbanization of Southern California. It was a lifestyle where they could live in houses on lots large enough for plenty of elbow room and a few horses as well. The City was incorporated in 1964 by Norco's citizens who believed the best way to protect the area from urbanization was to make it an independent city with control of its own destiny. Residential lots are one-half acre in size and are zoned for animal keeping. "City Living in a Rural Atmosphere" became the motto of Norco then and has been ever since.

Although Norco traces its history back to the Luiseno Indians who traveled over the land from their homes in the Temescal Valley, there was little development of the area until 1921 when most of the valley was sold to the North Corona Land Company. The name Norco is a contraction of North Corona. At the time, there were fewer than 100 families in the valley. A few years later, the North Corona Land Company, totaling 5,409 acres, was purchased by Rex B. Clark, who is considered the "founder" of Norco.

Clark believed Norco had the potential to become a luxury resort for the rich and famous, and in 1929 he opened the 700-acre Club Norconian Hotel and Spa, complete with mineral baths, an artificial lake and golf course, a huge swimming pool and a restaurant resplendent with marble and gold inlay. Although the resort enjoyed a period of popularity, the Depression took its toll. The club was sold in 1941 to the U.S. Navy who converted it to use as a military hospital. In 1962, the Navy sold a portion of the old resort to the State of California for use as a prison. The balance of the property, including Lake Norconian, is now the site of the Naval Warfare Assessment Station.

Norco has a city council/city manager form of government, its council consisting of five council members, elected at large for four-year terms. The City's mission statement is: "To serve Norco residents and businesses in a professional, ethical, and cost effective manner with excellent customer service and to provide a high quality of life in a community that values a rural atmosphere."

The City employs 82 persons who operate the City departments: Fire; Parks, Recreation and Community Services; Community Development; Economic Development; Administrative Services; and Public Works. Norco was the first city in Riverside County to contract with the Riverside County Sheriff's Department for police services and that contract arrangement is maintained to this day. In keeping with the rural tradition, Norco boasts 12 parks encompassing 381 acres, including a large equestrian park called Ingalls Park. The City also has 88 miles of improved horse trails.

Norco's 25,000 residents enjoy several annual events featuring family entertainment including the Norco Valley Fair, the Annual Western Art Show, a police rodeo sponsored by the HorseWeek Association and a professional rodeo sponsored by Norco Mounted Posse.

In addition to the California Rehabilitation Center (State prison) and the Naval Warfare Assessment Station, several high-tech industries such as DynCorp and Wyle Laboratories, the Norco Egg Ranch, and a successful auto mall and retail sector contribute to Norco's strong economic base and support the City's attractive lifestyle.

No city funds were used for this profile.

■ (Bottom Left) Lake Norconian, club and hotel, view looking north, taken in 1929.

■ (Bottom) Main dining room in the Norconian Hotel, looking north, taken in 1929. Dining room looks much the same today.

The Computer Edge

The Computer Edge of Corona helps keep the city's residents on the cutting edge of technology. Since its inception in 1992, this system integration and solutions provider for high-end PC users has provided training, supplies, repairs and upgrades for all IBM and IBM-compatible computer systems.

Owner Ahsan Baseer says his company caters strictly to high-end users and "prides itself on putting together computer systems with only the highest quality components."

Unlike many of his competitors who utilize assembly lines, Baseer builds his computer systems one at a time to maintain the highest level of quality available on the market.

A native of Hyderabad, India, Baseer emigrated to the US in 1974. He earned his undergraduate

degree in medical technology from Oklahoma's Northeastern University before completing his graduate studies in microbiology at the University of Arkansas in 1981.

Upon relocating to Southern California in 1986, this licensed clinical laboratory scientist served as the director of laboratory services at the Medical Center of La Mirada. He branched out on his own three years later to form the Anaheim Medical Research Institute.

In 1992, this young entrepreneur integrated his love of technology with the rapidly changing world of personal computers and launched The Computer Edge to meet a growing need for education and training.

The next year, Dastagir ("DA") Anwar sold a successful pair of grocery stores in Oklahoma to come to Corona and help his brother manage the booming new business.

Located on Green River Road in the Ralph's Shopping Center, The Computer Edge initially began as a children's training center. But as more and more adults requested Baseer's services, the program grew to include computer training for all ages.

Although the retail facility expanded to 2,800 square feet in 1996, the available space is already filled to brimming with boxes of state-of-the-art components and multimedia systems including scores of the latest in CD-ROM interactive games.

Baseer plans to expand the firm on a local level to other Corona locations as well as venturing into international markets.

"Since we meet such a growing need and because we only offer the highest quality components in our PC systems, there's no place for us to go but up in this industry."

The Computer Edge in Corona serves as a system integration and solutions provider for high-end PC users.

Ahsan Baseer (L), pictured with his brother Dastagir (DA) Anwar, take pride in putting together computer systems with only the highest quality components.

Corona Public Library

t the geographic center of Corona since the very beginning, the Corona Public Library has a proud tradition and dedication to being at the center of life in Corona. It continues to follow its mission:

"The Corona Public Library welcomes and supports all people in their enjoyment of reading and the pursuit of lifelong learning. Working together, we strive to provide equal access to information, ideas and knowledge through books, technology, programs, services and other resources. We believe in the freedom to read, to learn and to discover."

A number of volunteer groups were responsible in the early years for attempts to provide a lending library of books in Corona. The Womens Christian Temperance Union organized the first reading room library in 1893 and they were succeeded in those early efforts by the YMCA and Woman's Improvement Club.

In 1900, a ballot measure was passed by the citizens of Corona authorizing tax-supported public library services. A new location was secured in the First National Bank Building, which stood at the southeast corner of Sixth and Main streets. A successful appeal to the Carnegie Foundation brought funds to build the first library building which stood at the corner of Eighth and Main streets.

As the population of Corona continued to grow, reaching 27,599 people in 1970, a new 16,000-square-foot building was proposed and accepted by the community. This facility, built and dedicated in July 1971, contained 52,726 books, had a staff of 16, and an annual circulation of over 166,000 items. Just 15 years later, with a population of 44,843, a collection of 44,134 books and a staff of 40, an addition to that building was proposed. The community successfully passed a bond issue in 1988 and the present 62,300-

square-foot building was dedicated in June 1993 with a staff of 37 and 75,000 books.

The library established a Heritage Room in 1980 to collect, organize and make available for public use, information and artifacts relating to the history and development of the community. It serves as a primary resource for anyone doing research on this part of Southern California.

The Friends of the Corona Public Library was established in September 1964 and has been the primary support group for the library through many years. This organization provides volunteers, programs and funds for library materials. It operates a Book & Gift Shop which generates approximately $2,200 each month.

A Library Foundation (aka Corona Literary Society, Inc.) has been supportive of the library's

efforts since 1981 and is presently undertaking the development of permanent endowment funds for special projects for the library.

The Corona Public Library's vision for the future is to remain as the informational and educational center for the City of Corona. Staff will continue the policy of presenting programs for all ages, and provide cultural activities and educational resources that meet the needs of the community.

Corona United Methodist Church

Then and Now. Corona United Methodist Church as photographed in 1939 and as it stands today.

In 1886, attempting to attract land buyers in Corona (which was then called South Riverside), the South Riverside Land and Water Company donated one-quarter of a block of land to the Fletcher Methodist Episcopal Church and four other Christian denominations. The Fletcher Methodist Episcopal Church, forerunner of the Corona United Methodist Church, was named for a Boston resident named Fletcher who sent $250 to build a new church.

Consequently, the new church was organized in September, 1887, by Rev. S. P. Sowden who had been appointed to the Rincon Circuit, so named because the original meeting place was in the ballroom of the Rincon Hotel. In 1888, the church moved to its new two-room structure at the corner of 10th and Ramona. In 1889, the second largest audience gathered in South Riverside for the dedication of the new sanctuary. Reports at the time indicate that Rev. Colburn preached an "eloquent and powerful sermon which held the rapt attention of the congregation until he closed." The speech was so powerful that at its conclusion, when Elder Chase announced he had the "pleasure to permit those present to subscribe the amount still due to the contractors for building the church which amounted to $325." The people assembled donated the entire amount and the dedication services ended with a debt-free sanctuary.

Corona United Methodist Church has grown considerably over the years since its founding. In 1905 an addition was built to the 1889 sanctuary which provided Sunday School space and increased church seating by 300. By early 1909, Sunday School attendance had increased to the point where a new building was warranted. Dedication ceremonies for the new Sunday School were held on February 27, 1910, and the congregation gathered to admire the two-story structure, complete with bell tower. This building remains in use on the property today. By January 1917, a mortgage burning was held featuring the church choir who "sang especially well on this occasion and because of the importance of the event appeared in new Spanish costumes."

The church flourished under the leadership of Rev. Dr. Fletcher Watson and later Rev. Dr. Van Buskirk. Fifty years after the dedication of the first sanctuary, the present sanctuary was constructed and dedicated in 1939. The altar, pulpit and lectern were all hand carved by Rev. Van Buskirk and a church member.

There was very little change to the church until 1975 when a new structure to serve as the education building was dedicated at the corner of Main and Tenth streets. Church members themselves rolled up their sleeves and contributed much of the labor themselves.

Further building expansion occurred in 1984 consisting of refurbishing of the sanctuary. One of the first tasks was to remove the pipe organ which had been installed 45 years earlier. An organ specialist from Riverside did not offer much hope for reconstructing the 1938 instrument. In November 1985, without the aid of a manual and led by member Kenneth Whitcomb, 15 members volunteered to rebuild the organ themselves. It took the team six weeks to complete the project, but the organ sang again at the 1985 Christmas service.

Corona United Methodist Church will move into the 21st century in a new location suitable to accommodate its continually expanding congregation. Although there will be sadness at leaving their historical location, they will experience the same anticipation as that known by their first pastor, Rev. Sowden and the original 35 members who began the tradition of Methodists in Corona.

The 1928 Church Choir and Junior Choir are proudly on display.

Country Junction

Elmer Arnold, the proprietor of Country Junction, has been feeding locals and weary travelers alike hearty, down-home cooking for over 16 years. Situated at the corner of the Sixth Street exit and I-15, full parking lots are a testament to the popularity of this local eatery, and the four-foot-tall letters on the side of the building explain quite simply what the guiding spirit of the restaurant is all about — "Country Cookin'."

The building, built in 1922, is one of the oldest in the Corona area. Its colorful history marks an interesting link to the rustic past of the area. Starting life as a general store, it was then turned into a drinking establishment know as the Red Barn. It was known around the area as a rough-and-tumble cowboy bar, where Saturday nights were often the scene of pistols being fired into the ceiling and a paddywagon waiting outside to cart away those who got too unruly. The bar finally met its end when it was shut down by legal means.

A new and tamer establishment was opened in 1978 under the name Granny Lois' Old Red Wagon to serve the locals dinner. Two years later it was purchased by Mr. Arnold and his wife Marilyn, redecorated, and opened for business as Country Junction. The menu was changed to cater to the hearty appetites of the local crowd and breakfast, lunch and dinner were now offered. These changes made their mark in the hearts of the customers, and the restaurant has been going strong ever since. In late 1997 a patio was added to satisfy the growing number of diners, and patrons can now dine outside or just relax and discuss the ways of the world over a beer.

First time visitors often leave with memories of a satisfying, wholesome meal that more often than not brings them back for seconds the next time they're in the area. Repeat business is the bread and butter of Country Junction, a focus that fits with the eatery's appeal as a community landmark. The local community is vital to the success of the restaurant, and that success is illustrated by the fact that many of the regulars eat breakfast, lunch and dinner there. Another testament to the enduring hold of Country Junction over both memory and appetite is the picture hanging on the wall of the Dutch tour guide who brings his entire group there two or three times a year for a sampling of genuine American fare.

The food reflects the tastes of the owner and his customers. Biscuits and gravy, chicken fried steak and pork chops are just a few of the favorites that keep diners coming back for more. Where possible, all the ingredients come from local sources; both to ensure freshness and promote local ties. Further evidence of those ties is the artwork and crafts by local artisans displayed for sale throughout the main dining room.

Country Junction has built a reputation for good food and friendly service. This, coupled with a familiar atmosphere that brings customers back time and again, will undoubtedly ensure that the restaurant continues to grow and prosper along with the community it serves.

Country Side Inn

alking into a Country Side Inn is like walking into a charming French provincial hotel. The spacious European-inspired Inns offer a cozy, restful ambiance for guests from the moment they enter the gracious lobby to their elegant guest room, complete with the traditional four-poster bed and armoire.

The first Country Side Inn was built in 1985 in Cardiff-by-the-Sea. It was an immediate success and a second Inn was opened in 1987 in Newport Beach. The Country Side Inn in Corona opened its doors in 1989. The management company for the Inns is Ayres Group who are also the general contractors.

The Ayres Group is a family business. It began in 1905 when Frank H. Ayres moved from Ohio to Los Angeles. Ayres subdivided land and built houses in various locations in Los Angeles. His son, Don Ayres, Sr. worked with Frank and expanded the business into Newport Beach. Following the family tradition, his son, Don Ayres, Jr. worked with alongside him, learning the business from the ground up.

Ayres Group currently consists of Don Ayres, III, who oversees operations, Bruce Ayres, who handles processing and acquisition, Allyson Ayres, who is in charge of the decorating, and Doug Ayres, whose area is construction. The activities of Ayres Group has expanded so much since the early days that

the fourth generation has wisely subdivided each aspect of the operation into four areas of specialization. Although each of the four descendants of Frank Ayres has his own area of expertise, the family works as a team to focus on developing and operating new hotels.

As Bruce Ayres pointed out, "We're all hands-on people. We've grown up in the business, gone through the growing pains and now we've got a handle on the operation."

Country Side Inns are especially able to accommodate corporate business accounts, and many of their guests stay as long as a month at a time. Amenities for the business traveler have been added to the Inns, incorporating voice mail for messages, bigger desks and a second telephone line in the rooms for computer modem hookups. Comfortable conference facilities for groups up to 40 and audio-visual equipment are also available.

The Inns are mid-priced but high quality and include a hot breakfast in the room price for every guest.

The Corona Country Side Inn provides a heated pool and whirlpool spa for guests and for those who like to take relaxation to even greater heights, will make reservations for visits to nearby Glen Ivy Hot Springs just minutes away and a popular destination for guests. Exercise rooms and a small workout gym are also available.

Ayres Group is developing three new properties, one in Ontario near the new Ontario Mills Outlet, a refurbishing of the old Holiday Inn located in the city of Orange and a new Corona West. The Corona West Country Suites will feature bigger rooms, with a midroom countertop and sink, a microwave and refrigerator, and adjacent seating area in each room. Corona West is located at the end of Sixth Street and Maple and the 91 freeway.

The Ayres family has come a long way from their 1905 beginnings and look forward to even greater expansion in the future.

Dogloo, Inc.

When Aurelio F. Barreto III initially introduced his innovative concept in pet products to prospective buyers nearly a decade ago, they told him he was barking up the wrong tree.

Today, the same igloo-shaped doghouses that Southern California pet shop owners would only agree to take on consignment are among the highest revenue-generating canine abodes in the nation. Prominent Orange County businessman George Argyros so strongly believes in Barreto's vision that his Westar Capital investment fund purchased a 54 percent stake in Barreto's Corona-based corporation, Dogloo Inc.

Dogloo's genesis came in the early 1980s when Barreto decided to build a shelter for his Doberman pinscher, Baby. When the plywood structure he painstakingly created fell apart less than a year later, the design engineer decided to construct a doghouse from structural foam plastic instead. Unlike wood, it wouldn't absorb dog wastes and fleas couldn't burrow into it.

He called on the skills he'd honed as an engineer with Xerox and Hughes Aircraft to construct the original product. When his wife Peggy suggested the igloo shape, Barreto knew he was on to a good thing. The design was not only unique, but lent itself to a doghouse that was easy to manufacture, energy-efficient, impervious to acids, easy to clean and insulated to stay warm in winter and cool in the summer.

The couple mortgaged their home and scraped together $60,000 while Darrell Paxman, a founding partner, put in another $40,000. The trio hired contract manufacturers to build their first inventory, Barreto gave up a successful career in design consulting and Dogloo was born.

The Cuban immigrant quickly learned that building a better doghouse doesn't necessarily translate to instant success. When he finally got a pet store owner in Torrance to agree to take the doghouses on consignment, he was ecstatic. But the day Barreto and Paxman delivered their first Dogloos, the owner laughed in their faces.

Despite this discouraging start, the young entrepreneurs persisted and sold 1,800 Dogloos the first year. The company has grown by 20 percent each year since its inception in 1987 and has evolved through a major retail network that began with a list of independent pet stores and home improvement centers and grew to include mass merchandisers. In 1996, the company exceeded $60 million in sales and the Barreto's five-year plan is to quadruple that figure to over $250 million in annual sales.

Today, Dogloo sells in excess of one million doghouses and sports a line of over 260 different pet care products sold in 42 countries around the world. In addition to the trademark design, Dogloo also features more traditionally shaped doghouses, pet carriers, bowls, feeders and beds.

"I was born with an entrepreneurial spirit," says Barreto. "But the key to success in any business is persistence, persistence, persistence. I've always defined the word 'impossible' as something nobody can do until somebody else does it."

Fare's Industrial Tool & Supply

Fare's Industrial Tool & Supply dates back to the end of the 1940s when Corona was a little agricultural town surrounded by orange groves and packing plants. Originally the store was called Corona Hardware, but later it became known as Fare's Hardware. Fare's Hardware was a typical hardware store where you could buy tools, nuts and bolts and appliances.

When Minnesota Mining Company moved into Corona, they needed different items than the normal hardware. They had a big quarry and mining operation which required larger equipment, bigger nuts and bolts. As a result, Corona Hardware started stocking extraordinary supplies to support the new industry.

As the demand for such supplies grew, so did the amount of stock at Fare's Hardware. All the industrial supplies were moved to the back room of the hardware store, and then from the back room to a little building next door on Seventh Street. That little building became Fare's Industrial, named after the owner, Gerald Fare. Eventually, Fare's outgrew that little building and moved to a larger store on East Grand. That store is now occupied by Ace Lawnmower.

The actual introduction of Fare's Industrial was in 1957. The company was incorporated in 1963, and in 1971 Jack Kroonen, Gilbert Wilson and Charles Solomon became the owners, retaining the already known name of Fare's Industrial Tool & Supply.

President Jack Kroonen became involved with Fare's as the result of a conversation his mother had with her hairdresser. After his graduation from Corona High School, he went to work in the aerospace industry but by 1971, he was looking for a change. His family were long-time residents of Corona. His mother had had a women's dress shop called The Frock Shop since the early 1930s. When she heard that Mr. Fare would be selling either Fare's Hardware or Fare's Industrial, she told Kroonen. Kroonen's brother-in-law Wilson was also interested, and they decided to make the move. The third partner, Solomon had worked in the hardware store as far back as 1946 and

evolved with the business. Solomon and Wilson retired in 1991.

Fare's services the maintenance departments of various manufacturers in Corona, but its territory extends to Chino, includes Mira Loma, Riverside, Colton, Fontana and Lake Elsinore.

An example of the type of supplies Fare's provides would be Fender Musical, located in Corona. Fare's does not furnish them with anything they make the guitars out of but does furnish

them with things that are used to maintain the machinery that makes the guitars. Other manufacturers purchase products at Fare's that they use to maintain their assembly lines. Some of Fare's customers buy things for direct usage but a lot of sales are to the maintenance departments of other businesses.

All of Fare's inventory is housed on the premises which cover about 11,000 square feet. Approximately 20,000 different items are carried on the shelves at all times.

Fare's customers have changed as the city of Corona has changed. The packing plants they used to service have been replaced by gravel plants. The company has more competition these days including the big super stores.

Kroonen commented, "Fare's is tied closely to the housing industry so our future is linked to the expansion or reduction of that industry. We've seen a lot of companies come and go, but we've been here a long time and are still going strong."

Barth & MacGillivray.

DEALERS IN

Shelf and Heavy Hardware, Tinware, Stoves, Woodenware, Glassware, Crockery, Window Glass, Ammunition, Paints and Oils, and a full line of Farm Implements, and everything usually kept in a first-class Hardware.

Plumbing made a Specialty.

WE GUARANTEE ALL WORK.

We buy our goods from eastern markets and are giving you the benefit of low prices. Get our prices before buying. It will pay.

Don't Forget the Place.

Main Street,   Opposite Hotel.

Downs Oil

One of Corona's oldest family-owned operations, Downs Oil Co., Inc. is a familiar name for any area business that depends on heavy equipment or has a fleet of vehicles to operate.

The firm's founder, Elvin Downs, was extremely active in the Corona community. A member of the City Planning Commission for over a decade, he also served as president of the Chamber of Commerce and has the distinction of being one of the only presidents to serve for three consecutive terms.

In 1940, Elvin took over Standard Oil Co.'s (now Chevron) Corona Plant on Joy Street, across from the old Sunkist processing plant. He was Standard's first wholesale distributor in Corona, and sold oil and fuel products to businesses in the surrounding communities. Contemporary customers include corporations

such as 3M, Hamner Towing, Nature's Recipe Pet Foods and the City of Corona itself.

It seems Downs Oil was destined to be a family affair from the start. After his son John graduated from Corona High School, he honed his skills in the oil industry as a driver for Standard Oil Co. before joining his father's firm in 1962. Elvin's nephew, Richard, also signed on and the trio worked together until the elder Downs passed away in 1975, after more than 50 years in the oil business. John and his wife Catherine then took over the helm and moved the company to its new headquarters located just off the I-15 freeway at Magnolia Avenue. The

husband-and-wife team launched a key lock operation to sell fuel round-the-clock to trucking companies in 1976.

Sharon Downs Messner and Mike Downs, both Corona High School graduates, followed in their parents' footsteps, joined the company in the 80s and currently carry the company torch that has been passed down to the third generation.

Today, the company's three-fold operation includes sales of Chevron Lubricants (which are sold by the case, bucket and bulk), bulk gasoline and diesel fuel, and a card lock program. The latter venture began as an outgrowth of the key lock concept: selling fuel through the Card Lock program — similar to an automatic teller machine at a bank — allows businesses to track and control purchases made by their employees.

Downs Oil is also a member of the Commercial Fueling Network, which allows Downs Oil customers to use the fuel card at over 1,000 locations nationwide. Downs, which opened its first commercial fueling location over 20 years ago, now operates three such sites, two in Corona: the Magnolia Avenue headquarters and one on the corner of Railroad Street and Airport Circle. The third location is in the city of Lake Elsinore.

Customer service has been a hallmark of the company for all three generations, "In the commercial fueling business, you are in the business of building relationships with your customers and you want to be able to take care of their needs," says Mike Downs, president of the Corona-based company.

First Baptist Church of Corona

On April 13, 1891, George L. Joy, W.H. Jameson and Dr. J.C. Gleason gathered at the home of N.C. Hudson to discuss the organization of area Baptists.

At a second meeting a week later, the Rev. Charles Button D.D. joined the growing group to serve as moderator to create a resolution to organize the First Baptist Church of South Riverside. Hudson and S.W. Lockett were elected deacons, Dr. Gleason was named a clerk and Jameson became treasurer of the fledgling church.

The first meetings were held on the second floor of the original Lincoln School building with Rev. A.M. Petty as pastor. After four short months, he resigned due to ill health. The next month, on September 27, 1891, the First Baptist Church of South Riverside was declared properly organized and included in the fellowship of regular Baptist churches.

The first official church building was constructed in 1895 at the corner of Eighth and Main streets at a cost of $4,000. After a devastating fire destroyed the wooden building in 1937, the present New England-style structure was built on the same location at a cost of $40,000.

In 1913, a love of missions resulted in the founding of a Mexican Baptist mission in Corona. A decade later, Drs. Carol Jameson and Paul Gleason were commissioned as missionaries before Dr. Jameson moved on to the Velore Medical College in India, where she served for more than 40 years.

The educational building with its modern Sunday School facilities was added to the original structure in 1958. Colonial revival in style, the current sanctuary was designed by architect Douglas McClellan and constructed by Pinkerton & Jameson Co. to include steel-reinforced concrete walls, a gabled roof, steeple and arched windows.

In 1983, the church founded God's Kitchen to feed and clothe the needy and homeless until 1995, when the charitable organization moved to continue its work at the Circle of Hope Shelter.

Now known as the First Baptist Church of Corona, the church which started with a charter membership of only 25 residents has grown to over 350 active members today.

"By the power of the Holy Spirit, the purpose of the First Baptist Church of Corona is to celebrate the living God, cultivate growth in Christ, care for one another in Christ and communicate Christ to the world" — This is the vision of ministry and continues to be the mission of the First Baptist Church of Corona.

Maruhachi Ceramics of America, Inc.

Combining the art and ingenuity of the East with the creative and dynamic environment of the West, Maruhachi Ceramics of America, Inc. (MCA) has brought two cultures together to establish one of the world's premiere clay tile manufacturing facilities.

Whether the task is designing roof tile for a Hawaiian seaside estate, the Green River Golf Course Clubhouse in Riverside, or a shopping center in Rancho California, the timeless beauty of MCA's clay roof tile products create a unique style, color and design that leaves a mark wherever they are seen.

With its Natural Red, Blue CO1, Weathered Green Blend, Japanese Black and other glazed and matte finish tiles, MCA provides superior products to projects throughout the United States and the world. From Germany, Italy, Japan, Egypt and the Caribbean, this clay tile manufacturer has produced tile for the Walt Disney Company, Warner Bros. Studio in Burbank, locally at the Ralph's Shopping Center at the I–15 freeway and Magnolia in Corona, and the Mission Inn in Riverside, just to name a few. MCA's signature clay products can also be seen atop local police stations, schools, churches, medical centers and community buildings, as well as countless custom homes and historic renovation projects throughout the United States.

MCA was established over 85 years ago in Japan. Family-owned and operated, the company grew to become one of Japan's biggest tile manufacturers before deciding to expand in the West and test the market. With California's Spanish heritage, as well as the state's propensity for fires, company officials felt the roofing materials market was ripe for the introduction of its clay products.

Beginning as a clay tile importer in Norwalk in 1983, MCA established a factory in Corona in 1985. With a centralized Southern California site and easy access to transportation corridors, the company

bought an old factory and completely renovated it into a state-of-the-art production facility and office. Clay materials are mined in the nearby Temescal Canyon and then brought to the factory for processing. Mostly automated, the factory's assembly line crushes and moistens the clay before extruding it into the individual tiles which are then fired in a tunnel kiln. Turret Tile® was developed by MCA to provide tile for rounded or "turret" roof sections without the need to cut each individual tile. To better serve its customers, MCA provides high quality technical service to architects and contractors.

A strong believer in community participation, MCA is active in many business organizations, including the Corona Chamber of Commerce and the National Tile Roofing Manufacturers Association. But the company prides itself most on its local community involvement. Over the years, MCA has contributed to local schools and established a student exchange program with Gotsu City in Japan. Each year, a selected number of high school students from Corona and Gotsu travel to the other's country to study and learn about cuisine and culture.

By balancing social, economic and environmental needs, MCA brings professionalism, expertise and imagination to the tile industry by creating memorable products that cover rooftops in the local community, California and the world.

Republic Bag Inc.

Since its inception in 1976, Republic Bag Inc. has maintained a position as the innovative leader in polyethylene extruded products with a special focus on the varying needs of its customers. The company was started by Richard C. Schroeder.

Mr. Schroeder graduated from Miami University in Oxford, Ohio, with a degree in accounting. He followed this with a law degree, but when he graduated, he compared salaries of attorneys, accountants and salesmen, and sales won out. He was employed by Mobil Chemical and progressed to National Marketing Manager, where he was responsible for the sales of Mobilw's complete line of polystyrene and polyethylene products.

Having traveled for 15 years as both a Sales Representative and National Marketing Manager, Mr. Schroeder realized his family was of prime importance and decided to relocate to California to start his own business, with his investor

The Corona head-quarters of Republic Bag Inc.

partners who owned similar businesses throughout the United States. His alliance with his partners has enabled Republic Bag not only to market similar products nationally but to purchase bulk raw materials from national suppliers in larger quantities. Of course, as a company owner in Southern California, he no longer traveled as much and was able to enjoy his family.

Mr. Schroeder's son, Steve, joined the company in 1990 bringing his knowledge of computers as well as sales expertise to the Company. Steve's initial assignment to set up Republic Bag's complete company on computer has greatly improved the efficiency of the business. He currently concentrates on sales but does pinch-hit for his father.

Currently, the company is adding new equipment which will facilitate an expansion equal to several million dollars worth of sales from one new machine alone.

"Our slogan has always been 'immediate response to your specialized needs' and we strive to accomplish virtually anything our customer asks of us," commented Steve Schroeder. "We retain a lot of flexibility in our production. Even though we're now one of the major industrial plastic bag manufacturers in the Western Region, that's how we started and we intend to maintain that viewpoint."

Richard C. Schroeder and son, Stephen, lead Republic Bag Inc. in its steady expansion. *Courtesy John L. Blom*

St. Edward Catholic Church and School

t. Edward Catholic Church began in 1886 as a mission of St. Francis De Sales in Riverside when a priest came to Corona once a month to say Mass. There was no church building at that time so the monthly masses were held at the homes of two Corona families, the Cota family and the Lawson family. The Parish moved into its first church building, a small wooden structure, around 1898 or 1899 and later moved to a larger building which was dedicated in 1919. That church was used by the parish until 1951 when the present structure was constructed.

The Parish remained essentially the same size until Corona experienced the national population explosion after WWII. The changes in the Parish have always paralleled the changes in the city. Today, the Parish consists of some 5,400 families, and the church holds between 500-600 people. There are 11 masses on Saturday and Sunday, five are given in Spanish and six in English.

St. Edward was the first Catholic church in the town and has helped the expansion of the Church with the establishment of St. Mary Magdalene, St. Matthew and Corpus Christi Churches in Corona and St. Mel's in Norco.

In 1947, when Msgr. Matthew Thompson had been Pastor of St. Edward Church for about five years, he was able to realize his dream to have a Catholic school in Corona. He got together volunteers from the Parish and they started construction. The first building for the school consisted of four classrooms. Some years later, another section was added which greatly expanded the amount of classrooms and finally, a third extension was made which was actually a

second building. The construction of the school was a real community effort. Msg. Thompson continued to serve as pastor of St. Edward Church and mentor of St. Edward School for 33 years, and after his death in 1976, a memorial fund was established by friends to help the school.

St. Edward School opened with grades one through nine which enabled its students to go directly to high school upon graduation. The faculty consisted of all nuns, from the Franciscan Sisters, four of whom came originally to the Parish before the school was built to give religious instruction to public school children.

By the time St. Edward had been in existence 20 years, the school had a total of 549 students. The maximum enrollment in its history was about 580 and currently, St. Edward School is the largest Catholic elementary school in the diocese.

When the school was built, the Catholic parish for the area was St. Edward. As Corona expanded, St. Mel's of Norco was established, and when St. Mel's built its own school, the enrollment at St. Edward diminished for a period of time. The school also changed greatly when it moved from all Sisters as teachers to a combination of Sisters and lay teachers. By 1995, all classes were being taught by lay teachers.

Students at St. Edward's learn through a variety of programs and experiences: science fair, computer lab, spelling bees, math contests, sports programs and field trips.

The school draws its students from families of various socioeconomic and cultural backgrounds from all over Corona and prides itself on its multi-cultural population. St. Edward School accepts all denominations and has students who are practitioners of Catholicism, Christianity and, at times, such other religions as Hindu, Muslim, Janism, Jehovah's Witness, etc.

The continuing goal of the school is to aid students in developing or enhancing a positive self image and sense of morality in a stable environment. The motto of St. Edward School is "A Catholic education is an advantage for Life."

Starr Sign Design

hen Jennifer Starr graduated from California State University at Long Beach with a bachelor's degree in art, one of her teachers asked her, "What are you going to do now?" Jennifer thought it was a pretty odd question but answered, "I'm going to go out and get a job as an artist." The teacher responded pessimistically, "Good luck. You're never going to make any money or do anything as an artist. You might want to plan on something else."

Jennifer's first job out of college was doing layouts on the computer for a uniform emblem company. Her next position was in an art department for a decal company. From there it was off to Boise, Idaho, where she worked in a sign shop and learned all she needed to know to get started on her own business venture.

Starr Sign Design started out of the home with Jennifer working solo. Jennifer's husband, Tomas, helped her before work, after work and on weekends. In May of 1996, Tomas was able to devote his energies full time to the business which enabled Starr Sign Design to move out of its home and into its current quarters in Corona. Working side by side, Jennifer and Tomas have seen their efforts blossom into a successful venture.

Jennifer is the design expert and does all her designing on the computer utilizing the various sign programs which she knows inside and out. For a more innovative product, she often interchanges the programs to create something really spectacular for her client. Her programs are top of the line so she can offer her clients the very best.

Tomas is a fine craftsman, using his knowledge and abilities in carving and designing custom gold jewelry and applying it toward the three-dimensional pieces created at the sign shop.

Starr has branched out into utilizing a variety of materials and an astonishing array of signature. Their premier effort to date has been designing and carving an 8' x 8' three-dimensional display for Sunwest Sports, featuring two cut out palm trees with a blended sun behind the trees. On the face of the two trees is the name "Sunwest" in three-dimensional letters and underneath the word "Sports" in a three dimensional box which is mounted on clear plexiglass on top of the trees.

The business has produced graphics on boats, plexiglass faces, banners for trade shows, silkscreen on canopies, magnetic signs and vehicle graphics. One banner was so big they had to rent a lift to mount the sign. They recently enhanced a truck logo for a company based in Nevada. Originally, the logo had been limited to an outline of Nevada and the company name. Jennifer and Tomas designed buildings colored to appear lighted at night with mountains and a rising sun in the background, all within the outline of the state and including the company name, raising the level of a "logo" to "art."

"We do some things that are strictly professional, but we also do things that are more 'artsy,'" commented Jennifer. In the "artsy" area, they recently produced an airbrush banner for a children's teeball team. For professional signs, they have designed posts and supports so that the signs can be lifted out and refurbished on a regular basis. They have made signs for golf tournaments for the Corona Chamber of Commerce and are themselves members of the Chamber of Commerce.

When asked about future plans, Jennifer laughed. "I'm amazed every time we get a new client. I'm always surprised how things turn out. One company asked if we could find 700 teddy bears, put little T-shirts on them and print their logo on the front of the T-shirt. We did it. I could never have foreseen that project," she said.

Despite the ominous prediction of Jennifer's art instructor, in May, 1996, Jennifer and Tomas celebrated their fourth year in business as Starr Sign Design, and their young company continues to grow by leaps and bounds.

Tomas proudly displays Starr Sign Design's unique logo creation.

Starr Sign Design's premier three-dimensional display for Sunwest Sports.

W.B. Powell, Inc.

.B. Powell, Inc., is one of those low-profile companies with high-profile clients. The company is a full-service Architectural Milwork/ Contract Manufacturing facility that specializes in premium quality, custom fabricated products for hospitality, corporate and retail use, with resteraunts clients including Claim Jumper, Red Robin and virtually

When money is not a consideration.

every El Torito Mexican resteraunt throughout the United States.

Founder Dick Powell began his career in 1960 as a territory salesman for Dohrmann Hotel Supply Company and quickly took an interest in the contract side of the business. From there he joined a major supplier to Dohrmann, and three years later, started Pacific Commercial Interiors in Orange. In 1993 he moved the company to Corona where it occupies a 17,000-square-foot plant on Railroad Street.

W.B. Powell's country club projects include: Monterey, The Lakes and Palm Valley in Palm Desert, Oak Creek in Irvine and Coto de Caza. Recently Powell has made its presence felt in Las Vegas, hitting the jackpot with projects such as the MGM Grand, Flamingo Hilton, Caesar's Palace and Sam's Town.

Hans Prager, owner of The Ritz, a luxury restaurant in Newport

Corporate boardroom.

Beach's Fashion Island, was one of Powell's original two clients. When Prager decided to build The Ritz, Powell recalls, "It was fast track. They were drawing the plans as we were building. In fact, we were building faster than they were drawing the plans. And Prager, an absolute perfectionist, was involved in every detail."

Powell is currently widening its niche market to include hotels and casinos, and it has had several projects at the Hilton Hawaiian Village in Hawaii. Frequently, when a new tenant comes into the hotel's retail mall area, Powell is recommended for the tenant improvement work. As a result, Powell has completed projects for American Express, Bank of Hawaii and Louis Vuitton.

As times have changed at Powell, ownership and management have evolved, as well. These days, Steve Wimberly, Dick Powell's stepson, is handling the daily operations. He started working for the company right out of high school, literally learning the business "from the ground up," Powell remarked proudly. In April 1998, W.B. Powell was acquired by Foldcraft Co. of Minnesota, a 50-year-old manufacturer of seating, tables and related items serving the restaurant and hospitality markets. Foldcraft has earned a world-class reputation for product value, quality, customer service and uncompromising integrity – characteristics that have always been paramount at Powell. "I felt that if the company was going to be owned by someone other than me, Foldcraft was the kind of company I would want," stated Powell.

Dick Powell continues to advise and work with the company, but now on a limited basis. Word-of-mouth referrals continue to serve Powell as well today as they have throughout its 23 years of operation. When W.B.Powell is hired, the client is assured outstanding craftsmanship, meticulous attention to detail and hands-on project management by professionals dedicated to exceeding their clients' expectations.

Sunkist Growers

N̲o history of Corona would be complete without a look back at a company that helped turn the city into "The Lemon Capital of the World." The Lemon Products Division of Sunkist Growers, one of the largest and oldest agricultural marketing cooperatives in the country, was Corona's largest employer and the largest lemon processing plant in the world before closing its doors in 1984.

Originally known as Exchange By-Products Co., the company opened for business in 1915, operating in an old packinghouse. In 1921, Exchange By-Products changed its name to Exchange Lemon Products Company, processing an average of 10,000 tons of citrus annually. In 1948, the company took its owners' famous name as its own, Sunkist Growers. The timing was perfect — demand for lemon products was increasing, and Sunkist was ready to increase the visibility of its name brand.

By 1958, production had swelled to 200,000 tons annually (nearly eight million lemons were processed every 24 hours), and the plant employed an average of 700 to 1,000 people who worked among the 32 buildings sprawled along Joy Street. New homes, schools and shopping centers were built to accommodate the influx of employees who were packing lemon products for every major lemon juice processor in the country.

A freeze in the early 1960s destroyed much of Corona's lemon crop, forcing temporary cutbacks and layoffs. Production gradually increased, and by 1974 the Lemon Products facility was processing over 300,000 tons of lemons annually while employing 450 people who produced 350 different products that contained customer brand names, and another 350 products for specific customers that contained the Lemon Products brand name.

All major portions of the lemon were used, including the yellow outside part of the rind (called "flavedo"), from which lemon oil was extracted. The Corona plant produced about 80 percent of the lemon oil in the U.S., oil used for everything from perfume and soap to beverages, furniture polish, candy and bakery goods. The inside part of the rind (the "Albedo") was used for pectin in the making of bakery items, jams and candies.

Lemon juice was shipped in concentrate from throughout the country in everything from 50-gallon drums to tanker cars. Spent peel was dried and dehydrated for use as cattle feed. Efficiency was the watchword. Sunkist's Lemon Products Division took pride in its state-of-the-art facilities which utilized the latest technology to make lemon processing as efficient as possible.

The 1970s saw tremendous growth in Corona, with agricultural land making way for more housing and roads. The Lemon Products Division's output slowly decreased as production costs increased, and by 1980 the decision was made to move the processing closer to new fruit production. This meant closing the doors on one of the largest and most historic companies in Corona.

The famous "Sunkist Whistle," that was used to summon workers to their shift, blew its last blast on September 14, 1984. The whistle is on display at the Corona Public Library, a reminder of the role The Lemon Products Division of Sunkist Growers played in the agricultural heritage of Corona. But while groves and facilities have moved, Sunkist remains the world's largest and most famous citrus company.

■ Old aerial photos of the sprawling Sunkist plant on Joy Street in Corona.

T.B. Scott's Seafood Landing

There's an old adage that if you want something done right, you have to do it yourself. Scott Sherman and Tom Barnes have a different spin on this adage: If you want a great restaurant to go to, you have to open it yourself. Which is exactly what they have done with T. B. Scott's Seafood Landing.

Good friends, Sherman and Barnes found themselves driving regularly into Orange County for a relaxing meal after work and finally decided to build a restaurant themselves. Sherman and Barnes directed the renovations themselves without the assistance of any designers or architects. The project took much longer than they expected, and the builders thought it would be a perpetual construction project. By the time it was finished, nothing was left of the original structure other than supporting walls and some parts of the kitchen.

However, Sherman and Barnes got exactly what they wanted. In 1996, T.B. Scott's Seafood Landing, a beautiful and comfortable restaurant, christened with their own names opened for business.

The restaurant has many unique amenities including a full oyster bar, an open mesquite grill, and a handsome cocktail lounge complete with a big open hearth and fireplace. There is live entertainment five nights a week, ranging from comedy to karaoke, guitarists to bands, as well as a floor for dancing. Periodically, the restaurant has Las Vegas-style shows complete with costumes and big bands. A recent theme was "oldies"

T.B. Scott's Seafood Landing is proud of its beautiful and comfortable ambiance.

Oysters are only one of the 100-150 menu items featured in the spectacular Sunday brunch.

and groups such as The Drifters and The Coasters entertained guests.

In addition to a capacity of approximately 250 in the main dining room and 100 in the cocktail lounge, T.B. Scott's Seafood Landing has a banquet facility for about 200 where a tremendous number of banquets, corporate parties and weddings are held. A cozy outdoor patio is available for dining on those beautiful Southern California days and evenings.

The most outstanding feature, however, is the food. Fruits and vegetables are brought in fresh daily from Tom's Farms. Fresh seafood is brought in from local suppliers. There is a spectacular Sunday Brunch featuring 100-150 different menu items. Included is a pasta station where servers can custom-make any kind of pasta dish and an omelet station which provides similar service. There is cracked crab, oysters, clams, Mexican specialties, seafood specialties, a carving station with prime rib, leg of lamb and roasted turkey. Servers pour from bottomless bottles of champagne, included in the price of the brunch. There are mouth-watering desserts, all baked on the premises, as are the breads. The cioppino, a dish of fish and shellfish cooked with tomatoes, wine, spices and herbs, is probably the best anywhere. During the week, the executive chef provides about five specially designed features each day.

As Sherman proudly explained, "T.B. Scott's Seafood Landing is a great neighborhood place to be. It's the only place in the area that is somewhat

upscale without being expensive. You can go in jeans or suit and tie. This is the place in town where people go for a special occasion or just to relax in the cocktail lounge after work. It's comfortable, safe and friendly."

Thomas Miller Mortuary

homas Miller Mortuary of Corona has the distinction of being the next-to-oldest continuing business in the city. Not only does it claim longevity, it has also experienced great diversity having existed as a hardware and furniture store, a real estate office and a photography studio during the first quarter of a century of its operation.

The firm was founded in 1891 by David A. Sovereign who was primarily a furniture maker. Sovereign operated a hardware and furniture store and, since he was sometimes asked to construct coffins for the local citizenry, a mortuary was added to the services offered. It was located in a building later known as the Stanfield Bakery, but when William Farley purchased the business in 1896, he moved it to South Main Street. At that location, the mortuary operated in conjunction with the photography studio as well as the furniture store. By the turn of the century, the mortuary was owned by James L. Davis who not only ran the photo studio and the mortuary but also sold furniture and real estate.

The first formally trained mortician was J. C. ("Cy") Hoover, a graduate of the class of 1910 of Renaulds College of Embalming and Funeral Directors, in Chicago. Hoover took over the business in 1914 and added an annex on the same lot to operate exclusively as a mortuary for the first time. Two years later, he purchased the furniture "wing" of the business but moved it to separate quarters where it remained until 1936.

In 1931 Hoover added William R. Bell as a partner, and in 1942 Bell bought out Hoover. Ken Thomas became associated with the mortuary in 1948 and in 1949 the name changed to the Bell-Thomas Mortuary, the name it retained until it moved to its present location on East Sixth Street. The Thomas family ran the mortuary and were active participants in community affairs in Corona until their retirement in 1969 when Roger and Pat Miller purchased the business, at which time it became the Thomas Miller Mortuary.

Roger Miller came to California in 1959 to attend the San Francisco College of Mortuary Sciences. Prior to heading up Thomas Miller Mortuary, he worked for nine years in a Watsonville mortuary.

Both Roger and Pat Miller have involved themselves in many civic and community activities in Corona. Roger has served as president of the Corona Host Lions Club, as chairman of the Chamber of Commerce ambassador and as long-time director, drive chairman for the YMCA, chairman of the lay advisory council for the Corona Community Hospital, past Grand Knight of the local Knights of Columbus and past Commodore of the Corona Boat & Ski Club.

Pat Miller has served as president of the Soroptomists and is actively involved in the Women's Club, Corninos (Children's Home Society), Pink Ladies Hospital Auxiliary, Boys Club Auxiliary, Catholic Daughters, PTA and the Corona-Norco School District Advisory Committee.

The present day mortuary is an ultra-modern facility featuring a spacious chapel with a seating capacity of 250, adequate off-street parking and an attractively landscaped setting. The facility is a full-service mortuary, meaning that services and merchandise for every type of arrangement, budget and preference are available. The mortuary can also provide transportation arrangements to or from any part of the world and serves all faiths.

The second generation of Millers became part of the firm in 1992 when Roger and Pat's son, Chris, joined his parents as a director.

Thomas Miller Mortuary has the distinction of being a 55 year member and one of the earliest participants in the highly-respected Order of the Golden Rule. The mortuary is also active with various funeral directors' associations at the local, state and national levels. The firm still operates under its original mortuary license, number 66, issued by the State of California in 1896.

■ Roger and Pat Miller and son, Chris, are the proud owners of Thomas Miller Mortuary, the next-to oldest continuing business in Corona.

Troy Lee Designs

n the racing worlds of Indy Car, Formula One, Nascar, motorcycle and mountain biking, virtually every professional wears a helmet painted by Troy Lee Designs. Ranging from racers such as Jimmy Vasser, Paul Tracy and the Andretti family to celebrities such as Lyle Lovett, Vanilla Ice and Andy Pargh, Troy Lee Designs provides each individual with a helmet designed for his distinctive style. Because these drivers are moving at such incredible speeds, it is their helmets that identify them, so Troy Lee Designs strives to make them as memorable as possible.

Troy Lee's father, was and is a noted designer of racing paraphernalia, and taught Troy his craft including what paint to use, how to sand and prepare a transporter for color coat and how to coordinate a driving suit with a helmet. By the time he was 14, Troy was riding motocross bikes and painting helmets for himself, his friends and their friends. Word-of-mouth brought him more and more customers and by the age of 18, he was painting out of his mother's garage and racing full time.

In 1981, Troy was run out of his mother's garage. He then converted an old garage behind his sister's house into a little house where he could live and work. He also gave up pro motocross racing to paint helmets full time. The only thing lacking in this arrangement was an oven in which to heat-form his new helmet visors so he was sneaking into his mother's house to use her oven. Soon, however, the quantity of orders and his mother's complaints about plastic fumes inspired Troy to hire a mold builder for the first Troy Lee helmet visors.

Troy Lee Designs showroom.

Demand for the product continued and by 1985, Troy rented a small "hole-in-the-wall" shop at the Corona Airport. Actually, it was more like four walls with many holes. Within two years, business was good and the visors were a success, but the four walls and roof were leaking badly. More employees were hired and more products such as apparel, hats, sticker kits and other accessories were introduced. The company now occupied three leaky hangars at Corona Airport.

Troy Lee Designs celebrated a milestone event in October, 1990 when it moved into a 6,100-square-foot building of its own. New products were hatched and sales zoomed. By 1993, Troy Lee Designs' products were selling in over 30 countries. There was a full team of employees and the operation was really rolling and expanding into many different areas. Although helmet visors and sticker graphics kits have always been a main staple for the company, the apparel and accessory aspect of the operation became a huge part of sales. The company now offers a complete line of finer apparel shirts, hats, gear bags, mountain biking apparel and racing accessories.

Currently, Troy Lee Designs is the industry leader in custom helmet design. Their client list includes the top names in Formula One, Indy Car, Supercross, Motocross as well as in the fields of Superbike, Cross Country & Downhill mountain bike racing and even jet skis.

Troy Lee Designs' headquarters serves not only as its business and production center but also has a museum and showroom in-house which displays helmets, trophies, driving suits, jerseys, motorcycles and other mementos from the world's fastest racers.

The company continues to remain a small, tight-knit operation where family and friends work and play together. In a very competitive industry, Troy Lee Designs has dominated the racing world with its unique products and style. Although expansion may draw the company into many new areas, helmet design will always remain Troy Lee's first and abiding love.

Union Bank of California

It's Different Here

Just over seven years ago, Union Bank of California became the first major commercial bank in California to offer grocery store banking. In 1990, the bank opened 15 in-store branches in Southern California, including two in Corona located within Ralphs supermarkets. The bank now has 45 of these branches throughout the state, ranging in size from 300 to 400 square feet, with plans to open additional offices over the next 18 months.

Like all in-store offices, the Corona and Sierra del Oro branches are open 360 days a year, closing only on New Year's Day, Easter, Independence Day, Thanksgiving and Christmas. These seven-day-a-week banking offices offer all traditional banking services, including checking and savings accounts, certificates of deposit, individual retirement accounts, consumer loans and investment services. Both of Corona's in-store branches feature three teller stations, an ATM machine and a sit-down consulting area. Management and staff are cross-trained in a variety of services and instant identification systems at all teller windows allow for speedy transactions.

According to Corona branch manager Mike Stuart, the two Corona in-store branches are unique in that they offer customers a one-stop shopping opportunity at convenient hours and on especially busy weekend days. Sierra del Oro in-store manager Judi Ford said the banks' in-store location lends a hometown feel to the bank, adding that her staff members are on a first-name basis with many of their customers. Both Stuart and Ford noted that Union Bank of California's commitment to providing superior customer service has a positive influence on the Corona community through the bank's active corporate involvement.

"We believe that the best investment we can make is in the cities and towns where our customers raise their families and run their businesses," said Stuart. To that end, the Corona and Sierra del Oro in-store branches have participated in the popular Wings & Wheels event for the past two

years. Both branches are Chamber of Commerce members, while the Corona Office is also active in the Hispanic Chamber of Commerce. Since it opened almost eight years ago, the Sierra del Oro branch has donated to the Chad Zeller Memorial Walk/Run each year.

In addition to their community and philanthropic activities, Corona's in-store banking branches regularly feature special products and service promotions, such as Home Loan Days, which originated in the Corona office and is now a bank-wide promotion. Both branches also offer home equity, small business and auto loans, often in combination with other discounts and special offers.

Union Bank of California is proud to serve the Corona community. They invite all Corona residents to visit your local in-store banking branches to take advantage of UBOC's convenience and accessibility.

VIP Transport, Inc.

Based on the fundamental values of quality workmanship and excellent service, VIP Transport, Inc. offers relocation services to individuals, companies and conglomerates around the country and the world. With the motto "We make moving an art," no item is too small or large, too fragile or complicated to handle, from a family heirloom to delicate instruments destined for outer space.

VIP was started in January of 1982 by Dan Griffiths with the goal of providing full-service residential, commercial and special product door-to-door moving and shipping services. One of the country's largest Allied Van Lines agents, the company has additional offices in the San Francisco Bay Area and Washington D.C., as well as more than 1,000 domestic and international affiliate offices.

In 1995, the organization moved its corporate headquarters to the community of Corona. With its central location and access to freight and vehicle transport corridors, the city was geographically well suited for an all-service transportation company. In addition, the company tapped into the community as a labor source, hiring local residents to join its work force. Specialized packing and crating services include customized packaging and total logistics warehouse capabilities. The company also operates both a special distribution and production hub at its Corona center and has a state-of-the-art warehouse that includes a palletized storage system which provides a safe and secure environment for items as well as climate controlled storage.

With its adaptable, climate control storage vans, unique plug-in generators and specialized trained personnel, VIP is able to safely transport high value or sensitive materials from a doorstep in Los Angeles to a flat in Liverpool, England. The company has shipped everything from tissue samples from a college laboratory and museum artwork like the Abraham Lincoln exhibit to equipment for NASA's space shuttle program and Hubble telescope.

The company also transports many of Southern California's major professional sports teams in the Orange County and Los Angeles areas. Others, including local residents to Fortune 500 and entertainment companies, hospitals, high technology businesses and symphonies, have placed their perishables in the knowing hands of VIP for delivery all over the county and the world.

With a commitment to quality and caring, VIP strives to make moving easier at both the corporate and family level. VIP assists companies in moving materials for trade shows as well as office relocation. Along with its professional crew, VIP uses systematic color-coding location stickers, coordinating with office or house blueprints to facilitate a smooth, cost-efficient move. The transportation company will also pick up materials that are not fully complete or packaged, finish them up and then ship them around the globe. Computerized tracking also allows customers to know exactly where their possessions are throughout the entire moving process.

With some of the largest and widest vans available, VIP offers unmatched transport versatility and reliability for local, long-distance or international moves. A leader in the industry and friend of the community, the company's good fortunes can be traced to its professionalism and quality products. While growth and profitability are measures of accomplishments, at VIP Transport, the true gauge of success is the thousands of customers it serves.

Customized and climate controlled, VIP's versatile vehicles are able to transport delicate or durable items to one's doorstep with ease and efficiency.

Vision Photo Design

tew and Sheldon Ivester, the oldest and youngest of six children, are the owners and creative forces behind Vision Photo Design. The company is a full-service commercial photographic and design studio which specializes in producing all forms of creative materials geared toward every aspect of advertising, such as brochures, catalogs, flyers, posters, packaging and web page design.

Vision Photo Design was established in 1977, and Stew joined the staff in 1982, after working extensively in commercial photography. He studied advertising design at Biola University in La Mirada, California and also received an associates degree in photography at Cypress College. After several years as an employee at Vision, Stew was offered a partnership. Later, he became sole owner and just recently, Sheldon has become a partner in the company.

Sheldon's background is the perfect complement to his brother's. He studied accounting at Biola University and handles the financial end of the company, as well as doing a great deal of the day-to-day operations at the studio.

Vision Photo Design was originally based in Cerritos, but the Ivesters moved it to Corona in

When Vision Photo Design takes a photograph, you can taste the orange juice.

1994. As Stew explained, "Corona is becoming a hub for Los Angeles/Orange County/Inland Empire business, and we're right smack in the middle." In the past, companies who used to have to trek into Orange or Los Angeles counties for their photo and design work are now able to fulfill their needs locally with Vision Photo Design.

Vision has produced photographic advertising for a wide variety of clients including companies that specialize in sporting goods, the medical field, the paper industry and many others. Vision has recently moved into the realm of digital photography. With its new digital equipment, Vision can take a digital photo and drop it into the layout to show the client the very same day! There is no need for film or waiting for processing at a lab.

The Ivester brothers consider Vision Photo Design a professional resource for attention getting images and operate their company strictly on the idea expressed in their motto "You only get one chance to make that first impression." They make sure that first impression is outstanding.

A collage of advertisements done by Vision Photo Design.

Families in Corona

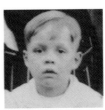

George Lewis Joy
May 31, 1832 – April 18, 1896

Without George Lewis Joy, Corona might have suffered the short life of many nearby fledgling towns. Good ideas and enthusiasm needed business experience, capital and integrity to succeed. As a successful 54-year-old business-man, George provided those along with wisdom and perseverance. He believed that founding a new town offered excitement and opportunity.

He was an entrepreneur, a tall portly man with a full grey beard who had learned farm-ing and the dry-goods business with his father in Townshend, Vermont. Soon after graduation from Leland Seminary in Townshend, where he studied Latin and Greek and developed a love for poetry, he opened his own store in Saxtons River, Vermont.

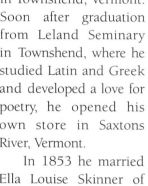

Ella Louise Skinner Joy (1832-1910), circa 1886.

In 1853 he married Ella Louise Skinner of nearby Windsor, when both were 21 years old. George and Ella had each been baptized earlier during the Second Great Awakening. Wherever they lived, they joined and were active in the Baptist church.

In 1859 the Joys moved to Pomeroy, Ohio, with their first daughter, Ella Maude. There George started a dry-goods store, and they had four more daughters. The second daughter, Hetty Mary, was the only one of the five who survived the typhoid epidemics that claimed lives all along midwestern rivers each summer.

Ella's brother, Benjamin Manning Skinner, operated a salt business in Pomeroy and Sioux City, Iowa, and asked George to join him. They prospered, and George extended their salt whole-saling to St. Louis, where he also developed several other businesses. His St. Louis Meat Packing Company necessitated frequent travel to Europe.

On one trip, the Joys took Hetty to Paris where she attended finishing school and studied art.

In 1885, they moved to Sioux City, Iowa where George, affluent by then, was both the owner of a loan company and the director of the Sioux National Bank. He joined his friend, former Iowa governor Merrill and three others to form the South Riverside Land and Water Company (SRL&W Co.) in California.

The Joys moved to South Riverside the following year to oversee the new venture and George, the primary investor ($200,000), became President of the new company. Within several years, he bought out other members of the syndicate and became the sole owner of South Riverside Land and Water Co. He continued to encourage new busi-nesses and provide services and leadership for the new community.

During the depres-sion of the 90s, his com-pany was left with fertile land and citrus nursery stock they couldn't sell. Necessity led them to solve their problem by planting the trees and entering the citrus business themselves.

In spite of successes and an imposing physique, George L. lived simply and believed that one should never seek public acclaim. He and Ella taught their daughter and grandchildren the importance of humility, generosity, kindness and appreciation of the talents and interests of others. Not only did the Joys set aside property for any church that wanted to build, they contributed generously to each building fund, but always asked that the gifts not be acknowledged publicly. They and several relatives were among eight founding members of Corona First Baptist Church.

Most new Californians came for either their health or to seek their fortune. For the Joys, both reasons applied. Ella had contracted tuberculosis as a child, and the deaths of four daughters from typhoid made them appreciate the healthy year-round climate. In addition, their investment in Corona — in the Golden State — promised financial rewards.

When George was dissatisfied with the work of the SRL&W Co. superintendent R.B. Taylor, he sent for his son-in-law, William Henry Jameson, to take the position. William Henry and Hetty arrived on the train with their son Joy in October 1887. Having their first grandson near-by and away from disease-ridden rivers pleased George and Ella.

Ella managed the home that they built at the southeast corner of Garretson Avenue and Grand Boulevard. She filled the yard with fruit trees and farm animals so she could share fruit, meat and produce with friends and relatives as well as anyone in need. Her grandson Joy said, "She could do anything." She sewed beautifully and was known for repairing her rental houses as well as her electric car. Her upbringing on her father's successful farm in Vermont, where relatives made extensive visits each summer, taught her not only practical skills, but enabled her to manage and entertain graciously.

With her daughter Hetty, she helped found the Women's Improvement Club, the Settlement House and the Women's Missionary Society of the Baptist Church. Because of her great interest in literature, especially poetry, she encouraged the founding of public schools soon after homes began to be built in Corona.

In the early 90s, the Joys built a new home on the south side of Grand Boulevard, between Palm and Victoria Streets. It was a tall Victorian house set back from the street with an expansive lawn.

After ten years in Corona, and less than a week before he died of apoplexy, George

was in the church he loved. He is quoted in the *South Riverside Bee* as responding to the roll call, "Dear friends, those of you who know me best know how almost impossible it is for me to express myself on an occasion like this. I can simply say I am trusting in my Savior; and I praise Him with the rising and setting of the sun. I love Him and shall love Him to the end."

In tribute to this great city father, children were dismissed from school for George Lewis Joy's funeral on the front lawn of his home. They formed two lines between which his casket was carried on its way to Sunnyslope Cemetery. Ella lived until 1910.

Only in recent years did the family learn that the Joys and Skinners were descended not only from seven who sailed on the Mayflower in 1620, but also from a long list of European royalty, including Charlemagne, Eleanore of Aquitaine and Edward the First.

George Lewis Joy, circa 1877.

William Henry Jameson
September 9, 1846 – November 21, 1912

Born in Boston in 1846 to William Henry and Mary Gilbert Jameson, whose Scottish ancestors came to Maine in the 1600s, William Henry II helped his father and his grandfather, Timothy Gilbert, in their piano business. When William was 16, his father was called to the Army in the Civil War as a paymaster, and took his son with him.

They came home four years later to find that the Timothy Gilbert Piano business had failed. The family then moved to Brooklyn, New York, where William, now tall and handsome with a large dark mustache, worked for six years.

In 1872, he followed two of his uncles to San Francisco, hoping to start a business. He stayed eight years, saving money for investment and spent his free time horseback riding, hiking and climbing in the Sierras. Then he moved to St. Louis to operate a successful wholesale hardwood lumber business.

Like his father and grandfather, serving his Lord was central in his life, and it was at the Second Baptist Church in St. Louis that he met George L. Joy and his family. Four years later, at 38, William married Hetty Mary Joy, George Joy's only daughter.

After the Joys moved to South Riverside, California, William and Hetty followed in 1887 with their 16-month-old son, Joy Gilbert. When they first moved to the home they built at the northwest corner of Joy Street and Grand Boulevard, Hetty had a little summer house made of twigs in the front yard for a bit of shade. Around them only cactus and sagebrush grew. The wind-driven dust had to be tamed, so they planted eucalyptus and sycamore trees, and within a year they had roses climbing over their front entrance.

William concentrated on managing the South Riverside Land & Water Company (SRL&W Co.) He also bought land to develop as citrus groves and built the Jameson Company Packinghouse adjacent to the railroad. The lemons, oranges and grapefruit they packed were boxed and labeled with colorful graphic art labels that have become collectors items. Jameson brand, Southland Beauties and WHJ were the top grades. Others were named Minerva, Justrite and Linwood. One label — the Leader — featured a beautiful bay horse because William always kept and rode fine horses.

The Jamesons had five more children: Eloise, Bernice, William Henry, Jr., Hetty and finally Adelaide, who later spoke of her father as, "... an extremely shy man, a perfectionist and an exacting father and employer."

With other relatives, William and Hetty helped start Corona First Baptist Church. Both of them had plans and ideas to enrich the community as well as their family and they wanted to promote education. Each served on the Corona School Board, and Hetty followed her husband as a Trustee of the University of Redlands, a Baptist college, which they helped establish.

Others considered William a wise, far-sighted financier with great integrity, but he was also a plain and unassuming man who disliked display.

Hetty had the outgoing personality in the family. She ran their home efficiently with the help of a Chinese cook and a gardener, as was the practice in that era. Her son, Joy, said that in the early days, groceries had to be bought in bulk, so until they finished a hundred pound sack of corn meal, they couldn't buy either wheat or oatmeal because storage attracted bugs.

Hetty was impressive both in size and character. With her mother, Ella Joy, she gave the land and helped establish the Women's Improvement Club, where women could learn child and home care, gardening, discuss books and have uplifting lectures and programs. The two women also gave the land and building for the Settlement House where they and their friends helped those who needed food, clothing and other necessities. They helped start and were active members of the Women's Missionary Society of the First Baptist Church.

Having seen the sad results of drinking among friends in Sioux City and St. Louis, Hetty became an avid Prohibitionist. Both she and William taught Sunday School and served on Church Boards. The statement in his obituary that, "He was as ready to help an enemy as a friend," was true of both the Jamesons and the Joys — always kind and generous.

After Hetty's mother Ella Joy died in 1910, William and Hetty hired the architect who had designed the Riverside Mission Inn to enlarge and remodel the Joys' Victorian home as a grand home for their family.

William loved travel and adventure and wanted to provide broad experiences and education for his children. He took each child on at least one special journey abroad in addition to the frequent family camping trips to Yosemite or other parts of the Sierras. They bought a house on the bluff in Corona Del mar so the family could enjoy the summer out of Corona's heat and learn to swim and handle kayaks and sailboats.

Probably knowing that he had cancer in 1909, William decided to take his entire family on a year-long trip around the world. Joy had just graduated from Stanford, so William assigned him to make all of the plans. The travel agent in Los Angeles much later told his granddaughter, Ann Dunham, she was "surprised by the unusually tall Jameson family, ... and shocked as Joy gave her a check for $20,000 (the biggest check she had ever seen) to cover ocean and land travel and most accommodations."

After they returned, William was bedridden most of the time. He had to give up his plans to build a magnificent hotel on Sixth Street. From his bed, he directed his eldest son so Joy could learn to manage all of the work of the ranch, packinghouse and community responsibilities. In 1912, he died of a sarcoma of the left leg.

Hetty survived as a grande dame until her death of cancer in 1927.

Hetty Joy Jameson (1863-1927), circa 1900.

oy Gilbert Jameson wished he had been born in Corona, but in 1887 at 16 months, he arrived from St. Louis with his parents. A letter his father wrote says "Joy ran all over the [railroad] car on the way out, but balanced himself so well that he did not get one bad knock … Hetty sometimes fears his brain is too active." Joy lived the rest of his life in the first home his parents built at the northwest corner of Joy Street and Grand Boulevard.

Joy loved to visit his grandmother Ella Joy, who had lost most of her sight. He read to her from her favorite poetry, Shakespeare, and the Bible and said that she frequently recited long passages from memory.

Watching his father and grandfather solve business problems, Joy, too, became known as a problem solver. His pioneering spirit met challenges with enthusiasm, persistence and ingenuity.

After his family bought the first big automobile in Corona (a Stanley Steamer) it became the town ambulance. Joy often drove, but feared he might have to deliver a baby or attend a death. Automobile racing soon became important to Corona, and Joy could watch the races on Grand Boulevard from his home.

Joy graduated from Corona High School, and then spent a year at Throop Academy in Pasadena (later California Institute of Technology) before he entered Stanford University to study geology and mining engineering, graduating in 1908. The great San Francisco Earthquake hit while he attended Stanford. Most important to him and his friends was the threat to the women's dormitory, so they dashed to see how they could help at Roble Hall, not realizing that their own dorm, Encina, suffered the worst damage on campus.

During the summers at Stanford, Joy hiked and camped with friends in the Sierras, following John Muir's trails. He learned not only about the rocks, minerals and natural history, but could identify nearly every tree and flower as well as most of the wildlife of California.

After graduation, Joy accepted an engineering job at a copper mine in South America, but was called back to Corona by his father to plan the year-long world tour for the family. When they returned to Corona, he had to take over the ranch and packinghouse operations because his father was dying of cancer.

Before he was 27 years old, Joy became the family patriarch and provided for his mother, two aunts and five siblings.

In 1912, he married Gladys Blickhahn, the niece of Mrs. T. C. Jameson. Joy and Gladys had one daughter, Elizabeth Joy, who died at three months, and two sons, Joy Gilbert, Jr. and Walter Thorndike. Tragically, Gladys died during the influenza pandemic in 1919.

Gladys' brother, who was stationed in Allentown, Pennsylvania in the Army, also died of influenza. He had written to his mother that he hoped to marry a "beautiful young teacher, Miriam Wagner — a small, blue-eyed brunette." Having lost both of her children, Mrs. Blickhahn wrote and asked Miriam to come to California to visit and comfort her.

During that visit, Joy got to know Miriam. After a two-year, long-distance correspondence with her, they were married in Allentown. Joy then took his city-girl bride on a two week pack trip honeymoon in the high Sierras. For her, that was an introduction into a life of adventure. They

(Bottom left)
Miriam Wagner
Jameson (1894 – 1977),
circa 1950.

(Bottom right)
Joy G. Jameson
(1886 – 1955),
circa 1950.

added four children to the family: Charles Henry, Miriam Margaret, David Wagner and Edith Ann.

In addition to managing family citrus operations and the Jameson Investment Co., Joy replaced his father on the board of Temescal Water Co. Upon becoming president, he searched and procured new water sources, planned and built Railroad Canyon Dam and bought water rights in the San Bernardino valley to assure plentiful water for Corona's future.

He helped establish and became lifelong President of the Exchange Lemon Products Company (Corona's biggest employer), was over 40 years on the Board of Trustees of the University of Redlands, served on the boards of the Queen Colony Fruit Exchange and Sunkist Growers Cooperative. He was active in the Corona Chamber of Commerce and the Rotary Club and served throughout World War II as chairman of War Bond sales. He was a leader of Corona's first Boy Scout Troop and received the Silver Beaver. A friend said, "Joy is a master at running committees and boards. He gets along with everyone."

The most important activity to him and his family was participation and service in Corona First Baptist Church where he and Miriam taught Sunday School. Their Christian faith guided their lives.

They traveled across the continent by both train and auto several times with their children —

and toured Europe. Joy wanted to study citrus culture and sales abroad, as well as provide their children with the broadening experiences his family had given him, including family pack trips in the Sierras.

In 1928, Joy and Miriam remodeled their home from the early bungalow into a Colonial style and Miriam surrounded it with a lovely garden. In addition to managing her household and family, she frequently entertained Joy's business associates, visiting ministers, missionaries and servicemen. She served on the Girls' Work Council, and was active in garden and book clubs, often sharing her artistic talents. During World War II, in addition to making clothing for her family, she sewed hundreds of heavy canvas citrus picking bags on her little Singer machine.

Joy, whose tall rugged looks claimed attention, became a distinguished looking older man with a full head of steel-gray hair atop his kind and friendly face. In 1955, Joy watched a football game on TV. He got up, went to the kitchen to tell Miriam, "Stanford's winning!" and dropped dead from ventricular fibrillation. The next day, the *Corona Independent* devoted the entire front page to Joy's life and death. Miriam lived to pursue her artistic interests and enjoy their 24 grandchildren, succumbing to heart failure in 1977.

The first daughter born to the Joy G. Jameson family was Miriam Margaret. She was the scion of George L. Joy and William H. Jameson, who had developed Corona into a major citrus growing area. Margaret Jameson Mellor followed in their footsteps and became a citrus rancher and her groves are still in production. They are managed by her son William Henry Jameson Mellor (Bill).

Margaret married Dr. Norman H. Mellor on June 28, 1947. They had four children: Peggy in 1948, Bill in 1949, Betsy in 1951, and Joanne in 1953.

On June 28, 1972 Norm and Maggie celebrated their 25th anniversary with nine family members when they went to Tahiti and Bora Bora. For their 50th anniversary, all 20 members of their family traveled to the north shore of Kauai. These two trips assured close family ties.

After Norm graduated from Stanford, he received his medical degree in 1942 from St. Louis University where he received the Alpha Omega Alpha (the Phi Beta Kappa of medicine). When Dr. Mellor opened his practice in August, 1947, he became the sixth physician in Corona. His 50 years of family practice (American Board, 1970), with a sub-specialty in cardiology, is the longest in Corona.

Maggie helped her husband in his office acting as a secretary-nurse. Her real forte was found in her work as a nutritionist and especially in her instruction to expectant mothers of how to breast-feed — this being done during the years when pediatricians and obstetricians actively opposed the practice. She had a B.A. from Stanford and an M.S. in nutrition from Cornell. She taught at colleges and universities, but was most proud of her weekly volunteer teaching in Spanish at the Riverside County Public Health Clinics.

Maggie was involved in the Del Taco restaurant chain. This business had been founded (including the idea of the drive-thru) by her brother, David Jameson, and Ed Hackbarth and Dick Naugle. Dr. Mellor and David Jameson still own the real estate of the first store established in 1964 at Third and Main streets in Corona.

The Mellors were avid birders. The American

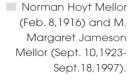

Norman Hoyt Mellor (Feb. 8, 1916) and M. Margaret Jameson Mellor (Sept. 10, 1923- Sept. 18, 1997).

Birding Association (ABA) listed them among those having seen the most birds in Mexico, South America and elsewhere. In their birding travels, they toured from Pt. Barrow, Alaska to Ushuaia, Tierra del Fuego (the southern tip of South America) and most tropical countries worldwide. Maggie stated, "I want to see this world before I see the next and I want to see the tropical birds before they are all gone." The Mellors led the Idyllwild Audubon Christmas Count for 30 years, and Norm published the "Checklist of the Birds of Idyllwild."

Scouting was big in the Mellor household. Dr. Mellor joined the Boy Scouts in 1929 and has attended or worked at Camp Emerson in Idyllwild, every year except when he was in the Army during two wars. He wrote *The 75-year History of Camp Emerson*, a record of the oldest continuously operating Boy Scout camp west of the Mississippi River. In his 69 years, he is the most honored Scouter in the Inland Empire Council (see: "The First Boy Scout Troop in Corona" profile). He established a Medical Explorer Post at Circle City Hospital — the first co-ed unit. His son Bill received his Eagle Rank in 1962.

In 1968, at Circle City Hospital, Dr. Mellor designed the first CCU-ICU built in California. It was his idea to have a nurse "eyeball monitor" the faces of all eight patients and the EKG monitors at the same time when seated at the nurse's desk. He was chief of the unit for 19 years and read almost all the electrocardiograms taken in the hospital. In the same year, he established a stress test and work evaluation unit in the hospital and helped start and run a cardiac rehabilitation class at the YMCA in Riverside. In 1984, Dr. Mellor was the Temescal District Citizen of the Year and also received the Distinguished Eagle Award for medicine in the Riverside County Council.

In the 1980s, Dr. Mellor developed two traveling doctor's offices in vans that served retirement communities with a doctor and nurse who traveled from Swan Lake in Mira Loma to Hemet. He has been a training physician for the Riverside Mountain Rescue Unit since 1965. For 25 years, he and Maggie hosted the RMRU technical practices on Tahquitz and Suicide Rocks at their cabin in Idyllwild, the Sky Yacht.

Beginning in 1975, the ABA published Dr. Mellor's "Health Hints for International Birding" articles. These articles covered everything from altitude illness to the iodination of water and vegetables. He considers his "Prevent Insect Bites Worldwide" as his best paper because it helps prevent all zoonoses from dengue fever to Lyme disease to malaria. He states, "My vocation and my avocation are the same — the prevention of disease." Maggie was always his secretary and editor. Dr. Mellor's current project is writing The 110-Year Practice of Medicine in Corona.

Maggie began painting in both oil and watercolors while recovering from poliomyelitis which she and the four children contracted at Christmastime 1954. At first, art provided therapy then later she proudly attained a Lifetime Artist Membership in the Laguna Art Association and helped to found the Corona Art Association. She always cut linoleum block prints of the most important family events of the year for her Christmas card. For the 50th Christmas, their grandson Tom Mellor printed a collage of all previous cards.

Her beautiful, almost-tropical garden reflected her artistry. She carried her art into the sewing that she and her three daughters did, which kept two machines busy. Norm still tells how she hemmed formal gowns while he drove her to parties.

In 1949, the Mellors built an indoor-outdoor home with the first gunited swimming pool in Corona. It was featured on the cover of the *Los Angeles Times Home Magazine* in its May 11th, 1952 issue. Maggie's kitchen, which she designed, reflected her knowledge of saving time and motion.

For Christmas 1996, Maggie published *Our Citrocado Ranch House — A Happy Home*. When they wrote history, both Maggie and Norm used what he calls the Mellor disclaimer — "History is the way each person remembers an event, and they never get the date right, either."

The First Troop of Boy Scouts
of America in Corona

he Prelude

The ideas that culminated in the Boy Scout movement began during the Boer War (1899-1902) in South Africa and later in England. Lt. General (later Lord) Baden-Powell had developed his thoughts during years of wartime and peacetime experiences on three continents. He had written the Scout Oath and the Scout Laws. His peacetime ideas were put into practice at a Boy Scout encampment on Brownsea Island off the coast of southern England in 1907. In 1908 he published the first handbook, *Scouting for Boys*. William D. Boyce brought Scouting to America in 1909. Congress chartered it on February 8, 1910.

When Scoutmaster Wilford Taylor established Boy Scout Troop 1 in the Riverside YMCA, it was the first unit in Riverside County. It was chartered directly by the National Council, BSA, on March 1, 1912.

The First Troop in Corona

In 1916 George Holt, pastor of the First Baptist Church, sponsored the first Boy Scout Troop in Corona. There was no Riverside County Council until 1921, so this troop was chartered directly by the National Headquarters, BSA.

The Scoutmaster of this troop in 1916 was a very impressive figure. Henry Jameson (William Henry Jameson III) had just graduated from Cornell University as an all-American football player. He

was six feet five inches tall, broad shouldered, and weighed 220 pounds (children called him "Uncle High-Knee"). He was assisted by his older brother, Joy Gilbert Jameson and friends Cecil Henson and H.Y. Reynolds. In 1919 Captain W.H. Jameson enlisted for WWI and Pastor Holt joined the Chaplain's Corps. The Scout Troop languished while the worldwide pandemic of influenza raged. Joy Jameson's wife died of it, and the troop folded.

Before 1916, the Jameson family had been going to Idyllwild. They took a train from Corona to Hemet, then a stagecoach up the Idyllwild Control Road. They drove when the road was improved for automobiles in 1909.

Upon formation of the Baptist Church Boy Scout Troop, the adults would drive the Scouts to Oak Cliffs at the bottom of the Idyllwild grade. They hiked the ten miles up the newly-named Toll Gate Road to Strawberry Valley to camp out. Automobiles carried the camping gear up the steep grade.

Carl J. (C.J.) Carlson, the Riverside Chief of Police during WWI, was the President of the Riverside Boy Scout Council in 1919. Ira Landis, later Superintendent of Schools, was Vice-President and Wilford Taylor was the Commissioner. This latter was the highest officer in a second-class council — equivalent to today's Scout Executive.

C.L. Emerson, owner of the Idyllwild Inn and President of Idyllwild Incorporated, a real estate company with 1,000 acres, allowed Boy Scouts from Riverside and San Jacinto-Hemet Councils to camp on his property in 1919. In keeping

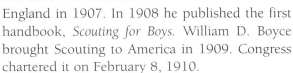

with his promise made at the closing campfire, he and C.J. Carlson rode horses down Strawberry Creek and picked out five acres on the flood plain for a permanent Boy Scout camp. They marked the boundaries of this best campsite in Strawberry Valley with cloth strips tied to trees. Named Camp Emerson, it became the first dedicated and permanent Boy Scout Camp west of the Mississippi River.

In October 1920 C.J. Carlson resigned as Chief of Police to become the paid professional Scout Executive for the new first-class Riverside County Council, BSA. A.M. Lewis was Council President and Wilford Taylor was commissioner.

The RCC Executive Board in 1920-21 from the area that would later become Temescal District included: Joy G. Jameson, Corona; B.N. Pratt, Elsinore; William Collier, Wildomar; Hugo Guenther, Murrietta Hot Springs; and Mr. Burnett of Temecula. When the RCC was chartered in 1921, it named Glen A. Calkins of Riverside as the president.

Thus the Executive Board contained the core of men who would later pick the name Temescal District for an area which has varied over the

years to extend as far north as Mira Loma and as far south as Temecula. Temescal District now includes only Corona and Norco. The Corona First Baptist Church has promoted Scouting since the beginning. Troop 54 continues a strong program of the "Outing in Scouting," with Scoutmaster Michael Downs, grandson of Cecil Henson.

The word Temescal came from combining the Aztec words "tema," to bathe, and "calli," house. This name had been brought to California from Mexico in the 1770s by Friar Junipero Serra when he established missions in California. Temescal was the name he gave to the unique Indian sweat lodges used for healing and purification of body and soul. In Temescal Canyon they are located beside the hot springs and creeks as they bubble up in artesian wells along the fault line of the Santa Ana Mountains, from Corona through Elsinore, Murrietta and Temecula.

The Berner Family

When Joy Berner looks out her living room window, she doesn't see just an attractively manicured lawn. She sees a yard extending for a long distance, unimpeded by other homes and four children playing football and other games. There is no paved road and no lights on the street. Dale Berner was a general contractor and builder in the city of Corona and in 1946, he built this family home which is still the bedrock of the Berner Family today. Joy and Dale's roots in Corona go back some 130 years, long before there was much of a city and long before they were born.

Dale Berner's Grandfather, John H. Baldwin, was born in 1864, approximately eight miles from present day Riverside in what was then called South Riverside. When John grew up, he met and married Lillie Wilson, a native of California, in 1891. John and Lillie made their home in the town of Auburndale, an area northwest of Corona en route to Norco. The Baldwins had a daughter named Mabel who grew up to marry George Berner, and their son, Dale Berner was born January 30, 1916 in Corona where he lived all his life until his death on January 6, 1996.

The Baldwins had a ranch consisting of 20 acres on the bluff of the Santa Ana River in Auburndale where John spent his early boyhood days. As a young man, he worked for a few years as a cowboy because much of the land of the area was devoted to cattle raising. When he was 22, he moved to San Diego County but after an absence of seven years, he returned to the ranch and married his sweetheart, Lillie. John and Lillie lived out their days on the ranch. John was a rancher, and he drove and grazed his cattle in the San Bernardino Mountains. He took an active interest in the development of Corona and served as a school trustee and as a road overseer.

While Mabel Baldwin was growing up in Auburndale, George Berner was being raised in

Portland, Oregon. He learned the building business and eventually immigrated from Oregon to California, settling in the Corona area. It is thought that George was hired by John Baldwin to do some work at the ranch, where he met Mabel. They fell in love and were married, making their home on the ranch for a while before moving into town. Their only child, Dale, was born in Corona in the Birthing House (the same maternity house where Terry Ware of the Ware Family was born) on January 30, 1916.

George Berner acquired a quarter of a block on Sixth Street where he built rental houses and a grocery store. In one corner of the grocery store Mabel and her cousin Ava Ridgeway ran an ice cream parlor which they named MAVA for Ma-bel and A-Va Ridgeway. On their opening day, they gave out free "lollipops," a dipper of ice cream

dipped in chocolate on a stick. Joy Berner was a little girl who enjoyed one of these free lollipops.

George built his family's home at 611 West Sixth Street and many other homes in Corona as well. He built the City Plunge, the building of *The Daily Independent*, a wing of Corona High School (which building is now the Civic Center), and the Spanish style building of Corona Junior High.

Joy Berner was born in Ethan, South Dakota but came to Corona at the age of one. Through her parents, Harry and Augusta Krick, Joy can

Joy and Dale Berner celebrate their 50th wedding anniversary.

trace her ancestry to the infamous Victoria Claflin Woodhull, the first woman candidate for President. Like Dale's father, Harry Krick was a carpenter and worked on many buildings in Corona.

Although both Joy and Dale attended kindergarten at Washington Elementary School, they entered Jefferson Elementary School the day it opened, over 70 years ago. At its opening, Jefferson had four classes: lst/2nd grade, 3rd/4th grade, 5th grade and 6th grade. Joy was a proud alumni at Jefferson's recent anniversary celebration. Joy and Dale went to Corona Junior High and Corona Senior High School. Dale went on to Riverside Community College and then to Occidental College. However, when his father became ill with cancer, he left school to be with his mother and complete his father's outstanding jobs.

Dale was very involved in sports, especially basketball and track. In honor of his achievements during his school years, in 1986 he was inducted into the Corona High School Hall of Fame where he still holds the Tri-County League record for low hurdles.

Joy also was an active sports enthusiast while in high school. She graduated with a Commercial Award and used her business knowledge to keep the books for Dale's contracting work and to serve as Director of Purchasing for the Corona-Norco Unified School District for 20 years.

When Dale and Joy were growing up, Corona was a very small town. But, although Dale and Joy knew each other, they didn't really "notice" each other until they were just out of high school. Joy's oldest brother was a friend of Dale's, and one day he and his girlfriend invited Dale and Joy to join them for a day in the mountains. Four years after that July 3 mountain picnic, Dale and Joy were married.

As newlyweds, Joy and Dale moved into one of the Berner homes on West 6th Street until Dale built their house in 1946 where Joy still lives. They had four children, Linda, Joan, Dale, Jr. and David, 11 grandchildren and ten great-grandchildren. As an item of interest, Dale, Jr. is married to Kathleen German of the German Family.

The Berner Family lst row (left to right) Joy Berner, Dale Berner 2nd row (left to right) David, Linda, Joan and Dale, Jr.

Joy looks back on the early days of Corona with heartfelt nostalgia. She remembers the town as being so small, she and her friends could hitch a ride with anyone going up to the top of Main Street where they could put on their roller-skates and glide on down. She recalls playing "Pussy Wants A Corner" in the middle of Buena Vista and Sixth Street. No traffic interfered with their game. When Joy and Dale were children, there was a red light that hung overhead at the intersection of Main and Sixth streets. When one of the several police officers were needed, the local telephone operator (who ran the city party line) would turn on the light which could be seen all over town. In those days, the Corona Fire Department consisted of one fire engine and one fireman who lived above the fire station. The rest of the firemen were volunteers. When the fire whistle blew, the volunteers say their password "Fourth of July" to the telephone operator who would then tell them where the fire was located.

The Berner Family built a good portion of the City of Corona, both literally and figuratively. Many of the buildings Dale Berner constructed still stand today. The children of Joy and Dale, their grandchildren and great-grandchildren have for the most part remained in the area, attending the same schools and participating in many of the same events as Dale and Joy. The Berner Family is rooted in the Corona past and building the Corona future.

The German Family, four generations strong in Corona, are a shining example of the stability and permanence enjoyed by families who have made their home in Corona. There were about 9,000 residents in the whole area when the Germans settled in Corona. Everyone knew everyone else. Residents could walk down the street and say hello to every single person they met. Housewives knew all the clerks in the stores they frequented. Main Street was just a little two lane road.

The German Family genealogy consists of some 1,600 pages in their family book. Their roots are in Germany and go back several centuries. When they immigrated to the United States, some of the family settled in Oakes, North Dakota. In the early years of the century, one branch of those immigrants produced 11 children, ten of whom were boys. Originally, there had been 12 children but one was lost during the great 1918 flu epidemic. It is five of the brothers of this branch of the large family that moved westward, settling

in Corona. They do attend the family reunion every three years to meet some of their more than 500 relatives.

In 1935, Larry German was the first of his family to settle in Corona. He lived in Alberhill (located between Corona and Lake Elsinore) and worked in the brick yards at Pacific Clay. After a short time, brother Frank joined him. When World War II ended, a third brother, Jerry, joined the group which now included Jerry's wife Carol. Jerry and Carol made their home in Alberhill, but Larry and Frank moved into Corona. Eventually, all three brothers and their families moved into Corona and the men "commuted" to work at the brick yard.

After several years at the brick yard, Jerry got a job working at Bear Collision Service, an auto body shop in Corona. Frank also got a job in town, working at a different auto repair shop and then joined brother Jerry. In 1948, Frank and Jerry were given an opportunity to lease the business which they did until 1955 when they bought the property, building and business for the grand sum of $13,500. Incidentally, the building which was constructed in 1945 was made completely of tin with a pipe frame. Because of the war effort, lumber was not available to private citizens at that time.

Brother Eugene came to Corona in 1953 and worked for Minnesota Mining for the next 26 years. His two sons are Corona residents. Finally, brother Edward made the trip west and worked for Pacific Clay for the next 30 years. The German brothers ran Bear Collision for many years. When Frank retired in 1984, Jerry's son, Jerry, bought Frank's share of the business, and the business was run by Jerry and Jerry. Later, when Jerry Senior retired, Jerry became sole owner and to date, is still running Bear Collision in its original building at 413 E. Grand.

Jerry and Carol German had six children, all of whom live in Corona: Donald, Kathleen, Jerry, Tom, Sarah and Jim. They attended St. Edward Catholic School and Corona High School.

While the children were growing up, Jerry and Carol were participants in their activities.

Jerry and Carol German loved the stability and permanence of their life in Corona.

Jerry was involved in Boy Scouts, Carol, in Brownies and Girl Scouts. Jerry attended Knights of Columbus and with brother Gene, helped with the construction and establishment of St. Matthews Church. All the Germans helped raise funds for the construction and furnishings of the new church. Carol did volunteer work for the County Health Department, helping in the well baby clinics and assisted in the health program at St. Edward School. She also worked on the Election Boards and helped senior citizens at the Corona Senior Center with their income taxes.

When Carol and Jerry bought their first home on Ontario Street, there were only three other houses in that area. Across the street was a railroad spur line which had been used for hauling citrus. The house was almost completely surrounded by orange groves. When the German kids had high school parties, no one else lived close enough to complain about noise.

Carol remembers the tarantulas ambling up the driveway as well as the rattlesnakes which came into the yard from the nearby gullies. When a rattlesnake was spotted, Carol would yell to the kids, "Run and get the hoe and kill the rattlesnake in the driveway." There were coyotes in the fields and hawks in the sky. The German's side yard was fenced in for a children's play yard, but frequently young Jerry would climb over from the fence and take off. The nearest neighbor, who irrigated the groves, would find the little boy lying in the groves, sound asleep and carry him home.

Corona had the traditional small-town friendliness. At Christmas, Santa Claus would sit at the top of the steps to the Courthouse (which was then across the street from the Library) and the kids would walk up the steps to see him. The Corona Fire station was located in the basement of the Courthouse and so was the jail.

Kathleen German Berner says to her, Corona is still a small town. She reminisces, "Many of my generation married within the Corona area community and still love going to the store and seeing familiar faces. My children attended the same schools I attended. When I go to a softball game to cheer one of my grandchildren, I see my classmates cheering on their grandchildren also. Corona was a wonderful place to grow up and is a wonderful place to grow old."

The six German children: (Row 1 left to right): Sarah and Kathleen; (Row 2 left to right) Jim, Tom, Don and Jerry

Frank and Jerry Sr. were proud of their business Bear Collision Services.

The Sam Markowitz Family

The Sam Markowitz story spans the twentieth century and stretches from sea-to-shining-sea. He was born July 16, 1906, in New York. In search of a better life, his parents left Budapest, Hungary, in the late 1800s and came through Ellis Island to emigrate to America.

Sam still recalls the East Coast street vendors selling roasted chestnuts and the thrill of finding a penny to buy one. But because members of their extended family lived on the West Coast, his family exited New York while Sam was still a youngster, traveled cross-country by train, settled for a time with relatives in Oakland, California, and there they sought to better their lives. Then, in a day when cars were few and roads were rough, Sam's family sailed south aboard a steam ship to reside in Los Angeles, a city of promising employment opportunities.

(Clockwise from-left) Al Klein, Sam Markowitz, Rose Markowitz, Bertha Markowitz, Mary Markowitz Klein, photo circa 1919.

The City of Angels presented new adventures for the hard working Markowitz Family. Soon a common early morning sight was young Sam delivering the morning newspaper house-to-house from a horse-drawn wagon. Then, Fox Studios hired Sam and his sister as extras in the cast for Jack in the Beanstalk. The two were paid four dollars per day, plus a box lunch and train fare. Today his family listens as Sam recalls that long ago movie experience. He chuckles while confessing that he believed the stage scene was quite real; then, he conveys how surprised he was when he peeked behind the movie set to discover nothing but an ugly hill. Thoughtfully he comments, "I learned a valuable lesson at that early age: Things are not always what they seem!"

In 1917 the Markowitz family was impressed as they visited relatives in the rural community of Corona. His aunt owned a citrus grove on Taylor Street; his uncle owned the only bakery in town. Sam's parents soon purchased citrus property and moved to the Circle City. That new chapter of Sam's life began as he was a ninth grader at the local high school where he became a member of the track team and ran the half-mile. He also worked after school and on weekends in the citrus industry for the Jameson Company, headed by Joy G. Jameson.

Sam reminisces about those years and reports that he became a jack-of-all-trades as he labored in the orange groves; he worked first as a fruit picker, then a blacksmith helper, and finally as a mule-skinner who had his own team. He describes, as if he had made the trip yesterday, the two and one-half hour trek from the groves on the south side of town all the way to the packing house located on Railroad Street. As Sam's experience increased, he was promoted to Foreman of the Southland Ranch groves.

Then Sam met Ruth Mabel Bush, a young Berkeley girl who was living in

Norco. They were married in 1928 when Sam was 22. The newlyweds began their lives together living in a house on the Jameson Southland Ranch on west Ontario Street; three of their four children were born in that house.

They were still living on the Ranch in 1932 when Sam accepted an offer to become a butcher at the Pepper Corner Store, which was a commissary at the Eastland Ranch for employees of the Jameson Company. That same year the Riverside Valley Home Gardens area on Magnolia Avenue parceled their land. Sam bought one acre and built a house for his family and later built two rental units plus a separate home for Ruth's parents. He always had a few horses as well as other animals, a large vegetable garden, flower gardens and fruit trees. While his children were growing up, Sam volunteered to become an assistant Scout Master of Troop 54. He was active in that role for a number of years.

When the Jameson Company purchased oil from General Petroleum for their equipment and used their own tanker, Sam was the deliveryman. Joy Jameson supplied the fuel for the construction of the Prado Dam in 1940. The route that had been started to simply supply the Jameson groves, soon spread throughout the district, and became a Mobile Oil Distributorship.

Sam and Ruth's youngest daughter, Kay, had three young children when she died of Leukemia at the age of 19. Near that same time Sam and Ruth divorced. Later Sam married Vivien Sheldon. Then in 1964 when Sam was the Foreman of the new Jameson Citrus Development in Horse Thief Canyon, he bulldozed a corner of the property, drilled a well and made a retreat for Boy Scout Troops and church groups. Throughout those years Sam was an active Mason and a Worthy Patron of Eastern Star.

(Left to Right) Patricia (Markowitz) Barker, Sam Markowitz and Donald Markowitz

After 51 years with the Jameson Company, Sam retired and moved to Arizona. Then, Sam and Ruth's youngest son, Paul, the father of three children, was killed by a drunk driver in an accident in San Bernardino.

Sam's daughter, Patricia, has been thoroughly involved for the last 42 years in various ministries at Crossroads Christian Church and has traveled extensively around the world. She is the widow of John L. Barker, who was a local building contractor and land developer. Patricia and John raised two daughters, Sherry and Trish. Sherry married Joe Panattoni and they have two sons, Joe and Danny. Trish and her husband, Wayne Denniston, also have two children, Roger and Crystal.

Sam's son, Donald and his wife, Anne, have four sons: Brad, Dean, Andy and Scott. Don served in the Navy and attained the rank of Petty Officer First Class. He then worked for the Edison Company as an instrument technician. Now retired, Don resides in Norco.

Sam returned to live in Corona in 1997. He resides in his daughter's guest home, spends time with his extensive family, grows vegetables, tends flowers, walks daily and every Wednesday attends Mid-Day Alive at Crossroads Christian Church. At 92 years young, he is in good health, has a twinkle in his eye and a zest for life.

The story of the Spiegel Family is a story of courage, patriotism and family love.

The First Generation

The Spiegel family story begins in Germany where both Herb Spiegel and Flora Hirsch Spiegel were born. During World War II, both families took steps to flee the Nazi horror.

Herb and his family escaped in May of 1939 and later that same year, Flora and four of her siblings fled to France, but her parents and the two youngest children of the family perished in the Holocaust. Flora entered the United States on Labor Day, 1941 through a program which was started by Eleanor Roosevelt. She was sent with her sister and three brothers to Atlanta. Herb settled with his family in New York City.

Herb and Flora met on a New Year's weekend in 1950. To say they had a whirlwind courtship is putting it mildly. Herb proposed on their very first date. At first, Flora told him he was crazy but said yes on their second date. Prior to their meeting, Herb had been in the U.S. Navy serving as a Seabee in Kodiak, Alaska, and when he was discharged in 1946, he had been offered a contract to work as a civilian in the same position he had held in the Navy, Electrician.

Herb and Flora were married on May 23, 1951, and Flora returned to Kodiak with Herb where they settled down to married life. As both of the Spiegels shared the philosophy that one has to participate and get involved in ones community, their home in Kodiak became the headquarters for all the Jewish events in the area. Sons Sam (1953) and Bob (1955) were born in Kodiak.

From Kodiak, the Spiegels moved to Albany, New York for two years, then to Corona, establishing Corona Industrial Electrical on October 11, 1958, and the family owned and operated the business for 36 years. At the time they settled in the area, there were only 14,000 people living in Corona.

Although the size of the projects handled by Corona Industrial Electric varied over the years, the personal contact and attention of the Spiegels to their customers never wavered.

Flora took on the financial end of the business from the start as her background was bookkeeping. She did take a brief time out in 1961 to give birth to son number three, Marc, and to learn to drive a car.

As a concerned citizen, Flora became active in politics and after one unsuccessful try, was elected to the City Council for a four-year term, from 1974-1978, serving as Mayor in 1976, during the United States Bicentennial. Flora chose not to seek a second term due to health reasons.

After her stint on the City Council, Flora served on the Riverside County Assessment Appeals Board for 13 years and as Chairman of the Board of Directors for Circle City Hospital. Flora was a past president of Soroptimist International of Corona, a member of Women's Improvement Club. She received many awards and commendations for all her work in the community, including the Boy Scouts of America Distinguished Citizen of the Year and Woman of Distinction Award from Soroptimist.

Herb has been active on both the Corona-Norco Unified School District's Vocational Guidance Committee and on the Statewide Apprenticeship Committee which establishes and monitors vocational education in California. Professionally, he remains active in the industry, serving since 1986 on the national code-making panel which set the rules and regulations for electrical codes in the United States.

Herb's community involvement includes being an active member of the Corona Host Lions, Corona Chamber of Commerce and Corona Public Library Foundation.

On March 8, 1992, Flora succumbed to a long-term battle with cancer. Family and friends recall her words at the America's Bicentennial, "Patriotism is not something you can legislate or proclaim. It is something right here in the heart."

The Next Generation Spiegels

Sam Spiegel is a Captain with the Corona Police Department. He started his career in law enforcement 25 years ago as a cadet. He holds a master's degree from Cal Poly and a bachelor's degree from Chapman College. Sam is a graduate of Corona Senior High, class of 1971. Charlene, Sam's wife since 1990, is an Administrative Manager for Hussman Corporation in Chino, California. They are both active in civic events and are members of Navy League. They divide their time between community, sharing time with their grandsons, and street-rod and motorcycle events.

Marc Spiegel is a 727 captain for Trans World Airlines, Inc. (TWA) based in St. Louis, Missouri. He and his wife Michelle have been married since 1992 and have a son, Jacob (1995). Marc is a graduate of Corona Senior High School, class of 1979 and holds a bachelor of science degree from Embry-Riddle Aeronautical University. Michelle is a full-time mom and a part-time cosmetologist. The "mid-continent" Spiegels enjoy being a family, traveling and participating in dog shows and working events with "Kodi," their Newfoundland breed dog.

After his graduation from Corona Senior High (1973), Bob Spiegel attended Fullerton College, leaving to become involved in his business career. He owned and operated a retail flower shop in Corona but left it to join his parents at Corona Industrial Electric in 1980.

Although Bob and Karen Gillerman had known each other for about a year, they became engaged within three weeks and were married in June 1985.

Bob and Karen worked with Herb and Flora in the family business with the idea that eventually they would take over the business and give the elder Spiegels the opportunity to retire and enjoy the fruits of their labors. For over seven years, all four Spiegels worked together

at Corona Industrial Electric sharing their work lives and their personal lives until Bob and Karen took over the business in 1992.

Bob and Karen have five children, Tanya (1986), Rebecca (1987), Rachel (1988), Isaac (1989) and Joshua (1991). Like Herb and Flora's children, these third generation Spiegels have always been actively involved in parents' activities. They know what their parents do and pitch in to help.

By 1994, the business picture changed, and Corona Industrial Electric was closed. Bob and Karen then began Spiegel Publications. Bob and Karen share the philosophy of the elder Spiegels of getting involved in one's community. They are extremely active in many organizations. Karen was elected to a four-year term as Treasurer for the city of Corona in November 1996.

Both have been recognized as Corona's Citizen of the Year, Bob in 1989 and Karen in 1995, as well as several other awards and commendations.

Out of the rubble of war-torn Germany came the Spiegels, a family of love, loyalty and patriotism to their family, their community and their country.

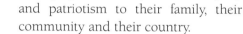

The Ware Family is one of the oldest families in Corona having been in the city for over 100 years. The first Ware to come to Corona was Andrew Jackson Ware who arrived in the area in 1893 when Corona was still known as South Riverside. This was the same year Riverside County was formed from parts of San Bernardino and San Diego Counties.

A. J. (as he was known) was born on July 26, 1860, in Steubenville, Ohio. As a young man, he had gone to the Sandwich Islands (now known as the Hawaiian Islands) to seek his fortune in the sugar cane industry. When he returned to the mainland, he became involved in the lumber business when ships transported lumber to Newport Beach from Northern California and Oregon. A. J. worked for a variety of lumber companies in the Corona area for the next ten years including the San Jacinto Land Company, Russ Lumber Company and the Newport Beach Wharf and Lumber Company. Early records show that in 1901, A. J. drew a salary of $50 per month from the Newport Lumber Company while his wife, Florence, received the princely sum of $25 for doing the bookkeeping.

On January 1, 1904, he opened his own business, Corona Lumber Company which played an integral role in the building of Corona. Corona Lumber Company was first established at Fifth and Main, and the horses used for the hauling of lumber were kept in a stable at Fourth and Washburn. Ware paid $5 a month to rent the building which had originally housed the town's first post office. The nail kegs that had served as mail boxes were replaced by lengths of lumber and

all the trappings that go with the lumber business.

Although he never entered the political arena, A. J. was dedicated to the development of the city. He organized the Corona National Bank which later became the First National Bank of Corona, serving as director and president. He was also secretary of the South Riverside Cemetery Association (now the Sunnyslope Cemetery) and was President of Corona Mutual Building & Loan Association.

A. J. and his wife never had any children of their own, but A. J. took a deep interest in helping local boys get a start in life. He would help boys who wanted to deliver newspapers buy their bicycles by loaning them the needed funds which they would repay at 25 cents or 50 cents a week.

A. J.'s brother Lewis had also immigrated to California, settling first in Pasadena where his oldest son, Frank and oldest daughter were born. The family moved from there to Fillmore in Ventura County. There Lewis attempted farming, and the family grew to a total of nine children. However, Lewis died unexpectedly when his wife Mary was pregnant with their last child. Unable to maintain the family by herself, Mary moved to Corona where the last child was born. It is thought that A. J. took care of Mary Ware and the ten children, and he raised his niece Florence Ware as his own even providing her with a college education.

Lewis Ware's two oldest sons, Frank and Howard, joined Corona Lumber Company in their teen years. At the age of 14, Howard helped his uncle with deliveries. Corona Lumber had three delivery horses and Howard was given responsibility for Molly who drew the smaller of the wagons. None of

Andrew "A. J. Ware" arrived in Corona in 1893.

the wagons were fitted with a driver's seat, so Howard could either sit on the load of lumber itself or on the frame of the wagon. When Howard and Frank delivered loads of lumber to the Glen Ivy Hot Springs Hotel in Temescal Canyon, it would take them from 7:30 a.m. to 1:30 p.m. to make the delivery and return.

Like their Uncle A. J., both Frank and Howard were active members of the Corona community. Frank was President of the Chamber of

Commerce, President of the Rotary Club and served on the school board. Howard served on the Corona City Council.

After Corona Lumber was well established, A. J. acquired several other lumber companies, Perris Valley Lumber Company, Elsinore Pioneer Lumber Company (which still exists) and Antelope Valley Lumber Company. As a young man, Frank was sent to run the Elsinore Pioneer Lumber. By this time, he had married Mary Inez Kirby Ware who was born in Corona on Christmas Day, 1892. He worked at Elsinore Pioneer Lumber until 1923 when he and his branch of the Ware Family returned to Corona where they have been ever since.

Frank's oldest son, Terence "Terry" Robert Ware was born August 14, 1916, in a large house on West 6th Street which had maternity facilities, there being no hospital in Corona at the time. Terry carried

on the family tradition and went to work at Corona Lumber. Terry was the innovator of the Corona Lumber Company trademark "Lum B-u-r-r-r." Following the Ware Family tradition of involvement in civic affairs, Terry Ware served a term as President of the Corona Chamber of Commerce.

When A. J. passed away, he left his share of Corona Lumber to Frank and Howard. When Frank died, his share passed to Terry which left Terry and his Uncle Howard running the company. When Howard retired, he sold his portion of the company to two men outside the family. Then Terry and one of his partners bought out the other partner and when Terry retired he sold his remaining share. Although Terry and his wife still owned the building and the property, eventually they sold that also, and the Ware Family's involvement with Corona Lumber finally ended as did Corona Lumber Company.

Many of the buildings built by the Ware Family through their family business, Corona Lumber Company, are still standing today including the Post Office, the Featherston building, the Citizens National Bank, the Methodist Church and parsonage, St. Edwards Catholic Church and School and Dr. Munn's medical-dental building. They also built hundreds of homes for residents of Corona. Without the hard work and industry of the Ware Family and Corona Lumber Company, the city of Corona would not enjoy the expansion and growth it does today.

A. J. Ware and his nephews Howard Ware and Frank Ware at their desk at Corona Lumber in 1942.

Corona Lumber Company in 1904.

The Kroonen Family

The Kroonen Family is one of the oldest families still living in Corona. The first Kroonen in the area was Leo Kroonen, a Dutch architect and builder, who was hired to build Temescal and Rincon schools. He married Mary L. Walkinshaw on June 30, 1889. Mary was born on the site where the Good Samaritan Boys Home was located near the Santa Ana River, just a short distance northwest of Corona.

Mary Kroonen's parents, grandparents and great-grandfather immigrated from Scotland, arriving by covered wagon via Salt Lake City in 1853. Mary was one of ten children. Her Grandfather Walkinshaw, along with others, took up land along the Santa Ana River, but had to surrender their farm when found to be on early Spanish grants. Her stepfather W.B. Roberds had one of the first dairies supplying settlers of the area.

When Mary was a little girl, Corona was just a place where sheep and cattle grazed on foothigh grass. The small settlement was part of San Bernardino County until 1893. Mary's family moved to Rincon and later settled in an area called Auburndale which ran along the Santa Ana River. They made their first trip into the sleepy, dirty town of Los Angeles in 1877.

Mary and Leo Kroonen planned to live in a home they had built near Mary's parents in Auburndale, but when the railroad wasn't extended to Pomona Road, they moved their house to Buena Vista and Olive in the first orange orchard in South Riverside and were among the first to sell oranges. They had the first indoor bathtub.

(Top photo) Mary L. and Leo Kroonen Sr. in 1921.

(Bottom photo) Mary and Leo Kroonen's children: (l. to r.) Leo Kroonen, Jr.; Mary Kroonen Savage and William Oscar "Dutch" Kroonen.

Leo Kroonen designed and built many buildings and houses in Corona including several schools, the City Hall and the Plunge. Mary's life centered around her family. Aunt May (as she was known to most Coronans then) was considered one of the best cooks in town. Her daughter Mary said "She always left cookies out." In 1926 she made her daughter Mary's wedding veil. That same veil was worn in 1947 by granddaughter Elma, and by great-granddaughters Marilyn in 1979 and Patty in 1981.

Three children were born to Mary and Leo: Leo Jr., William Oscar and Mary. Leo Jr. was the youngest agricultural inspector appointed for the State of California but spent most of his life as a beekeeper and part-time carpenter. William Oscar was known as "Dutch" throughout his life. His son Jack Kroonen later became the owner of Fare's Industrial Tools. Daughter Mary had her own memories of delivering milk in pint jars to her cousins because the family had a cow. She was the first in the family to fly in an airplane. She attended Riverside Junior College and married George Savage. Granddaughter Dollie Johnson was Director of Food Services for Corona Unified School District for 19 years.

Mary Kroonen lived to be 101. In 1969 she was honored as the oldest county native. Her son, Leo Kroonen, Jr. received the same award in 1996. Descending from these three children are six grandchildren, nine great-grandchildren, nine great-great-grandchild, and two great-great-great grandchildren — five generations of Kroonens in Corona and eight generations in California. Memories from generation to generation overlap and blend into a century of Kroonens.

Although Corona has grown tremendously since those early days, the Kroonen family name persists in the children, grandchildren and great-grandchildren who have made this area their home. As grandson William Kroonen commented when describing his grandfather's name inscribed on the City Hall cornerstone, "As a child my whole world was Corona. It was a neat and tidy little world we lived in." And it still is.

ears ago when the summer of 1965 was warming and moving closer, the lives of Tom Miter and Carol Cooke were changed forever on May 29th. The morning woke in Corona as the day's activities marched like a parade. Carol, an extremely quiet child, midway through her 15th year, became a bride. Tom, a 19-year-old rowdy, rambunctious boy, was the groom.

In the midst of the preparation, ceremony and celebration, parental disappointment submerged beneath a veneer of pride and pleasure. The audience smugly knew that innocence had been erased; so, they gathered to repair a wrong, to pretend these two could transform their condition into something the family could present as right. But failure loomed large as their "shouldn't have" was rewritten and legally recorded as two "I do's."

One white canvas, a palette with seven colors, and two wooden handled brushes were handed to the young couple. They passionately believed they could paint; even though, they didn't know what the "could" might be. With white shirts, blue jeans and bare feet, they began to apply color to their path.

They had not a notion of the rickety, broken bridges they would cross, the washed-out roads they would traverse, and that occasionally the landscape would provide no path, so they would have to build as they traveled. An eight-lane well-used highway would never be found. Lack of fear allowed them to proceed because they didn't know what to be afraid of.

On their tenth anniversary, Tom and Carol decided to renew their marriage vows and have the formal wedding that had not happened in 1965. The unexpected guest at that 1975 anniversary celebration was Jesus Christ. Again their lives changed forever as they promised to continue their life together with the addition of the God of the universe as the Lord of their lives.

Today, Tom is an Associate Pastor at Crossroads Christian Church. He graduated from Pacific Christian College in 1979 and has been full time on the Crossroads staff since January 1, 1980. The Miter legacy began in Corona in the 1930s when Tom's grandmother, Belle Miter became the proprietor of the fashionable women's clothing store, "The Town Shop." Tom's father, Bill, returned to Corona at the conclusion of World War II with a wife, Mary, and infant Tom. They still live in Corona.

Carol moved to Corona with her mother and stepfather in the summer of 1963, preceding her ninth grade year at Corona Junior High School. At the end of her sophomore year, she quit high school to marry Tom. Their first child, a son, Shawn, was born on her 16th birthday; daughter, Deidre, was born in 1968.

In 1985, after a 20-year recess from education, Carol enrolled at Riverside Community College. She earned an associate's degree, transferred to California State University at San Bernardino, earned a bachelor's degree in English, and then a master's degree in Composition. Since the autumn of 1991 Carol has been a Professor of English at the Norco Campus of RCC.

Their adult children reside in Corona. Shawn has one daughter, Desiree. Deidre is married to John Dunn and has two children, a daughter and son, Ashly and Emerson.

Next May 29th, Tom and Carol Miter will conclude another 12 months of history. Panel after panel they've painted the Miter mural into a multicolored narrative that's stamped "Made in Corona!"

anuel Rico was born in 1887 in El Valle de Santiago, Guanajuato Mexico. In 1904 at age 16, he emigrated to the United States. He came to this "Land of Opportunity," learned English phonetically, learned the American customs, worked hard and used his keen mind to prosper.

Manuel and a cousin, Jesus Rico, traveled and worked together. They landed jobs with the Santa Fe Railroad which served as a revolving door for many immigrants. They worked in Utah and in California.

In 1904, still only 16, Manuel went to work for Mr. Alex Barnes baling hay.

In 1910 Manuel and his cousin, Jesus, went into business together. With a team of horses and a hay baler they sought work with local ranchers. The business was successful and grew so that after several years, Manuel was able to buy his

first home on Sheridan Street. Now he had a place to keep his horses and also to marry the former Bernarda Martinez.

In 1912 Manuel brought his parents and two sisters to Corona. There were no restrictions to crossing the Mexican border at that time. They bought some property on Sheridan Street and on Merrill Street and settled in. The property is still owned by family members. By 1918 he and his cousin had parted company. Manuel then bought another team of horses, known locally as "The Black Beauties," and a new wagon and started hauling manure from area ranches to the citrus groves.

Manuel and Bernarda started a family and had two daughters, Concepcion and Consuelo as

well as three sons, Santos, Margarito and Frank. They were all born in Corona. Bernarda died at age 40 in 1928. Manuel and his third wife, Lena Vasquez, had eight children; Lupe Guzman of Ontario, Nellie Garcia, Bea Bravo, Johnny Rico, Helen Costello, Manuel and Ralph Rico, all of Corona and Esther Hernandez of Riverside. Lena died in 1956 at age 33. Ralph, the youngest was three years old.

In 1920 Manuel bought his first truck, a REO Speedwagon. He bought and traded in Dodge trucks for the next 30 years.

Despite the crash of 1929 and the great Depression of the 30s, Manuel's business continued to grow. Fertilizer was necessary to grow the citrus and helped Corona become "The Lemon Capital of The World." During WWII he was allowed to build a storage tank and install a gas pump for his vehicles. This was during the time of strict rations on many commodities, including gasoline. By the early 40s, the married sons and daughters with families were living at "The Ranch," 12 acres Manuel had bought some years before. "The Ranch" was sold in 1995 and a Target store is located at that site.

Eldest son Santos helped his father run the business for many years, then branched out on his own. He has his own fleet of trucks based in Calexico, California. Frank, the third son, also had his own trucking company and is now retired. Margarito, having returned from the Army, returned to the family business.

By the time Manuel died in 1963, Margarito was rebuilding. Now with youngest son, Ralph as president, business is good and they have 20 trucks and seven cat loaders.

It's a funny thing that fertilizer could be the commodity for a family's success, but there you have it.

The Rico Family are not only fourth generation Americans, and Californians, but Coronans as well. Here to stay, there are 40 grandchildren, 65 great-grandchildren and 42 great-great grandchildren.

In 1968, when Steve Nathan retired from the Air Force after 26 years of service, he set out to create a whole new life for himself, his wife Doris and their sons, Steve and Dennis. To the great benefit of the citizens of Norco, he accomplished this goal and beyond.

When Nathan settled in Norco, he found his new home a mecca for the electronics industry. He worked for several different companies and then founded his own company, Norco Alarms, which installed alarm systems throughout Riverside County and surrounding areas. Nathan was the 27th person to qualify for the State of California Manager's license. Doris contributed her bookkeeping skills to the company for many years. When Steve "retired" again, Norco Alarms was sold for a seven-figure price.

However, founding, developing and running a successful business was not enough for Steve's boundless energy. He turned his attention to Norco politics. In the 1970s Steve headed a committee to recall three city councilmen who opposed the interstate freeway going through Norco. Although this victory was one of many, it certainly was not his last.

In 1978 Steve was elected to City Council. During his 12-year stint with the City Council, he served as Mayor of Norco twice and Vice-Mayor three times. Two accomplishments he is especially proud of are his work to open a campus of Riverside Community College in Norco and implementing a D.A.R.E. (a drug education program) in the Norco schools. Also, he was appointed by the warden to the Citizens Advisory Committee for the state prison in Norco.

The enormous variety of committees and activities in which Steve is involved include serving as Chairman of the Riverside Transit Authority,

Steve and Doris Nathan have played a major role in the development of the City of Norco.

the County Grand Jury and the Board of Directors of the California Grand Jurors. Steve's contributions to Norco were recognized at the 57th annual Norco Chamber of Commerce banquet where he was named Man of the Year. He was president of the Corona AARP Club.

Steve is an active member of the Lions Club and the American Legion. For the past five years, he has gone every year to England to dig with archeological teams for relics and old coins. His pride and joy is a Roman coin he found dating back to 31 B.C. He was elected to the Board of Directors of the Riverside Treasure Hunter's Club.

Steve and Doris have been married 51 years. "Don't know how we ever did it!" exclaimed Doris. The Nathans have had a life filled with travel and diversity during their Air Force years and civic accomplishments and personal happiness during their "second life" in Norco.

Chapter 1

Bancroft, Hubert Howe. *History of California.* There are several volumes of California history by Bancroft. They are divided into specific years and contain much valuable information.

Cleland, Robert Glass. *The Cattle on a Thousand Hills: 1850-1880.* San Marino: Huntington Library 1951.

Ormsby, Waterman. *The Butterfield Overland Mail: Only Through Passenger on the First Westbound Stage.* Huntington Library: San Marino, CA 1960. The author wrote eight articles which appeared in the New York *Herald* from September 26 to November 19, 1858.

Wilkinson, David. *History of the Yorba-Slaughter Adobe.* Thesis for the University of California, Riverside. June 1983.

The ancient Temescal Road, which crossed the sloping alluvial plain where Corona would some day be built, began as a trail used by the Luiseño and Gabrielino Indians. There are several books which tell about the life of the Gabrielino and Luiseño people:

Boscana, Gerononimo. *Chinigchinich: Historical Account of the Belief, Usages, Customs, and Extravagancies of This Mission of San Juan Capistrano.* First published 1836. 1933 edition: Fine Arts Press, Santa Ana.

Johnston, Bernice. *California's Gabrieleno Indians.* Los Angeles, CA: Southwest Museum. 1962.

McCawley, William. *The Gabrieleno Indians of Los Angeles.* Malki Museum Press, Morengo Indian Reservation. 1996

Sparkman, Philip Stedman and Lyle Whitcomb Smith *The Culture of the Luiseño Indians.* Ramona, CA: Ocoma Books. 1971.

Smith, Lyle Whitcomb. *The Big Yellow Bus.* Corona, CA 1990

There are numerous old books about the missions of California. They clearly show the love and fascination each author felt for the missions. Some particularly interesting ones are:

Englehart, Fr. Zephyrin. *The Missions and Missionaries of California.*

Hall, Trowbridge. *California Trails, An Intimate Guide to the Old Missions.* McMillan Co. 1920

James, George Wharton. *In and Out of the Old Missions of California.* Little, Brown, and Co. 1905 *Old Franciscan Missions of California.* 1913.

Newcomb, Rexford. *The Old Mission Churches and Historic Houses of California; Their History, Architecture, Art, and Lore.* J. B. Lippincott and Company. 1925

Miscellaneous Notes

The *Corona Daily Independent* printed special editions to celebrate the 50th Anniversary (May 1936) and 75th Anniversary (May 1961) of the founding of the city. They have recorded valuable information about the years when the Indians traversed the mesa and the families that owned the large ranchos that occupied the territory.

For several months in 1939 Watt Bonfoey wrote a special column in the *Corona Daily Independent.* He remembered many of the early pioneers and passed on personal stories that would have been lost to history if it had not been for his efforts. Especially interesting are his stories about the people who lived in the hills and canyons surrounding Corona. These rugged pioneer families were here even before the colony was founded.

A particularly valuable tool in the study of the Spanish ranching families, *Saddleback Ancestors, Rancho Families of Orange County, California* was written and published by the Orange County Geneological Society in 1969. Although it is principally about Orange County's ranchos and old families, there are some connections with Riverside County families.

The Yorba-Slaughter Adobe, now owned by the San Bernardino County Museum, is located on Highway 71, a few miles north of Prado Dam. Make a right turn off of the first off ramp, and turn left on the Old Pomona-Rincon Road, the first road to the left. The adobe and winery are on the right, a short distance from the intersection. It is best to call ahead to make sure they will be open.

Chapter 2

Board of Trade. *Corona, California, The Queen Colony.* Corona Publishing Co. 1902. High-quality photographs convey a sense of the Corona at the turn of the century.

Bonfoey, Watt. "History of Early Corona Days." A scrapbook of Watt Bonfoey's newpaper columns, appearing in 1939 in the *Corona Daily Independent.*

Brown, John Jr. and James Boyd. *San Bernardino and Riverside Counties: With Selected Biography of Actors and Witnesses of the Period of Growth and Achievement.* Chicago: Lewis Publishing Co. 1922.

Dumke, Glenn S. *The Boom of the Eighties in Southern California.* San Marino: Huntington Library 1944.

Fitch, Robert. *Profile of a Century.* Riverside: Riverside County Historical 1993.

Gabbert, John Raymond. *History of Riverside City and County.* Riverside: 1935.

Industrial Edition, *Corona Courier,* Corona, California. March 1909. Many clear photographs of local buildings are included.

Kellogg, H. Clay. *History of the Founding of Corona, California.* September 9, 1913.
Mellor, Betsy. *The Beginnings of Corona.* U. S. History paper 1968

Reynolds, Stanley, and Fred Eldredge. *Corona, California Commentaries.* Los Angeles: Sinclair Printing Company. 1986. This well-detailed book, sponsored by the Heritage Committee of the Friends of the Corona Public Library, gives an overview of Corona history. There are sections about every facet of Corona history. Of particular interest are the chapters that tell the stories of the Italian and Hispanic pioneers of the area.

Rolfe, Frank. *A Sketch in the Life of R. B. Taylor and the Story of the Development of Ida Grove, Iowa, Wayne, Nebraska, and the Founding of Corona, Riverside County.*

Miscellaneous Notes

Invaluable material is available in the microfilms of the *Corona Daily Independent,* located in the Publications section of the Corona Public Library. Of special note are the important articles about the colony's history which appear in the May 1936 (50th Anniversary) and the May 4, 1961 (75th Anniversary) issues.

A letter to the citizens of Corona from Robert B. Taylor, the founder of South Riverside, appears in the May 4, 1961 edition of the *Corona Daily Independent.* Written on April 14, 1913, it was found hidden in the back of a framed drawing of South Riverside by Rudy Ramos 48 years later.

To do further research the individual churches, businesses, persons, and organizations, go to the Heritage Room of the Corona Public Library and ask for the folder containing information on that particular subject.

Chapter 3 & 4

Adams, Keith, Badich, McClellan, and Smith. *Step Into the Past.* The Corona Unified School District. 1992.

Chamber of Commerce.1912 Promotional Book.

Chase, Ethan Allen. *The Eightieth Birthday of Ethan Allen Chase.* January 1912.

Galbert, John Raymond. *History of Riverside City and County; Events Affecting the Development of the Inland Empire, Growth of Cities and Industry.* 1935.

Gould, Janet Williams. *Corona Source Book,* Volumes I, II, III. This set includes several rare original documents relating to area history.

Gunther, Jane Davies. *Riverside County, California Place Names, Their Origins and Their Stories.* Rubidoux Printing Company. 1984.

Reynolds, Stanley, and Fred Eldridge. Corona California Commentaries. Corona, CA. 1986. This comprehensive book contains information on almost every facet of Corona's history.

————-. *Corona La Mesa.* Corona High School Annual. Contains an illustrated section about the town's history.

————-. *History and Directory of Riverside County* (1893-1894).

————-. *Corona, California.* The Board of Trade. 1908.

Miscellaneous Notes

To get a true feeling for the history of the Circle City, drive around Grand Boulevard and take a good look at the many historic houses. Original pie-shaped parks are located at Tenth and Merrill (Maple Park) and Tenth and Joy (Joy Park).

The Corona Daily Independent and the *Corona Courier* contain detailed information regarding the day-to-day history and events of the city. It is available on microfilm in the Publications section of the public library.

Chapter 5

Coffin, Helen Lockwood. *California Southland.* Article available in the Heritage Room of the Corona Public Library.

Farr, John and Gloria Scott Freel. *Corona: Citrus, races and more...* Corona Historic Preservation Society 1992.

Kovacik, Bob. *Corona Road Races 1913, 1914, and 1916.* This seven-part series about road racing in Corona, written for the *Riverside Press Enterprise* by sports editor Bob Kovacik, is published in an illustrated booklet.

Reynolds, Stanley and Fred Eldridge. *Corona, California Commentaries.* Corona, CA. 1986.

Miscellaneous Notes

The 1920s was a time of prosperity for Corona and Southern California. Some of the landmarks of the era still surviving include:
- In 1923, the City built a picturesque new state-of the-art high school in a dramatic Spanish Colonial Revival style at 800 West Sixth St. It has been beautifully preserved and now serves as the City Hall.
- The Landmark/Corona Theatre Building at 211 E. Sixth Street, built in 1928-29, is a fine example of 1920s Spanish Colonial Revival architecture.
- Jefferson School, located at Vicentia and Tenth streets, was built in 1927-28. It is known for its dramatic Spanish Colonial Revival architecture.

Houses built during the 1920s in Spanish Colonial, English Tudor, Colonial, and other Revival styles are sprinkled throughout the older sections of Corona. They are known for their romantic architecture, popular in the 1920s.

Files containing specific information on subjects contained in this chapter, such as road races or World War I, are available in the Heritage Room of the Corona Public Library.

Take a drive around the Grand Boulevard Circle and picture the excitement that must have occured on race days in 1913,1914, and 1915. Can you imagine the cars going almost 100 miles an hour?

Chapter 6

Cobb, Sue, Ron Snow and Linda Bruinsma. *Norco Remembers*. The citizens of Norco published this charming community history in 1989. It has a lot of valuable information about Norco and the families and events that have shaped the city.

Greenwood, Roberta. *Historical and Archaeological Evaluation: Rincon Townite and Environs*. U. S. Army Corp of Engineers 1987.

Langenwalter, Paul and James Buck. *Phase II: Archaeological Studies of the Prado Basin and Lower Santa Ana River*. (Note: this study contains a history of each ranch in detail).

Norco Historical Society. *A Brief History of Rex B. Clark's Lake Norconian Club*. 1989. The Norco Historical Society has a large collection of important historical photographs. It has more than 50 of the photos taken by a professional photographer during the 1920s of almost every phase of the Lake Norconian Club during the 1920s.

Rolfe, Frank. *The Beginnings of Glen Ivy*. Unpublished. Available in the Heritage Room, Corona Public Library.

Miscellaneous Notes

Tour of Lake Norconian Club:
The Norco Historical Society has been conducting fascinating tours of the Lake Norconian Club, led by Steve Nathan, but will probably not be able to do so again until after the seismic work on the main building is finished. Steve Nathan, Norco historian, has been heavily involved in Norco affairs, serving as a Mayor in 1981-82, and on the City Council for many years. He is president of the Norco Historical Society.

Grant documents and maps for the Rancho La Sierra Sepulveda were supplied by Phil Brigandi.

To truly understand the story of Norco, you should drive the streets of the City. The older section is on the east of Hamner Avenue, along the foothills. If you look closely you can find some of the houses from the 1920s, 30s, and 40s among the newer homes. They are mostly single-storied, have wood siding, and wood-sash windows.

The horse trails, small barns, large lots, and variety of animals tell you that Norco is a special place to live. In the late 1960s, a new section to the west of Hamner Avenue opened for the development of new homes and mini-ranches, some of which overlook the Santa Ana River. El Cerrito, to the east and south of Corona, has a special country atmosphere. The Glen Ivy Hotel is now a private facility, but the bathhouse and the campgrounds are open to the public. The Fuller RanchO is now a private school for boys.

Chapter 7

Karr, John and Gloria Scott. *Corona, Citrus, races, and more...* Corona Historic Preservation Society. 1993.

—————. *Guide to Historic Landmarks of Riverside County, California*. Several Corona historic site and landmarks, along with their locations, are described in this book. Gloria Scott Freel researched and wrote the material on the Corona sites.

Stadelbacher, Valerie and Dorothy Laird. *A Historic and Architectural Driving Tour to a Splendid Assortment of Corona's Homes*. Corona Public Library. 1993.

—————. *Corona, California*. Corona Chamber of Commerce. 1958

—————. *Corona, California*. Corona Chamber of Commerce. 1964

Miscellaneous Notes

To reach the Old Temescal Road, go south on Main Street, turn east (left) on Ontario, pass under the I-15 Freeway, and continue south on Old Temescal Road. There are monuments at the sites of the Third Serrano Adobe and the tanning pits. Glen Ivy Hot Springs is near by.

The Heritage Room and museum are on the second floor of the Corona Public Library, 630 S. Main Street. Call the Heritage Room to check their hours. The museum section is open the same hours as the library.

The Norco Historical Society has an interesting array of memorabilia and pictures, including over 50 professional photographs of the Lake Norconian Club as it was being built.

Harvey Mack is Curator of the Forest Service History Center. It is located at 1147 E. Sixth Street, Corona.

The Yorba-Slaughter Adobe, operated by the San Bernardino County Museum, is open Wednesday through Saturday, during selected hours. It is located at 17127 Pomona Rincon Road in Chino, and can be reached from Highway 71.

Corona Heritage Park—Within the next few years, the Old Foothill Ranch will be developed into an active historical park, depicting the rich agricultural background of the area. It is located on the Foothill Parkway.

Index

Partners Index

Photos not otherwised marked are Courtesy Heritage Room, Corona Public Library